Instant Pot Air Fryer Lid Cookbook

800 Easy and Healthy Air Fryer Recipes to Help You Master Your Instant Pot Air Fryer Lid on a Budget

William L. Rowell

Table of Content

Chapter 5 Rice and Grains......45

Chapter 6 Fish and Seafood .. 60

Chapter 7 Snacks and Appetizers................................76

Chapter 8 Vegan 90

Chapter 9 Vegetables and Side Dishes......................................104

Introduction

When you buy an Instant pot air fryer lid, it is very important to have a cookbook. Because it is a unique device, that's why I am writing this book. First of all, congratulations! You made an excellent choice when you bought an Instant pot air fryer lid! If you are still sitting at the fence, this cookbook is also for you! This cookbook introduces the different models, explains how to use your Instant pot air fryer lid, briefly describes the cooking functions and gives some tips. Then we start with the Instant pot air fryer lid.

So this book is suitable for the working mom, Instant pot and vegetarian beginners, working professionals and cooking lovers who want to learn cooking with Instant pot air fryer lid.

If you are going to cook some Instant pot air fryer lid recipes, then get this book. This great learning book, which are highly recommended, will guide you in an absolute way with some important approaches This is such a great book. Simple as it is, but it gives you a great understanding. I am sure you will enjoy reading this book.

Instant pot air fryer lid opens up a world of cooking options. It does not just make your favourite recipes easy, but also shorten the preparation time significantly. I recommend you to prepare your dishes. Extend the boundaries of what your Instant pot air fryer lid can do and you will be happier in the long run.

The Air Fryer Lid is the Instant Pot's best bud. It uses super-heated, fast-blowing air to cook and crisp food. You can use it to cook food from fresh or frozen, or, to crisp up an item after it's been cooked in the Instant Pot.

This book help reader the things that affect day-to-day life - such as your job, taking care of your family, getting errands done, etc. – the life that can sometimes make it impossible for you to find the time to cook a decent dinner.

Chapter 1 About the Instant Pot Air Fryer Lid

Expand your culinary collection with the new Instant Pot Air Fryer Lid and turn your normal Instant Pot into a powerful deep fryer. Our innovative Even Crisp™ technology ensures a crunchy crunch and a golden finish every time. Air frying, roasting, baking, roasting, reheating and dehydrating directly in the inner pot of the instant pot to save time, space and cleanliness. Finally, you can combine the delicate results of pressure cooking and the crisp browning of air roast with a quick lid change.

The air fryer lid brings a host of new features to your kitchen so everyone can have fun preparing great, healthy meals quickly and easily. Whip tender ribs or a nice big chicken in your instant casserole, then use the air fryer lid to add a nice finish to each bite.

Conveniently, the air fryer lid stays loose on the bottom of the pan, making it easy to manoeuvre, easy to clean, and comes with a protective pad for safe and easy storage. The cover control panel has buttons for your different needs. The display is clear and easy to read. With the 6 smart present programs, you can cook at the touch of a button or adjust settings for a fully personalized cooking experience. After many rigorous tests, the results are ready ... and they are delicious.

The Specs

The Air Fryer Lid
Length: 10.7 inches
Width: 11.6 inches
Height: 6.2 inches
Weight: 5.95 lbs / 2.7 kg
Power: 1500W
Warranty: 1 Year
Programs: Air Fry, Broil, Bake, Roast, Reheat, and Dehydrate
Max Temperature: 400°F (204°C)
Min Temperature: 125°F (52°C)

The Air Fryer Basket
Diameter: roughly 7.5 inches (air frying works best when you arrange your ingredients in a single layer)

Settings

To do this...	Do this!
Change the temperature scale (°F and °C).	When in standby, press and hold the + button over **Temp** until Fahrenheit **(°F)** or Celsius **(°C)** appears on the display.
Turn sounds on and off.	**Sound On:** When in Standby mode, press and hold the + button over Time until S On appears on the display. **Sound Off:** When in Standby mode, press the — button beneath **Time** until **SOFF** appears on the display. Error alerts cannot be silenced.
Adjust and save custom cooking times and temperatures.	Once a Smart Program is selected, changes to the cooking time and temperature are saved once the Smart Program begins.
Reset an individual smart program.	When in standby, press and hold one Smart Program button until the appliance beeps. The Smart Program has been restored to the factory default setting.
Reset all smart programs.	When in standby mode, press and hold Cancel until the appliance beeps. All Smart Programs have been restored to the factory default settings.

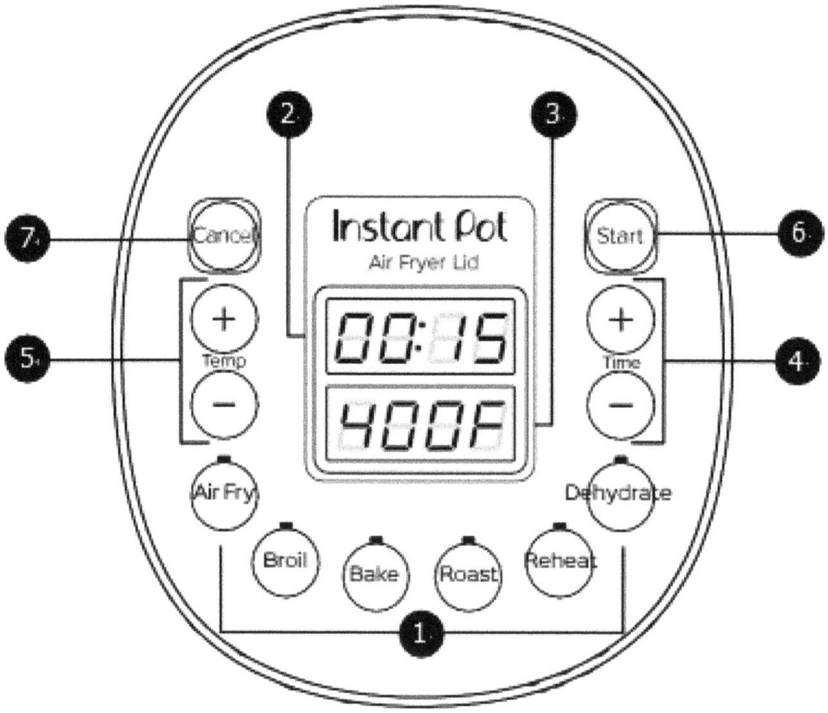

Control Panel and Buttons

1	**Smart Programs**	◉ Air Fry ◉ Broil ◉ Bake ◉ Roast ◉ Reheat ◉ Dehydrate
2	**Time Display**	The Time Display shows the time in HH:MM format. It counts up or down, depending on the Smart Program.
3	**Temperature Display**	The Temperature Display shows the set temperature in °C or °F.
4	**+ / – Time**	Press to adjust the time.
5	**+ / – Temp**	Press to adjust the cooking temperature in °C or °F.
6	**Start**	Begins the selected Smart Program.
7	**Cancel**	Stop a Smart Program at any time.

Functions (Pre-Programmed Settings)

Air Fry: Crisp up pressure-cooked dishes and frozen foods

Default Time*	Time Range	Default Temperature*	Temperature Range
20 minutes (00:20)	1 to 45 minutes (00:01 to 00:45)	205°C 400°F	150 to 205°C 300 to 400°F

Air frying is an amazing way to bring out a lot of flavour using only a little oil. Crisp up previously cooked dishes or use the Air Fryer Lid to cook a dish from start to finish. Ideal for fresh or frozen fries, chicken wings, shrimp and more.

While the Air fryer settings should be compatible with most recipes, when cooking vegetables at 450 degrees, we found that the maximum temperature in both modes was 400 degrees. As convection improves heating performance, we refined the recipe and it worked well despite cooking at a lower temperature than recommended.

On the lower side of the temperature scale is the dehydration mode, which can reach 105 degrees. However, the frying basket couldn't hold more than a handful of fruit slices, not even with the two-tier pan, so we didn't like that feature.

Roast: Use to finish meats with a nice crust or crispy skin

Default Time*	Time Range	Default Temperature*	Temperature Range
40 minutes (00:40)	1 to 45 minutes (00:01 to 00:45)	380°C 193°F	121 to 193°C 250 to 380°F

The Roast Smart Program is perfect for beef, lamb, pork, poultry, vegetables and more. Give your roast a beautiful crust, crisp up poultry skins or give your vegetables a golden exterior.

Broil: Great for melting cheese on top of pastas

Default Time*	Time Range	Default Temperature*	Temperature Range
10 minutes (00:10)	1 to 20 minutes (00:01 to 00:20)	205°C 400°F	Not Adjustable

Broiling involves direct top-down heating, and broiled foods benefit from being placed close to the element. Perfect for melting cheese on French onion soup.

We used the broiler tray and broiler for cheese-topped chicken sandwiches on bagel halves. While the sandwiches were nicely warmed and the cheese melted well, our creations were so tall that they were perched on the broiler tray, so a bit of cheese touched the heating element. The cheese came off the element easily once it cooled, but next time we'll pay more attention to food height. As for width, we had to squish the two bagel halves a bit to make them fit side-by-side. A third half wouldn't have fit.

Bake: Works just like an oven and can be used for brownies and cakes

Default Time*	Time Range	Default Temperature*	Temperature Range
30 minutes	1 to 1 hour	185°C	82 to 193°C
(00:30)	(00:01 to 01:00)	365°F	180 to 380°F

Like a tiny oven, the Bake Smart Program can be used to create delicious brownies, fluffy cakes, pastries, buns and much more. Bake with the provided multi-level air fryer basket or any oven-safe baking dish, such as a spring form pan. Unless specified in your recipe, do not cover your batter when baking. If baking in the air fryer basket, line the interior of the air fry basket with aluminium foil or parchment paper, then pour in loose batter. If using a baking dish, make sure to elevate the dish with a steam rack when cooking. The bake option isn't as intuitive as the other programs. A chart in the included booklet said the air fryer basket should be used for baking, with the food under the broiler rack. It makes sense since hot air blowing strongly on a cake probably isn't good, and the rack would provide a baffle. One problem we had with baking was to find a suitably small baking pan and to find a recipe to fit the pan. We ended up using a 6-inch spring-shaped pan that was about the largest possible choice, and we baked cornbread from a box mix. The cornbread baked well, but it's doubtful we'd be baking cakes in this unless it was our last option.

Reheat: Warm up leftovers without drying them out

Default Time*	Time Range	Default Temperature*	Temperature Range
15 minutes	1 to 1 hour	138°C	49 to 182°C
(00:15)	(00:01 to 01:00)	280°F	120 to 360°F

We used the reheat setting to warm up leftover chicken and vegetables using the broiler tray. While it worked well, we only had room for a single serving. Taking the food out of the hot pot wasn't very neat. We ended up turning the frying basket over onto a plate, and the food spilled out with the tray following. It wasn't a pretty presentation, but our lunch was nicely warm. Because of the holes in the broiler tray, it wouldn't be useful for reheating small foods like rice, and sauces would drain away. It's also a lot to clean for reheating a single plate of food.

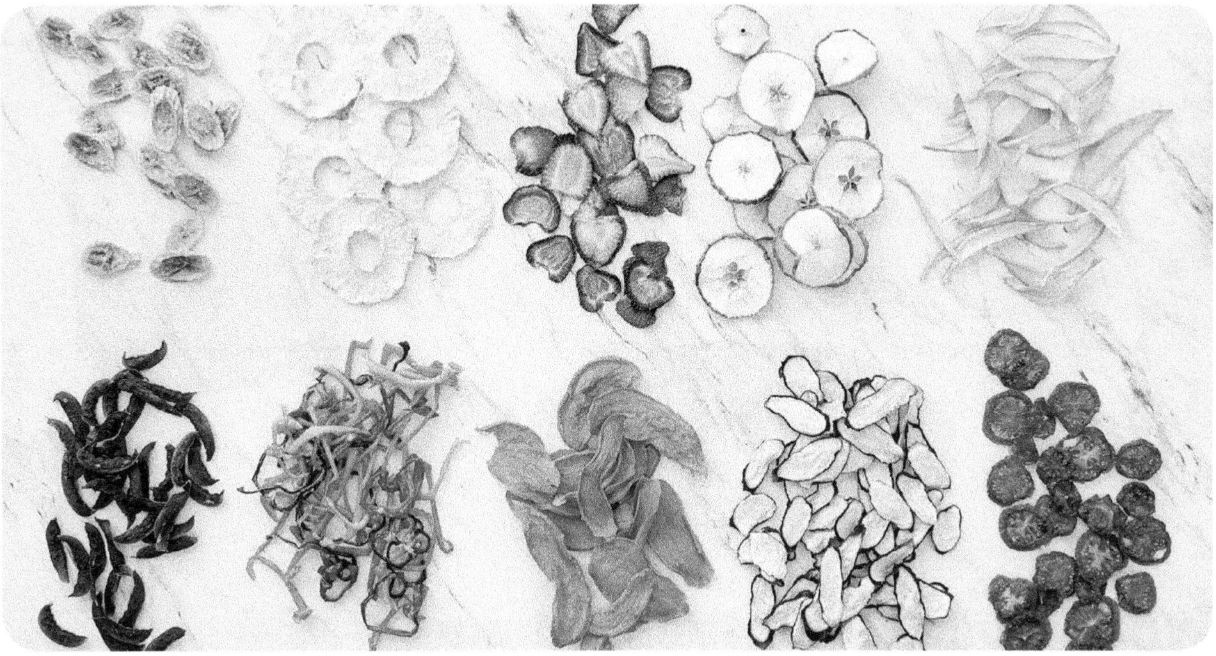

Dehydrate: Low-heat over a long time to make your own apple chips and dried fruit.

Default Time*	Time Range	Default Temperature*	Temperature Range
6 hours	1 to 72 hours	52°C	41 to 74°C
(06:00)	(01:00 to 72:00)	125°F	105 to 165°F

The Dehydrate Smart Program applies low heat over a long period of time to safely dry out foods.

Make dried fruit, dehydrated vegetable chips and all kinds of jerky. Always follow a trusted recipe when dehydrating meat.

For items that have NOT been pressure cooked, the manual provides a few general suggestions for cooking times and temperatures:

Food	Air Fry Temperature	Time
French Fries (from frozen)	400ºF (205ºC)	22 minutes
Quartered Chicken	400ºF (205ºC)	38 minutes
Chicken Wings	400ºF (205ºC)	19 minutes
Carrots	400ºF (205ºC)	8 minutes
Asparagus	400ºF (205ºC)	4 minutes

What Comes with the Package

The package includes the air fryer lid, a multi-level air frying basket, a base for the air frying basket, a broil/dehydrating tray, a protection pad to set the lid on when it's hot, and instruction materials.

Accessories

	**Casserole Dish:** A casserole (French: diminutive of casse, from Provençal cassa 'pan') is a variety of a large, deep pan or bowl, typically with a glass lid, used for oven-cooking a variety of dishes, as well as referring to the category of foods cooked inside it.
	**Baking Gloves:** An oven glove, or oven mitt, is an insulated glove or mitten usually worn in the kitchen to easily protect the wearer's hand from hot objects such as ovens, stoves, cookware, etc. They are similar to pot-holders.
	**6*6*2-Inch Baking Pan:** This pan use for baking cake, etc.
	**Aluminium Foil:** At home, people use aluminum foil for food storage, to cover baking surfaces and to wrap foods, such as meats, to prevent them from losing moisture while cooking. People may also use aluminum foil to wrap and protect more delicate foods, like vegetables, when grilling them.

	**Non-Stick Cooking Spray:** Put less elbow grease into grating cheese by using a non-stick cooking spray on your cheese grater for smoother grating. The spray also makes for easier and faster clean-up.
	**Parchment Paper:** Baking paper – also known as bakery paper or parchment paper, as it is often called especially in the US – is grease-proof paper that is used in baking and cooking as it provides a heat-resistant, non-stick surface to bake on.
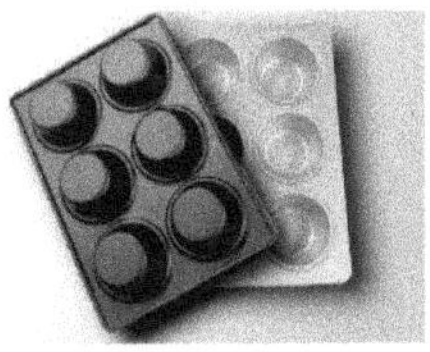	**Muffin Tin:** A type of pan used for baking muffins. ... The muffin batter is poured into the individual pockets and as the muffin bakes, a top forms over the pocket while the base of the muffin is baked in the shape of the cup.
	**Tongs :** Tongs are a type of tool used to grip and lift objects instead of holding them directly with hands. There are many forms of tongs adapted to their specific use.
	**Broiler Pan :** In simple words, a broiler pan is a pan that is used for broiling food. Broiling is a method of cooking in which food is cooked by being exposed to heat directly. Many people confuse broiling with roasting.

Compatible Devices Models

- The 6 Quart Air Fryer Lids are made for use with 6 Quart Instant Pot Multi-Use Pressure Cookers, respectively.

Duo 60 (IP-DUO60, IP-DUO60 V2, IP-DUO60 V2.1, IP-DUO60-ENW, IP-DUO60 V3, Duo 60 V3, Duo Frontier Rose 60, Duo Dazzling Dahlia 60, Duo White 60, Duo Teal 60, Duo Red 60, Duo Black SS 60, Duo Red SS 60, Duo Nova Black SS 60).

Lux 60 (IP-LUX60, Lux Blue 60, Lux Red 60, IP-LUX60 V2, IP-LUX60-ENW, IP-LUX60-ENWMM, IP-LUX60 V3, Lux Breezy Blossoms 60, Lux Vintage Floral 60, Lux Black SS 60, Lux Red SS 60, Lux 60 V3).

Duo Plus 60 (Duo Plus 60, Duo Plus Cinnamon SS 60, Duo Plus Blue SS 60, Duo Plus Copper SS 60, Duo Plus Black SS 60). Ultra 60 (Ultra 60).

Viva 60 (Viva, Viva 60, Viva Cinnamon 60, Viva Cobalt 60, Viva Eggplant 60, Viva Red SS 60, Viva Black SS 60).

Nova Plus 60 (Nova Plus 60).

Duo Nova 60 (Duo Nova 60).

- It is not compatible with the Smart WiFi 60, Duo Evo Plus 6, Duo Evo Plus 60, Duo SV 60, or Max 60. It also is not compatible with 3-quart or 8-quart Instant Pots or with electric pressure cookers made by other companies. In addition, it should only be used with stainless steel inner pots, and not with ceramic non-stick coated inner pots.

Pros and Cons

Pros:

1. It's easy to use and clean: It's super easy to use because the buttons are easy to push and everything about it is very intuitive. Just take a damp towel and wipe!
2. The jingle that you hear with the Instant Pot when you put the lid on correctly is the same with the air fryer lid.
3. I love that halfway through the cooking process, it starts beeping at you and the screen tells you to flip the food. A great reminder to shake that basket!
4. The insert is non-stick and it is a separate, removable bucket that makes for easy washing.
5. I was actually VERY surprised at how much it could fit into the basket. It looks small but when I started using this, it was able to fit 16 ounces of tofu and a lot of chicken wings at once.
6. I actually like the distance between the basket and the air fryer element. It's not right up under the element so some food you cook that may splatter won't get onto the element, which as a result may make clean-up harder.
7. You can use it on several 6-quart Instant Pot
8. It has 6 different pre-set programs
9. It is easy to use and clean

10. You can store it away when not in use
11. Air drying works well - food comes out crispy and even throughout, nothing is burned or under-cooked.
12. The dehydrating feature worke well too - it doesn't seem to get too hot and burn the garlic, and I suspect it works about as fast as a normal dehydrator, albeit with a smaller quantity.
13. While it's bulky, the protective pad is a welcome accessory and makes storing it much easier.

Cons:

1. The temperature doesn't go higher than 400 degrees. I guess I don't know why I'd want it to go higher but I would like at least up to 450 degrees.
2. It's big and bulky BUT it is far better than having another machine.
3. Since the air fryer basket goes into the stainless steel Instant Pot insert, you have to wash both when you're done cooking.
4. That beeping sound (when the lid is off) can be annoying.
5. You must handle it with extra care because of the extreme heat.
6. Does not fit 8-quart pressure cookers (or bigger)
7. Does not fit 4-quart or pressure cookers (or smaller)
8. Particularly for us in the RV, we have to be very cautious about running it at the same time with other big appliances so that we don't trip a breaker.
9. The cord is short, so you'll have to have an outlet that is easily accessible. (This is a safety feature.) It's about the same length as the cord on the Instant Pot itself, but because it sits higher above the counter, it feels a little shorter. DO NOT use the Air Fryer Lid with an extension cord.
10. Sometimes difficult to turn foods. When using the air fryer basket, the upper layer browns the food on top, while the lower layer browns food on the bottom. While you can turn food on the top of the tray easily, I found it difficult to remove the broil tray to turn the food on the bottom rack.

Chapter 2 Using the Instant Pot Air Fryer Lid

How to Start

1. Place the air fryer lid on the instant pot cooker base.
2. Connect air fryer lid power cord to a 120v power source.
3. Select a smart program (air fry, broil, bake, roast, reheat, dehydrate).
4. Time display: The time display shows the time in HH:MM format. It counts up or down, depending on the Smart Program. e + or - to adjust time.
5. Temperature display: The temperature display shows the set temperature in ^{o}C or ^{o}F.
6. + / – Time Press to adjust the time.
7. + / – Temp Press to adjust the cooking temperature in ^{o}C or ^{o}F.
8. Start: Begin the selected Smart Program.
9. Cancel: Stop the Smart Program at any time.
10. About halfway through, the Air Fryer Lid beep loudly, with the words "Turn Food" on its display. I then removed the lid and proceeded to, well, turn the food. From reading other air fryer recipes, this seems to be unique to the Air Fryer Lid.
11. Lift the lid off the instant pot cooker base and place it on the protection pad provided.
12. Turn flip, or rotate your food, then place the air fryer lid on the instant pot cooker base to resume cooking.
13. When the smart program completes, the lid beeps, and the display indicates "end" and "cool". The fan will continue to run for 5 minutes or stop immediately when you lift the lid off.
14. Lift the lid off the instant pot cooker base and place it on the protective pad, or let the air fryer lid keep your food warm for up to 1 hour.
15. Carefully remove your food, serve and enjoy!
16. Including the "turn food" msg and the 'end cool 'msg

How to Clean

1. **Disassemble Before Cleaning:** Always unplug the appliance and let it cool to room temperature before cleaning. Never use metal scouring pads, abrasive powders or harsh chemical detergents on any part or accessory.
2. **Multi-Level Air Fryer Basket:** Dishwasher safe if placed on top rack, otherwise clean with a damp cloth and mild dish soap and rinse well with clear, warm water.
3. **Protective Pad and Storage Cover:** Dishwasher safe if placed on top rack, otherwise clean with a damp cloth and mild dish soap and rinse well with clear, warm water. Use the reverse side of the protective pad to cover the Air Fryer Lid when storing.
4. **Air Fryer Lid:** Clean with a barely-damp cloth and mild dish soap, then use a clean, barely-damp sponge to remove the soap residue. DO NOT wash or submerge in water or other liquid.
    - Always check the element cover for oil spatter and food debris and remove them before turning on the air fryer lid.
    - To remove baked-on grease and food residue, spray the element cover with a mixture of baking soda and vinegar and wipe clean with damp cloth.
    - For stubborn stains, allow the mixture to sit on the affected area for several minutes before scrubbing clean.
5. **Make sure not to use anything more abrasive than a toothbrush to scrub the element cover.**
    - DO NOT remove the element cover.
    - DO NOT rinse or immerse the Air Fryer Lid in water or other liquid.
6. **Outer Body:** Clean with a barely-damp cloth and mild dish soap, then use a clean, barely-damp sponge to remove the soap residue. DO NOT machine-wash.
    - Wipe dry with a soft cloth.
    - DO NOT rinse or immerse the Air Fryer Lid in water or other liquid.
7. **Power Cord:** Wipe clean with a barely-damp cloth as needed.

* *To avoid risk of electrical shock and personal injury:*

- Do not immerse the appliance in water or any liquid.
- Do not rinse the appliance under a tap.
- Do not wet the prongs of the power cord.

Suggestions

The Air Fryer Lid makes your Instant Pot multi cooker even more versatile — whether you want to pressure cook first and use the Air Fryer Lid to crisp up your dish, or if you'd prefer to cook your meal just using the Air Fryer Lid — you can!

Depending on your recipe, you can use the multi-level air fryer basket or any oven-safe cookware to cook or crisp your meal, or, you can place food right in the inner pot. Just make sure you always have the stainless-steel inner pot inserted first!

Here are some suggestions:

1. Remember to preheat the instant pot before cooking, which only takes a few minutes.
2. You can use the air fry lid to fry meat and vegetables, to dehydrate fruit, and to reheat leftovers.
3. Keep a little distance between the chunk food to leave the space for hot air.
4. Remember to spritz the air fryer basket with cooking spray before putting the food in the basket unless the food have the oil already.
5. Air frying works best when you arrange your ingredients in a single layer.
6. Allow the food to cool after cooking.
7. If food could not be made at a single time, try to work in batches.

Conclusion

If you're in the market for an air fryer and already have a compatible 6 quart Instant Pot, I'd highly recommend considering the Instant Pot Air Fryer Lid instead of buying another machine.

I am very happy with mine and although I don't think I'll use it every day, it is definitely something I am happy to have in my cabinets for those days that I do want to use it.

I haven't used all the functions on it (such as broil, bake, roast, dehydrate) but I can see the reheat function work well (if you don't have a microwave) or the broiling option for crisping stuff up quickly.

I do appreciate that the basket is non-stick (but I still spray it a little with cooking spray) and for storage, it's easy to store everything into the stainless steel insert.

Chapter 3 Beef

Beef Roast with Thyme

Prep time: 5 minutes | Cook time: 55 minutes | Serves 4

1½ pounds (680 g) beef eye round roast
1 tablespoon olive oil
Sea salt and ground black pepper, to taste
1 onion, sliced
1 rosemary sprig
1 thyme sprig

1. Toss the beef with the olive oil, salt, and black pepper; place the beef in the air fryer basket.
2. Put the air fryer lid on and roast in the preheated instant pot at 390ºF (199ºC) for 45 minutes. Flip the beef when the lid screen indicates TURN FOOD.
3. Top the beef with the onion, rosemary, and thyme. Continue to cook an additional 10 minutes.
4. Enjoy!

Beef Burgers

Prep time: 5 minutes | Cook time: 15 minutes | Serves 3

¾ pound (340 g) ground beef
2 cloves garlic, minced
1 small onion, chopped
Kosher salt and ground black pepper, to taste
3 hamburger buns

1. Mix the beef, garlic, onion, salt, and black pepper until everything is well combined. Form the mixture into three patties. Place the patties in the air fryer basket.
2. Put the air fryer lid on and air fry in the preheated instant pot at 380ºF (193ºC) for 15 minutes. Flip the burgers when the lid screen indicates TURN FOOD.
3. Serve the burgers on the prepared buns and enjoy!

Garlicky Porterhouse Steak

Prep time: 5 minutes | Cook time: 12 minutes | Serves 4

1½ pounds (680 g) Porterhouse steak
1 tablespoon olive oil
Kosher salt and ground black pepper, to taste
½ teaspoon cayenne pepper
1 teaspoon dried parsley
1 teaspoon dried oregano
½ teaspoon dried basil
2 tablespoons butter
2 garlic cloves, minced

1. Toss the steak with the remaining ingredients; place the steak in the air fryer basket.
2. Put the air fryer lid on and air fry in the preheated instant pot at 400ºF (205ºC) for 12 minutes. Flip the steak when the lid screen indicates TURN FOOD.
3. Bon appétit!

Beef Brisket with Thyme

Prep time: 5 minutes | Cook time: 1 hour | Serves 4

1½ pounds (680 g) beef brisket
2 tablespoons olive oil
1 teaspoon onion powder
1 teaspoon garlic powder
Sea salt and ground black pepper, to taste
1 teaspoon dried parsley flakes
1 teaspoon dried thyme

1. Toss the beef with the remaining ingredients; place the beef in the air fryer basket.
2. Put the air fryer lid on and roast in the preheated instant pot at 390ºF (199ºC) for 15 minutes. Flip the beef when the lid screen indicates TURN FOOD.
3. Reduce the temperature to 360ºF (182ºC). Continue to cook the beef for 55 minutes more. Bon appétit!

Glazed London Broil

Prep time: 5 minutes | Cook time: 28 minutes | Serves 3

1 pound (454 g) London broil
¼ cup soy sauce
¼ cup fresh lemon juice
2 garlic cloves, minced
1 tablespoon paprika
Sea salt and ground black pepper, to taste

1. Toss the beef with the remaining ingredients and let it marinate for an hour.
2. Place the beef in a lightly oiled air fryer basket and discard the marinade.
3. Put the air fryer lid on and roast in the preheated instant pot at 400ºF (205ºC) for 28 minutes. Flip the beef when the lid screen indicates TURN FOOD.
4. Bon appétit!

Garlicky Beef with Mustard

Prep time: 5 minutes | Cook time: 1 hour | Serves 4

1½ pounds (680 g) beef brisket
2 tablespoons olive oil
3 garlic cloves, pressed
Sea salt and ground black pepper, to taste
1 teaspoon crushed red pepper flakes
2 tablespoons tomato ketchup
2 tablespoons Dijon mustard

1. Toss the beef brisket with the olive oil, garlic, salt, black pepper, and red pepper; now, place the beef brisket in the air fryer basket.
2. Put the air fryer lid on and roast in the preheated instant pot at 390ºF (199ºC) for 15 minutes. Flip the beef brisket when the lid screen indicates TURN FOOD.
3. Reduce the temperature to 360ºF (182ºC). Continue to cook the beef brisket for approximately 55 minutes or until cooked through.
4. Shred the beef with two forks; add in the ketchup and mustard and stir to combine well. Bon appétit!

Beef Cheeseburgers Buns

Prep time: 5 minutes | Cook time: 15 minutes | Serves 3

¾ pound (340 g) ground chuck
1 teaspoon minced garlic
2 tablespoons BBQ sauce
Sea salt and ground black pepper, to taste
3 slices cheese
3 hamburger buns

1. Mix the ground chuck, garlic, BBQ sauce, salt, and black pepper until everything is well combined. Form the mixture into four patties.
2. Arrange the patties in the air fryer basket.
3. Put the air fryer lid on and air fry in the preheated instant pot at 380ºF (193ºC) for 15 minutes. Flip the burgers when the lid screen indicates TURN FOOD.
4. Top each burger with cheese. Serve the burgers on the prepared buns and enjoy!

Butter London Broil

Prep time: 5 minutes | Cook time: 28 minutes | Serves 4

1½ pounds (680 g) London broil
Kosher salt and ground black pepper, to taste
¼ teaspoon ground bay leaf
3 tablespoons butter
1 tablespoon Dijon mustard
1 teaspoon crushed garlic
1 tablespoon chopped fresh parsley

1. Toss the beef with the salt and black pepper; place the beef in a lightly oiled air fryer basket.
2. Put the air fryer lid on and roast in the preheated instant pot at 400ºF (205ºC) for 28 minutes. Flip the beef when the lid screen indicates TURN FOOD.
3. In the meantime, mix the butter with the remaining ingredients and place it in the refrigerator until well chilled.
4. Serve warm beef with the chilled garlic butter on the side. Bon appétit!

Strip Steak with Butter

Prep time: 5 minutes | Cook time: 15 minutes | Serves 4

1½ pounds (680 g) New York strip steak
2 tablespoons butter, melted
Sea salt and ground black pepper, to taste
1 teaspoon paprika
1 teaspoon dried thyme
1 teaspoon dried rosemary

1. Toss the beef with the remaining ingredients; place the beef in the air fryer basket.
2. Put the air fryer lid on and air fry in the preheated instant pot at 400ºF (205ºC) for 15 minutes. Flip the beef when the lid screen indicates TURN FOOD.
3. Enjoy!

Beef Cheese Muffins

Prep time: 10 minutes | Cook time: 25 minutes | Serves 4

Meatloaves:
1 pound (454 g) ground beef
¼ cup seasoned bread crumbs
¼ cup grated Parmesan cheese
1 small onion, minced
2 garlic cloves, pressed
1 egg, beaten
Sea salt and ground black pepper, to taste

Glaze:
4 tablespoons tomato sauce
1 tablespoon brown sugar
1 tablespoon Dijon mustard

1. Thoroughly combine all ingredients for the meatloaves until everything is well combined.
2. Scrape the beef mixture into lightly oiled silicone cups and transfer them to the baking dish.
3. Place the baking dish in the air fryer basket. Put the air fryer lid on and bake in the preheated instant pot at 380ºF (193ºC) for 20 minutes.
4. In the meantime, mix the remaining ingredients for the glaze. Then, spread the glaze on top of each muffin; continue to cook for another 5 minutes.
5. Bon appétit!

Beef Brisket Carnitas

Prep time: 5 minutes | Cook time: 1 hour | Serves 4

1½ pounds (680 g) beef brisket
2 tablespoons olive oil
Sea salt and ground black pepper, to taste
1 teaspoon chili powder
4 medium-sized flour tortillas

1. Toss the beef brisket with the olive oil, salt, black pepper, and chili powder; now, place the beef brisket in the air fryer basket.
2. Put the air fryer lid on and roast in the preheated instant pot at 390ºF (199ºC) for 15 minutes. Flip the beef brisket when the lid screen indicates TURN FOOD.
3. Reduce the temperature to 360ºF (182ºC). Continue to cook the beef brisket for approximately 55 minutes or until cooked through.
4. Shred the beef with two forks and serve with tortillas and toppings of choice. Bon appétit!

Shallots Beef Meatloaf

Prep time: 10 minutes | Cook time: 25 minutes | Serves 4

1½ pounds (680 g) ground chuck
1 egg, beaten
2 tablespoons olive oil
4 tablespoons crushed crackers
½ cup minced shallots
2 garlic cloves, minced
1 tablespoon chopped fresh rosemary
1 tablespoon chopped fresh thyme
Sea salt and ground black pepper, to taste

1. Thoroughly combine all ingredients until everything is well combined.
2. Scrape the beef mixture into a lightly oiled baking dish.
3. Place the baking dish in the air fryer basket. Put the air fryer lid on and bake in the preheated instant pot at 390ºF (199ºC) for 25 minutes.
4. Bon appétit!

Red Wine Chuck Roast

Prep time: 5 minutes | Cook time: 55 minutes | Serves 5

½ cup red wine
1 tablespoon Dijon mustard
1 tablespoon minced fresh garlic
1 teaspoon crushed red pepper flakes
Sea salt and ground black pepper, to taste
2 pounds (907 g) chuck roast
1 tablespoon corn flour

1. Place the wine, mustard, garlic, red pepper, salt, black pepper, and chuck roast in a ceramic bowl. Cover the bowl and let the meat marinate for 3 hours in the refrigerator.
2. Toss the roast beef with the corn flour; place the roast beef in the air fryer basket.
3. Put the air fryer lid on and roast in the preheated instant pot at 390ºF (199ºC) for 55 minutes. Flip the roast beef when the lid screen indicates TURN FOOD.
4. Enjoy!

Lemony London Broil

Prep time: 10 minutes | Cook time: 28 minutes | Serves 4

1 pound (454 g) London broil
Kosher salt and ground black pepper, to taste
2 tablespoons olive oil
1 small lemon, freshly squeezed
3 cloves garlic, minced
1 tablespoon chopped fresh parsley
1 tablespoon chopped fresh coriander

1. Toss the beef with the remaining ingredients and let it marinate for an hour.
2. Place the beef in a lightly oiled air fryer basket and discard the marinade.
3. Put the air fryer lid on and roast in the preheated instant pot at 400ºF (205ºC) for 28 minutes. Flip the beef when the lid screen indicates TURN FOOD.
4. Bon appétit!

Ribeye Steak with Rosemary

Prep time: 5 minutes | Cook time: 15 minutes | Serves 4

1 pound (454 g) ribeye steak, bone-in
2 tablespoons butter, room temperature
2 garlic cloves, minced
Sea salt and ground black pepper, to taste
2 rosemary sprigs, leaves picked and chopped

1. Toss the ribeye steak with the butter, garlic, salt, black pepper, and rosemary; place the steak in the air fryer basket.
2. Put the air fryer lid on and air fry in the preheated instant pot at 400ºF (205ºC) for 15 minutes. Flip the ribeye steak when the lid screen indicates TURN FOOD.
3. Bon appétit!

Beef with Oregano

Prep time: 10 minutes | Cook time: 1 hour | Serves 4

1½ pounds (680 g) beef brisket
2 tablespoons olive oil
Sea salt and freshly ground black pepper, to taste
1 teaspoon dried oregano
1 teaspoon mustard powder
½ teaspoon ground cumin
2 cloves garlic, minced
2 tablespoons chopped chives
2 tablespoons chopped cilantro

1. Toss the beef brisket with the rest of the ingredients; now, place the beef brisket in the air fryer basket.
2. Put the air fryer lid on and roast in the preheated instant pot at 390ºF (199ºC) for 15 minutes. Flip the beef brisket when the lid screen indicates TURN FOOD.
3. Reduce the temperature to 360ºF (182ºC). Continue to cook the beef brisket for approximately 55 minutes or until cooked through.
4. Shred the beef with two forks and serve with toppings of choice. Bon appétit!

Mushroom and Beef Patties Rolls

Prep time: 5 minutes | Cook time: 15 minutes | Serves 4

1 pound (454 g) ground chuck
2 garlic cloves, minced
1 small onion, chopped
1 cup chopped mushrooms
1 teaspoon cayenne pepper
Sea salt and ground black pepper, to taste
4 brioche rolls

1. Mix the ground chuck, garlic, onion, mushrooms, cayenne pepper, salt, and black pepper until everything is well combined. Form the mixture into four patties.
2. Arrange the patties in the air fryer basket.
3. Put the air fryer lid on and air fry in the preheated instant pot at 380ºF (193ºC) for 15 minutes. Flip the patties when the lid screen indicates TURN FOOD.
4. Serve the patties on the prepared brioche rolls and enjoy!

Tenderloin Steaks with Mushrooms

Prep time: 10 minutes | Cook time: 15 minutes | Serves 4

1½ pounds (680 g) tenderloin steaks
2 tablespoons butter, melted
1 teaspoon garlic powder
½ teaspoon mustard powder
1 teaspoon cayenne pepper
Sea salt and ground black pepper, to taste
½ pound (227 g) cremini mushrooms, sliced

1. Toss the beef with 1 tablespoon of the butter and spices; place the beef in the air fryer basket.
2. Put the air fryer lid on and roast in the preheated instant pot at 400ºF (205ºC) for 10 minutes. Flip the beef when the lid screen indicates TURN FOOD.
3. Add in the mushrooms along with the remaining 1 tablespoon of the butter. Continue to cook for an additional 5 minutes. Serve warm.
4. Bon appétit!

Steak Buns with Mustard

Prep time: 5 minutes | Cook time: 15 minutes | Serves 4

1½ pounds (680 g) skirt steak
1 teaspoon steak dry rub
½ teaspoon cayenne pepper
Sea salt and ground black pepper, to taste
2 tablespoons olive oil
2 tablespoons Dijon mustard
8 Hawaiian buns

1. Toss the beef with the spices and olive oil; place the beef in the air fryer basket.
2. Put the air fryer lid on and air fry in the preheated instant pot at 400ºF (205ºC) for 15 minutes. Flip the beef when the lid screen indicates TURN FOOD.
3. Cut the beef into slices and serve them with mustard and Hawaiian buns. Bon appétit!

Basil Butter Steak

Prep time: 10 minutes | Cook time: 12 minutes | Serves 5

2 pounds (907 g) ribeye steaks, bone-in
Kosher salt and freshly ground black pepper, to taste
3 tablespoons butter
1 tablespoon minced fresh basil
1 tablespoon minced fresh parsley
2 tablespoons minced fresh scallions
2 cloves garlic, minced
Kosher salt and freshly ground black pepper, to taste

1. Toss the steak with the salt and black pepper; place the steak in a lightly oiled air fryer basket.
2. Put the air fryer lid on and air fry in the preheated instant pot at 400ºF (205ºC) for 12 minutes. Flip the steak when the lid screen indicates TURN FOOD.
3. In the meantime, mix the butter with the remaining ingredients and place it in the refrigerator until well chilled.
4. Serve the warm steak with the chilled herb butter and enjoy!

Butter Short Loin

Prep time: 10 minutes | Cook time: 14 minutes | Serves 5

2 pounds (907 g) short loin, sliced
2 tablespoons butter, room temperature
1 tablespoon dark brown sugar
1 teaspoon coarse sea salt
1 teaspoon ground black pepper
1 teaspoon cayenne pepper
1 teaspoon ground coriander

1. Toss the short loin with the remaining ingredients; place the short loin in the air fryer basket.
2. Put the air fryer lid on and air fry in the preheated instant pot at 400ºF (205ºC) for 14 minutes. Flip the short loin when the lid screen indicates TURN FOOD.
3. Bon appétit!

Lemony London Broil

Prep time: 5 minutes | Cook time: 28 minutes | Serves 4

1 pound (454 g) London broil
¼ cup freshly squeezed lemon juice
¼ cup olive oil
2 tablespoons tamari sauce
1 tablespoon stone-ground mustard
1 teaspoon mixed peppercorns
3 tablespoons cold butter
2 tablespoons fresh Italian herbs
1 teaspoon garlic powder
½ teaspoon kosher salt

1. Toss the beef with the lemon juice, olive oil, tamari sauce, mustard, and peppercorns; let it marinate for an hour.
2. Place the beef in a lightly oiled air fryer basket and discard the marinade.
3. Put the air fryer lid on and roast in the preheated instant pot at 400ºF (205ºC) for 28 minutes. Flip the beef when the lid screen indicates TURN FOOD.
4. Meanwhile, mix the butter, herbs, garlic powder, and salt. Serve warm beef with the chilled herb butter on the side.
5. Bon appétit!

Steak Salad with Tomato

Prep time: 10 minutes | Cook time: 12 minutes | Serves 5

2 pounds (907 g) T-bone steak
1 teaspoon garlic powder
Sea salt and ground black pepper, to taste
2 tablespoons lime juice
¼ cup extra-virgin olive oil
1 bell pepper, seeded and sliced
1 red onion, sliced
1 tomato, diced

1. Toss the steak with the garlic powder, salt, and black pepper; place the steak in the air fryer basket.
2. Put the air fryer lid on and air fry in the preheated instant pot at 400ºF (205ºC) for 12 minutes. Flip the steak when the lid screen indicates TURN FOOD.
3. Cut the steak into slices and add in the remaining ingredients. Serve at room temperature or well chilled.
4. Bon appétit!

Spicy Beef Meatloaf

Prep time: 10 minutes | Cook time: 25 minutes | Serves 4

1½ pounds (680 g) ground chuck
½ onion, chopped
1 teaspoon minced habanero pepper
¼ cup crushed tortilla chips
1 teaspoon minced garlic
Sea salt and ground black pepper, to taste
2 tablespoons olive oil
1 egg, whisked

1. Thoroughly combine all ingredients until everything is well combined.
2. Scrape the beef mixture into a lightly oiled baking dish.
3. Place the baking dish in the air fryer basket. Put the air fryer lid on and bake in the preheated instant pot at 390ºF (199ºC) for 25 minutes. Flip the meatloaf when the lid screen indicates TURN FOOD.
4. Bon appétit!

Beef Filet Mignon with Mustard

Prep time: 5 minutes | Cook time: 14 minutes | Serves 4

1 pound (454 g) beef filet mignon
Sea salt and ground black pepper, to taste
1 teaspoon cayenne pepper
3 tablespoons olive oil
1 tablespoon Dijon mustard
4 tablespoons dry French wine

1. Toss the filet mignon with the rest of the ingredients; place the filet mignon in the air fryer basket.
2. Put the air fryer lid on and air fry in the preheated instant pot at 400ºF (205ºC) for 14 minutes. Flip the filet mignon when the lid screen indicates TURN FOOD.
3. Enjoy!

Beef Brisket with Ketchup

Prep time: 5 minutes | Cook time: 1 hour | Serves 4

1½ pounds (680 g) beef brisket
2 tablespoons tomato ketchup
1 tablespoon brown mustard
1 teaspoon chili powder
2 tablespoons salt
1 teaspoon garlic powder
1 teaspoon onion powder
1 tablespoon ground black pepper
1 tablespoon brown sugar

1. Toss the beef with the remaining ingredients; place the beef in the air fryer basket.
2. Put the air fryer lid on and roast in the preheated instant pot at 390ºF (199ºC) for 15 minutes. Flip the beef when the lid screen indicates TURN FOOD.
3. Reduce the temperature to 360ºF (182ºC). Continue to cook the beef for 55 minutes more or until cooked through.
4. Bon appétit!

Beef Roast Rolls

Prep time: 5 minutes | Cook time: 50 minutes | Serves 4

1½ pounds (680 g) bottom round roast
2 tablespoons olive oil
2 garlic cloves, minced
1 teaspoon rosemary
1 teaspoon parsley
1 teaspoon oregano
Sea salt and freshly ground black pepper, to taste

1. Toss the beef with the spices, garlic, and olive oil; place the beef in the air fryer basket.
2. Put the air fryer lid on and roast in the preheated instant pot at 390ºF (199ºC) for 50 minutes. Flip the beef when the lid screen indicates TURN FOOD.
3. Cut the beef into slices and serve them with dinner rolls. Bon appétit!

Mushroom and Beef Muffins

Prep time: 5 minutes | Cook time: 25 minutes | Serves 4

1 pound (454 g) ground beef
1 egg, beaten
1 teaspoon Dijon mustard
Sea salt and ground black pepper, to taste
½ onion, minced
½ cup mushrooms
¼ cup seasoned bread crumbs
1 teaspoon Italian seasoning mix
½ cup ketchup

1. Thoroughly combine all ingredients , except for the ketchup; mix until everything is well combined.
2. Scrape the beef mixture into lightly oiled silicone cups and transfer them to the baking dish.
3. Place the baking dish in the air fryer basket. Put the air fryer lid on and bake in the preheated instant pot at 380ºF (193ºC) for 20 minutes.
4. Then, spread the ketchup on the top of each muffin and continue cooking for another 5 minutes.
5. Bon appétit!

Broccoli and Beef Patties

Prep time: 10 minutes | Cook time: 15 minutes | Serves 4

1 pound (454 g) beef
½ pound (227 g) broccoli, minced
1 small onion, chopped
2 garlic cloves, minced
Sea salt and ground black pepper, to taste
1 tablespoon tamari sauce

1. In a mixing bowl, thoroughly combine all ingredients . Shape the mixture into four patties. Arrange the patties in the air fryer basket.
2. Put the air fryer lid on and air fry in the preheated instant pot at 380ºF (193ºC) for 15 minutes. Flip the burgers when the lid screen indicates TURN FOOD.
3. Serve the warm patties with the topping of choice. Bon appétit!

Coulotte Roast with Garlic

Prep time: 10 minutes | Cook time: 55 minutes | Serves 5

2 pounds (907 g) Coulotte roast
2 tablespoons olive oil
1 tablespoon finely chopped fresh parsley
1 tablespoon finely chopped fresh cilantro
2 garlic cloves, minced
Kosher salt and ground black pepper, to taste

1. Toss the roast beef with the remaining ingredients; place the roast beef in the air fryer basket.
2. Put the air fryer lid on and roast in the preheated instant pot at 390ºF (199ºC) for 55 minutes. Flip the roast beef when the lid screen indicates TURN FOOD.
3. Enjoy!

Garlicky Roasted Beef

Prep time: 5 minutes | Cook time: 55 minutes | Serves 4

1½ pounds (680 g) eye round roast
4 cloves garlic, peeled and thinly sliced
2 tablespoons olive oil
Kosher salt and ground black pepper, to taste

1. Pierce the beef with a sharp knife and insert the garlic slices into the holes.
2. Toss the meat with the oil, salt, and black pepper and transfer it to the air fryer basket.
3. Put the air fryer lid on and roast in the preheated instant pot at 390ºF (199ºC) for 55 minutes. Flip the beef when the lid screen indicates TURN FOOD.
4. Enjoy!

Paprika Beef Rolls

Prep time: 5 minutes | Cook time: 15 minutes | Serves 4

1 pound (454 g) ground beef
½ teaspoon garlic powder
½ teaspoon onion powder
1 teaspoon paprika
Sea salt and ground black pepper, to taste
8 dinner rolls

1. Mix all ingredients , except for the dinner rolls. Shape the mixture into four patties. Arrange the patties in the air fryer basket.
2. Put the air fryer lid on and air fry in the preheated instant pot at 380ºF (193ºC) for 15 minutes. Flip the burgers when the lid screen indicates TURN FOOD.
3. Serve the burgers on the prepared dinner rolls and enjoy!

Butter Filet Mignon

Prep time: 5 minutes | Cook time: 14 minutes | Serves 4

1½ pounds (680 g) filet mignon
2 tablespoons soy sauce
2 tablespoons butter, melted
1 teaspoon mustard powder
1 teaspoon garlic powder
Sea salt and ground black pepper, to taste

1. Toss the filet mignon with the remaining ingredients; place the filet mignon in the air fryer basket.
2. Put the air fryer lid on and air fry in the preheated instant pot at 400ºF (205ºC) for 14 minutes. Flip the filet mignon when the lid screen indicates TURN FOOD.
3. Enjoy!

Beef Burgers Buns

Prep time: 5 minutes | Cook time: 15 minutes | Serves 3

¾ pound (340 g) ground beef
2 tablespoons minced onion
1 teaspoon minced garlic
1 teaspoon cayenne pepper
Sea salt and ground black pepper, to taste
1 teaspoon red chili powder
3 hamburger buns

1. Mix the beef, onion, garlic, cayenne pepper, salt, black pepper, and red chili powder until everything is well combined. Form the mixture into three patties. Place the patties in the air fryer basket.
2. Put the air fryer lid on and air fry in the preheated instant pot at 380ºF (193ºC) for 15 minutes. Flip the burgers when the lid screen indicates TURN FOOD.
3. Serve the burgers on the prepared buns and enjoy!

Beef Roast with Carrot

Prep time: 10 minutes | Cook time: 55 minutes | Serves 5

2 pounds (907 g) top sirloin roast
2 tablespoons olive oil
Sea salt and ground black pepper, to taste
2 carrots, sliced
1 tablespoon fresh coriander
1 tablespoon fresh thyme
1 tablespoon fresh rosemary

1. Toss the beef with the olive oil, salt, and black pepper; place the beef in the air fryer basket.
2. Put the air fryer lid on and roast in the preheated instant pot at 390ºF (199ºC) for 45 minutes. Flip the beef when the lid screen indicates TURN FOOD.
3. Top the beef with the carrots and herbs. Continue to cook for an additional 10 minutes.
4. Enjoy!

Filet Mignon with Basil

Prep time: 5 minutes | Cook time: 14 minutes | Serves 4

1½ pounds (680 g) filet mignon
Sea salt and ground black pepper, to taste
2 tablespoons olive oil
1 teaspoon dried rosemary
1 teaspoon dried thyme
1 teaspoon dried basil
2 cloves garlic, minced

1. Toss the beef with the remaining ingredients; place the beef in the air fryer basket.
2. Put the air fryer lid on and air fry in the preheated instant pot at 400ºF (205ºC) for 14 minutes. Flip the beef when the lid screen indicates TURN FOOD.
3. Enjoy!

Ribeye Steak with Butter

Prep time: 5 minutes | Cook time: 15 minutes | Serves 4

1½ pounds (680 g) ribeye steak, bone-in
2 tablespoons butter
1 Montreal seasoning mix
Sea salt and ground black pepper, to taste

1. Toss the ribeye steak with the remaining ingredients; place the ribeye steak in a lightly oiled air fryer basket.
2. Put the air fryer lid on and air fry in the preheated instant pot at 400ºF (205ºC) for 15 minutes. Flip the ribeye steak when the lid screen indicates TURN FOOD.
3. Bon appétit!

Beef Brisket with BBQ Sauce

Prep time: 5 minutes | Cook time: 1 hour | Serves 4

1½ pounds (680 g) beef brisket
¼ cup barbecue sauce
2 tablespoons soy sauce

1. Toss the beef with the remaining ingredients; place the beef in the air fryer basket.
2. Put the air fryer lid on and roast in the preheated instant pot at 390ºF (199ºC) for 15 minutes. Flip the beef when the lid screen indicates TURN FOOD.
3. Reduce the temperature to 360ºF (182ºC). Continue to cook the beef for 55 minutes more.
4. Bon appétit!

Red Wine Rump Roast

Prep time: 5 minutes | Cook time: 55 minutes | Serves 4

1½ pounds (680 g) rump roast
2 tablespoons olive oil
Sea salt and ground black pepper, to taste
1 teaspoon Italian seasoning mix
1 onion, sliced
2 cloves garlic, peeled
¼ cup red wine

1. Toss the rump roast with the rest of the ingredients; place the rump roast in a lightly oiled air fryer basket.
2. Put the air fryer lid on and roast in the preheated instant pot at 390ºF (199ºC) for 55 minutes. Flip the rump roast when the lid screen indicates TURN FOOD.
3. Bon appétit!

Skirt Steak with Garlic

Prep time: 5 minutes | Cook time: 12 minutes | Serves 4

1½ pounds (680 g) skirt steak
Kosher salt and freshly cracked black pepper, to taste
1 teaspoon cayenne pepper
¼ teaspoon cumin powder
2 tablespoons olive oil
2 garlic cloves, minced

1. Toss the steak with the other ingredients; place the steak in the air fryer basket.
2. Put the air fryer lid on and air fry in the preheated instant pot at 400ºF (205ºC) for 12 minutes. Flip the steak when the lid screen indicates TURN FOOD.
3. Bon appétit!

Filet Mignon with Herb

Prep time: 5 minutes | Cook time: 14 minutes | Serves 4

1½ pounds (680 g) filet mignon
2 tablespoons olive oil
2 cloves garlic, pressed
1 tablespoon Italian herb mix
1 teaspoon cayenne pepper
Kosher salt and freshly ground black pepper, to taste

1. Toss the beef with the remaining ingredients; place the beef in the air fryer basket.
2. Put the air fryer lid on and air fry in the preheated instant pot at 400ºF (205ºC) for 14 minutes. Flip the beef when the lid screen indicates TURN FOOD.
3. Enjoy!

Flank Steak with Paprika

Prep time: 5 minutes | Cook time: 12 minutes | Serves 5

2 pounds (907 g) flank steak
2 tablespoons olive oil
1 teaspoon paprika
Sea salt and ground black pepper, to taste

1. Toss the steak with the remaining ingredients; place the steak in the air fryer basket.
2. Put the air fryer lid on and air fry in the preheated instant pot at 400ºF (205ºC) for 12 minutes. Flip the steak when the lid screen indicates TURN FOOD.
3. Bon appétit!

Rump Roast with Paprika

Prep time: 5 minutes | Cook time: 50 minutes | Serves 4

1½ pounds (680 g) rump roast
Ground black pepper and kosher salt, to taste
1 teaspoon paprika
2 tablespoons olive oil
¼ cup brandy
2 tablespoons cold butter

1. Toss the rump roast with the black pepper, salt, paprika, olive oil, and brandy; place the rump roast in a lightly oiled air fryer basket.
2. Put the air fryer lid on and roast in the preheated instant pot at 390ºF (199ºC) for 50 minutes. Flip the rump roast when the lid screen indicates TURN FOOD.
3. Serve with the cold butter and enjoy!

Beef Sausage with Peppers

Prep time: 5 minutes | Cook time: 15 minutes | Serves 4

1 pound (454 g) smoked beef sausage
2 bell peppers, sliced
2 garlic cloves, pressed
2 tablespoons olive oil
1 teaspoon sage
1 teaspoon thyme
Sea salt and red pepper, to taste

1. Toss all ingredients in a lightly oiled air fryer basket.
2. Put the air fryer lid on and air fry in the preheated instant pot at 380ºF (193ºC) for 15 minutes. Flip the sausage when the lid screen indicates TURN FOOD.
3. Serve warm and enjoy!

Rosemary Beef Roast

Prep time: 10 minutes | Cook time: 55 minutes | Serves 5

2 pounds (907 g) top round roast
2 tablespoons extra-virgin olive oil
2 cloves garlic, pressed
1 tablespoon chopped fresh rosemary
1 tablespoon chopped fresh parsley
1 teaspoon red chili powder
Kosher salt and freshly ground black pepper, to taste

1. Toss the beef with the remaining ingredients; place the beef in the air fryer basket.
2. Put the air fryer lid on and roast in the preheated instant pot at 390ºF (199ºC) for 55 minutes. Flip the beef when the lid screen indicates TURN FOOD.
3. Enjoy!

Coulotte Roast with Butter

Prep time: 5 minutes | Cook time: 55 minutes | Serves 5

2 pounds (907 g) Coulotte roast
2 tablespoons butter
Kosher salt and ground black pepper, to taste
1 teaspoon ground allspice
1 teaspoon minced garlic

1. Toss the beef with the remaining ingredients; place the beef in the air fryer basket.
2. Put the air fryer lid on and roast in the preheated instant pot at 390ºF (199ºC) for 55 minutes. Flip the beef when the lid screen indicates TURN FOOD.
3. Enjoy!

Beef Sausage with Potato

Prep time: 10 minutes | Cook time: 15 minutes | Serves 4

8 baby potatoes, scrubbed and halved
4 smoked beef sausages
1 teaspoon Italian seasoning mix

1. Toss all ingredients in a lightly oiled air fryer basket.
2. Put the air fryer lid on and air fry in the preheated instant pot at 400ºF (205ºC) for 15 minutes. Flip the sausage when the lid screen indicates TURN FOOD.
3. Serve warm and enjoy!

Chuck Eye Steak

Prep time: 5 minutes | Cook time: 12 minutes | Serves 4

1½ pounds (680 g) chuck eye steak
2 tablespoons olive oil
1 teaspoon paprika
1 tablespoon Dijon mustard
Kosher salt and ground black pepper, to taste

1. Toss the steak with the remaining ingredients; place the steak in the air fryer basket.
2. Put the air fryer lid on and air fry in the preheated instant pot at 400ºF (205ºC) for 12 minutes. Flip the steak when the lid screen indicates TURN FOOD.
3. Bon appétit!

Scotch Tender with Mustard

Prep time: 5 minutes | Cook time: 55 minutes | Serves 4

1½ pounds (680 g) Scotch tender
2 garlic cloves, pressed
1 tablespoon stone-ground mustard
2 tablespoons balsamic vinegar
2 tablespoons soy sauce
2 tablespoons olive oil
1 teaspoon garlic powder
Kosher salt and ground black pepper, to taste

1. Toss the Scotch tender with the remaining ingredients; place the Scotch tender in the air fryer basket.
2. Put the air fryer lid on and roast in the preheated instant pot at 390ºF (199ºC) for 55 minutes. Flip the Scotch tender when the lid screen indicates TURN FOOD.
3. Enjoy!

Panko Beef Rolls

Prep time: 8 minutes | Cook time: 15 minutes | Serves 4

1 pound (454 g) ground beef
1 cup seasoned bread crumbs
1 tablespoon finely chopped fresh cilantro
1 tablespoon finely chopped fresh parsley
8 Hawaiian butter dinner rolls

1. Mix all ingredients , except for the rolls. Shape the mixture into four patties. Arrange the patties in the air fryer basket.
2. Put the air fryer lid on and air fry in the preheated instant pot at 380ºF (193ºC) for 15 minutes. Flip the burgers when the lid screen indicates TURN FOOD.
3. Serve the burgers on the prepared rolls and enjoy!

Beef Steaks with Fish Sauce

Prep time: 5 minutes | Cook time: 14 minutes | Serves 4

1½ pounds (680 g) Tomahawk steaks
2 bell peppers, sliced
2 tablespoons butter, melted
2 teaspoons Montreal steak seasoning
2 tablespoons fish sauce
Sea salt and ground black pepper, to taste

1. Toss all ingredients in the air fryer basket.
2. Put the air fryer lid on and air fry in the preheated instant pot at 400ºF (205ºC) for 14 minutes. Flip the steak when the lid screen indicates TURN FOOD.
3. Bon appétit!

Ribeye Steak with Cheese

Prep time: 5 minutes | Cook time: 15 minutes | Serves 4

1 pound (454 g) ribeye steak, bone-in
Sea salt and ground black pepper, to taste
2 tablespoons olive oil
½ teaspoon onion powder
1 teaspoon garlic powder
1 cup crumbled blue cheese

1. Toss the ribeye steak with the salt, black pepper, olive oil, onion powder, and garlic powder; place the ribeye steak in the air fryer basket.
2. Put the air fryer lid on and air fry in the preheated instant pot at 400ºF (205ºC) for 15 minutes. Flip the ribeye steak when the lid screen indicates TURN FOOD.
3. Top the ribeye steak with the cheese and serve warm. Bon appétit!

Garlicky Beef Tenderloin

Prep time: 10 minutes | Cook time: 20 minutes | Serves 4

1½ pounds (680 g) beef tenderloin, sliced
2 tablespoons sesame oil
1 teaspoon five-spice powder
2 garlic cloves, minced
1 teaspoon peeled and grated fresh ginger
2 tablespoons soy sauce

1. Toss the beef tenderloin with the remaining ingredients; place the beef tenderloin in the air fryer basket.
2. Put the air fryer lid on and air fry in the preheated instant pot at 400ºF (205ºC) for 20 minutes. Flip the beef tenderloin when the lid screen indicates TURN FOOD.
3. Enjoy!

Beef Shoulder with Onion

Prep time: 5 minutes | Cook time: 55 minutes | Serves 4

1½ pounds (680 g) beef shoulder
Sea salt and ground black pepper, to taste
1 teaspoon cayenne pepper
½ teaspoon ground cumin
2 tablespoons olive oil
2 cloves garlic, minced
1 teaspoon Dijon mustard
1 onion, cut into slices

1. Toss the beef with the spices, garlic, mustard, and olive oil; place the beef in a lightly oiled air fryer basket.
2. Put the air fryer lid on and roast in the preheated instant pot at 390ºF (199ºC) for 45 minutes. Flip the beef when the lid screen indicates TURN FOOD.
3. Add in the onion and continue to cook for an additional 10 minutes.
4. Bon appétit!

Chuck Eye Roast with Tomato

Prep time: 10 minutes | Cook time: 55 minutes | Serves 4

1½ pounds (680 g) chuck eye roast
Sea salt and ground black pepper, to taste
1 teaspoon crushed red pepper flakes
2 tablespoons olive oil, melted
1 jalapeño pepper, chopped
1 large-sized tomato, sliced

1. Toss the roast beef with the salt, black pepper, salt, red pepper flakes, and olive oil; place the roast beef in a lightly oiled air fryer basket.
2. Put the air fryer lid on and roast in the preheated instant pot at 390ºF (199ºC) for 45 minutes. Flip the roast beef when the lid screen indicates TURN FOOD.
3. Top the roast beef with the tomato and jalapeño pepper. Continue to cook for 10 minutes more. Enjoy!

Buttery Ribeye Steak

Prep time: 5 minutes | Cook time: 15 minutes | Serves 4

1½ pounds (680 g) ribeye steak
Sea salt and freshly ground black pepper, to taste
1 tablespoon olive oil
2 garlic cloves, minced
½ stick cold butter, cut into cubes

1. Toss the ribeye steak with the salt, black pepper, olive oil, and garlic; place the ribeye steak in the air fryer basket.
2. Put the air fryer lid on and air fry in the preheated instant pot at 400ºF (205ºC) for 15 minutes. Flip the ribeye steak when the lid screen indicates TURN FOOD.
3. Top the ribeye steak with the butter and serve warm. Bon appétit!

Beef Shoulder with Garlic

Prep time: 5 minutes | Cook time: 1 hour | Serves 5

2 pounds (907 g) beef shoulder
Kosher salt and ground black pepper, to taste
2 garlic cloves, minced
1 tablespoon Italian seasoning mix

1. Toss the beef shoulder with the remaining ingredients; now, place the beef shoulder in the air fryer basket.
2. Put the air fryer lid on and roast in the preheated instant pot at 390ºF (199ºC) for 15 minutes. Flip the beef shoulder when the lid screen indicates TURN FOOD.
3. Reduce the temperature to 360ºF (182ºC). Continue to cook the beef shoulder for approximately 55 minutes or until cooked through.
4. Shred the beef shoulder with two forks and serve with toppings of choice. Bon appétit!

Chapter 4 Pork

Smoked Paprika Pork Loin Chops

Prep time: 5 minutes | Cook time: 15 minutes | Serves 4

1 pound (454 g) pork loin chops
1 tablespoon olive oil
Sea salt and ground black pepper, to taste
1 tablespoon smoked paprika

1. Place all ingredients in a lightly greased air fryer basket.
2. Put the air fryer lid on and air fry in the preheated instant pot at 400ºF (205ºC) for 15 minutes. Flip the pork loin chops when the lid screen indicates TURN FOOD.
3. Bon appétit!

Bacon Salad with Croutons

Prep time: 15 minutes | Cook time: 16 minutes | Serves 5

1 pound (454 g) bacon, cut into thick slices
1 head lettuce, torn into leaves
1 tablespoon chopped fresh chives
1 tablespoon chopped fresh tarragon
1 tablespoon chopped fresh parsley
2 tablespoons freshly squeezed lemon juice
2 garlic cloves, minced
Coarse sea salt and ground black pepper, to taste
1 teaspoon crushed red pepper flakes
2 cups bread cubes

1. Place the bacon in the air fryer basket.
2. Put the air fryer lid on and air fry in the preheated instant pot at 400ºF (205ºC) for 10 minutes. Flip the bacon when the lid screen indicates TURN FOOD. Reserve.
3. Reduce the temperature to 390ºF (199ºC). Add the bread cubes and air fry for approximately 6 minutes or until the bread is toasted.
4. Toss the remaining ingredients in a salad bowl; top the salad with the bacon and croutons. Bon appétit!

Scallions Pork Dinner Rolls

Prep time: 10 minutes | Cook time: 15 minutes | Serves 4

1 pound (454 g) ground pork
Sea salt and freshly ground black pepper, to taste
1 teaspoon crushed red pepper flakes
½ cup chopped scallions
2 garlic cloves, minced
1 tablespoon olive oil
1 tablespoon soy sauce
8 dinner rolls, split

1. In a mixing bowl, thoroughly combine the pork, spices, scallions, garlic, olive oil, and soy sauce. Form the mixture into four patties.
2. Arrange the patties in the air fryer basket.
3. Put the air fryer lid on and air fry in the preheated instant pot at 380ºF (193ºC) for 15 minutes. Flip the patties when the lid screen indicates TURN FOOD.
4. Serve the patties in dinner rolls and enjoy!

Pork Roast with Paprika

Prep time: 5 minutes | Cook time: 55 minutes | Serves 4

1½ pounds (680 g) center-cut pork roast
1 tablespoon olive oil
Sea salt and freshly ground black pepper, to taste
1 teaspoon garlic powder
1 teaspoon hot paprika
½ teaspoon dried parsley flakes
½ teaspoon dried rosemary

1. Toss all ingredients in a lightly greased air fryer basket.
2. Put the air fryer lid on and roast in the preheated instant pot at 360ºF (182ºC) for 55 minutes. Flip the pork when the lid screen indicates TURN FOOD.
3. Serve warm and enjoy!

Pork Spareribs

Prep time: 5 minutes | Cook time: 35 minutes | Serves 4

2 pounds (907 g) pork spareribs
1 teaspoon coarse sea salt
1/3 teaspoon freshly ground black pepper
1 tablespoon brown sugar
1 teaspoon cayenne pepper
1 teaspoon garlic powder
1 teaspoon mustard powder

1. Toss all ingredients in a lightly greased air fryer basket.
2. Put the air fryer lid on and roast in the preheated instant pot at 350ºF (180ºC) for 35 minutes. Flip the pork ribs when the lid screen indicates TURN FOOD.
3. Bon appétit!

Pork Cheese Burgers

Prep time: 8 minutes | Cook time: 15 minutes | Serves 4

1 pound (454 g) ground pork
Sea salt and ground black pepper, to taste
1 tablespoon Italian herb mix
1 small onion, chopped
1 teaspoon minced garlic
¼ cup grated Parmesan cheese
¼ cup seasoned bread crumbs
1 egg
4 hamburger buns
4 teaspoons Dijon mustard
4 tablespoons mayonnaise

1. In a mixing bowl, thoroughly combine the pork, spices, onion, garlic, Parmesan, bread crumbs, and egg. Form the mixture into four patties.
2. Arrange the patties in the air fryer basket.
3. Put the air fryer lid on and air fry in the preheated instant pot at 380ºF (193ºC) for 15 minutes. Flip the burgers when the lid screen indicates TURN FOOD.
4. Serve the burgers with hamburger buns, mustard, and mayonnaise. Enjoy!

Cheese Pork with Mushrooms

Prep time: 10 minutes | Cook time: 15 minutes | Serves 4

1½ pounds (680 g) pork tenderloin
Sea salt and ground black pepper, to taste
2 tablespoons olive oil
1 pound (454 g) mushrooms, sliced
2 ounces (57 g) blue cheese

1. Toss the pork with salt, black pepper, and olive oil. Transfer the pork to a lightly greased air fryer basket.
2. Put the air fryer lid on and air fry in the preheated instant pot at 400ºF (205ºC) for 10 minutes. Flip the pork when the lid screen indicates TURN FOOD.
3. Top the pork with the mushrooms. Continue to cook for about 5 minutes longer. Top the warm pork with blue cheese.
4. Bon appétit!

Pork Cheese Sandwich

Prep time: 10 minutes | Cook time: 55 minutes | Serves 4

1½ pounds (680 g) pork butt
1 teaspoon stone-ground mustard
½ teaspoon ground cumin
2 cloves garlic, crushed
Kosher salt and freshly ground black pepper, to taste
½ teaspoon ground allspice
2 tablespoons fresh pineapple juice
2 ounces (57 g) Swiss cheese, sliced
16 ounces (454 g) Cuban bread loaf, sliced

1. Toss all ingredients , except for the cheese and bread, in a lightly greased air fryer basket.
2. Put the air fryer lid on and air fry in the preheated instant pot at360ºF (182ºC) for 55 minutes. Flip the pork butt when the lid screen indicates TURN FOOD.
3. Using two forks, shred the pork; assemble the sandwiches with cheese and bread. Serve warm and enjoy!

Pork Sausage with Brussels Sprouts

Prep time: 5 minutes | Cook time: 15 minutes | Serves 4

1 pound (454 g) sausage links, uncooked
1 pound (454 g) Brussels sprouts, halved
1 teaspoon dried thyme
1 teaspoon dried rosemary
1 teaspoon dried parsley flakes
1 teaspoon garlic powder

1. Place the sausage and Brussels sprouts in a lightly greased air fryer basket.
2. Put the air fryer lid on and air fry in the preheated instant pot at 380ºF (193ºC) for 15 minutes. Flip the sausage and Brussels sprouts when the lid screen indicates TURN FOOD.
3. Bon appétit!

Pork Patties with Teriyaki Sauce

Prep time: 10 minutes | Cook time: 15 minutes | Serves 4

1 pound (454 g) ground pork
Kosher salt and ground black pepper, to taste
1 tablespoon chopped fresh parsley
1 tablespoon chopped fresh coriander
1 teaspoon sliced habanero pepper
1 tablespoon teriyaki sauce
1 small onion, chopped
1 clove garlic, minced
4 brioche hamburger buns, lightly toasted

1. In a mixing bowl, thoroughly combine the pork, spices, habanero pepper, teriyaki sauce, onion, and garlic. Then, roll the mixture into four patties.
2. Arrange the patties in the air fryer basket.
3. Put the air fryer lid on and air fry in the preheated instant pot at 380ºF (193ºC) for 15 minutes. Flip the pork patties when the lid screen indicates TURN FOOD.
4. Serve the patties with the brioche hamburger buns. Enjoy!

Glazed Ham

Prep time: 5 minutes | Cook time: 1 hour | Serves 4

1½ pounds (680 g) smoked and cooked ham
¼ cup honey
1 small-sized orange, freshly squeezed
1 tablespoon balsamic vinegar
1 tablespoon stone-ground mustard
½ teaspoon crushed red pepper flakes
Freshly ground black pepper, to taste

1. In a mixing bowl, whisk all the remaining ingredients to make the glaze.
2. Wrap the ham in a piece of aluminum foil and lower it into the air fryer basket.
3. Put the air fryer lid on and air fry in the preheated instant pot at 375ºF (190ºC) for 30 minutes.
4. Remove the foil, increase the temperature to 400ºF (205ºC), and continue to cook for an additional 15 minutes, coating the ham with the glaze every 5 minutes.
5. Bon appétit!

Pork Loin Ribs with Zucchini

Prep time: 10 minutes | Cook time: 37 minutes | Serves 4

1½ pounds (680 g) pork loin ribs
2 cloves garlic, minced
1 tablespoon olive oil
4 tablespoons whiskey
1 teaspoon onion powder
Sea salt and ground black pepper, to taste
½ pound (227 g) zucchini, sliced

1. Toss the pork ribs with the garlic, olive oil, whiskey and spices; place the ingredients in a lightly greased air fryer basket.
2. Put the air fryer lid on and roast in the preheated instant pot at 350ºF (180ºC) for 25 minutes. Flip the pork ribs when the lid screen indicates TURN FOOD.
3. Top the pork ribs with the sliced zucchini and continue cooking for an additional 12 minutes. Serve immediately.
4. Bon appétit!

Picnic Ham with Garlic

Prep time: 5 minutes | Cook time: 1 hour | Serves 4

1½ pounds (680 g) picnic ham
2 tablespoons olive oil
2 garlic cloves, minced
2 tablespoons rice vinegar
1 tablespoon tamari sauce

1. Toss the ham with the remaining ingredients; wrap the ham in a piece of aluminum foil and lower it into the air fryer basket.
2. Put the air fryer lid on and air fry in the preheated instant pot at 375ºF (190ºC) for 30 minutes.
3. Remove the foil, increase the temperature to 400ºF (205ºC), and continue to cook for an additional 15 minutes or until cooked through.
4. Bon appétit!

Sirloin Chops with Cheese

Prep time: 5 minutes | Cook time: 15 minutes | Serves 3

1 pound (454 g) sirloin chops
1 egg
2 tablespoons butter, at room temperature
Sea salt and ground black pepper, to taste
3 tablespoons grated Pecorino cheese
½ cup bread crumbs
1 teaspoon paprika
1 teaspoon garlic powder

1. Pat the pork sirloin chops dry with kitchen towels.
2. In a shallow bowl, whisk the egg until pale and frothy.
3. In another shallow bowl, thoroughly combine the remaining ingredients. Dip the pork chops into the egg, then the cheese and crumb mixture.
4. Place the pork sirloin chops in a lightly oiled air fryer basket.
5. Put the air fryer lid on and air fry in the preheated instant pot at 400ºF (205ºC) for 15 minutes. Flip the pork sirloin chops when the lid screen indicates TURN FOOD.
6. Bon appétit!

Pork Burgers

Prep time: 15 minutes | Cook time: 15 minutes | Serves 4

1 pound (454 g) ground pork
1 small onion, chopped
1 garlic clove, minced
4 tablespoons crushed tortilla chips
1 teaspoon minced fresh sage
1 teaspoon minced fresh coriander
1 tablespoon minced fresh parsley
1 egg, beaten
½ teaspoon smoked paprika
Sea salt and freshly ground black pepper, to taste

1. In a mixing bowl, thoroughly combine all ingredients . Form the mixture into four patties. Arrange the patties in the air fryer basket.
2. Put the air fryer lid on and air fry in the preheated instant pot at 380ºF (193ºC) for 15 minutes. Flip the burgers when the lid screen indicates TURN FOOD.
3. Bon appétit!

Pork with Applesauce

Prep time: 5 minutes | Cook time: 55 minutes | Serves 5

1 tablespoon olive oil
2 tablespoons soy sauce
2 pounds (907 g) pork butt
Kosher salt and freshly ground black pepper, to taste
2 cloves garlic, smashed
2 sprigs fresh sage, chopped
1 cup applesauce

1. Toss all ingredients , except for the applesauce, in a lightly greased air fryer basket.
2. Put the air fryer lid on and air fry in the preheated instant pot at 360ºF (182ºC) for 45 minutes. Flip the pork butt when the lid screen indicates TURN FOOD.
3. Top the pork butt with the applesauce and continue cooking for a further 10 minutes.
4. Let it rest for a few minutes before slicing and serving. Bon appétit!

Syrupy Ham with Apple

Prep time: 10 minutes | Cook time: 1 hour | Serves 5

2 pounds (907 g) cooked ham
1 apple, cored and chopped
¼ cup maple syrup
2 garlic cloves, crushed
¼ cup Madeira wine

1. In a mixing bowl, whisk all the remaining ingredients to make the glaze.
2. Wrap the ham in a piece of aluminum foil and lower it onto the air fryer basket.
3. Put the air fryer lid on and air fry in the preheated instant pot at 375ºF (190ºC) for 30 minutes.
4. Remove the foil, increase the temperature to 400ºF (205ºC), and continue to cook for an additional 15 minutes, coating the ham with the glaze every 5 minutes.
5. Bon appétit!

Pork Muffin Burgers

Prep time: 8 minutes | Cook time: 15 minutes | Serves 4

1 pound (454 g) ground pork
1 egg
½ cup seasoned bread crumbs
1 teaspoon dried oregano
½ teaspoon dried basil
Sea salt and ground black pepper, to taste
1 small red onion, chopped
1 teaspoon minced garlic
1 tablespoon olive oil
4 English muffins

1. In a mixing bowl, thoroughly combine the pork, egg, bread crumbs, spices, onion, garlic, and olive oil. Form the mixture into four patties.
2. Arrange the patties in the air fryer basket.
3. Put the air fryer lid on and air fry in the preheated instant pot at 380ºF (193ºC) for 15 minutes. Flip the burgers when the lid screen indicates TURN FOOD.
4. Serve the burgers with English muffins and enjoy!

Bacon with Cauliflower

Prep time: 10 minutes | Cook time: 12 minutes | Serves 4

1 pound (454 g) bacon, cut into thick slices
1 pound (454 g) cauliflower, cut into florets
1 tablespoon maple syrup
1 teaspoon paprika
Kosher salt and ground black pepper, to taste
2 cloves garlic, minced

1. Toss all ingredients in the air fryer basket.
2. Put the air fryer lid on and air fry in the preheated instant pot at 400ºF (205ºC) for 12 minutes. Flip the bacon and cauliflower when the lid screen indicates TURN FOOD.
3. Serve immediately. Bon appétit!

Glazed Ham with Lime

Prep time: 5 minutes | Cook time: 1 hour | Serves 4

1½ pounds (680 g) ham
¼ cup sherry wine
2 tablespoons dark brown sugar
2 tablespoons freshly squeezed lime juice
1 tablespoon stone-ground mustard
A pinch of grated nutmeg
½ teaspoon ground cloves
¼ teaspoon ground cardamom
½ teaspoon ground black pepper, or more to taste

1. In a mixing bowl, whisk all the remaining ingredients to make the glaze.
2. Wrap the ham in a piece of aluminum foil and lower it into the air fryer basket.
3. Put the air fryer lid on and air fry in the preheated instant pot at 375ºF (190ºC) for 30 minutes.
4. Remove the foil, increase the temperature to 400ºF (205ºC), and continue to cook for an additional 15 minutes, coating the ham with the glaze every 5 minutes.
5. Bon appétit!

Pork and Beef Burgers

Prep time: 8 minutes | Cook time: 15 minutes | Serves 5

1 pound (454 g) ground pork
½ pound (227 g) ground beef
½ cup chopped scallions
1 teaspoon minced garlic
1 tablespoon Sriracha sauce
5 tablespoons crushed tortilla chips
2 tablespoons olive oil
Sea salt and ground black pepper, to taste
5 ciabatta rolls

1. In a mixing bowl, thoroughly combine the meat, scallions, garlic, Sriracha sauce, tortilla chips, olive oil, salt, and black pepper. Form the mixture into four patties.
2. Arrange the patties in the air fryer basket.
3. Put the air fryer lid on and air fry in the preheated instant pot at 380ºF (193ºC) for 15 minutes. Flip the burgers when the lid screen indicates TURN FOOD.
4. Serve the burgers with ciabatta rolls. Bon appétit!

Pork Loin Roast

Prep time: 10 minutes | Cook time: 15 minutes | Serves 4

1½ pounds (680 g) top loin roasts, sliced into 4 pieces
2 tablespoons olive oil
1 teaspoon hot paprika
Sea salt and ground black pepper, to taste
1 tablespoon Dijon mustard
1 teaspoon crushed garlic

1. Place all ingredients in a lightly greased air fryer basket.
2. Put the air fryer lid on and air fry in the preheated instant pot at 400ºF (205ºC) for 15 minutes. Flip the pork when the lid screen indicates TURN FOOD.
3. Bon appétit!

Ham Steaks with Butter

Prep time: 5 minutes | Cook time: 12 minutes | Serves 4

1 pound (454 g) ham steaks
2 tablespoons butter, room temperature
1 teaspoon paprika
2 tablespoons agave syrup

1. Place the ham in a lightly greased air fryer basket.
2. Mix the butter, paprika, and agave syrup in a small bowl.
3. Put the air fryer lid on and air fry in the preheated instant pot at 380ºF (193ºC) for 8 minutes. Flip the ham steaks and baste them with the butter glaze when the lid screen indicates TURN FOOD.
4. Baste the ham steaks and cook for an additional 4 minutes or until cooked through.
5. Bon appétit!

Bacon and Tomato Sandwich

Prep time: 8 minutes | Cook time: 10 minutes | Serves 3

6 ounces (170 g) thick-cut bacon
2 tablespoons brown sugar
2 teaspoons chipotle chile powder
1 teaspoon cayenne pepper
1 tablespoon Dijon mustard
1 heads lettuce, torn into leaves
2 medium tomatoes, sliced
6 (½-inch) slices white bread

1. Toss the bacon with the sugar, chipotle chile powder, cayenne pepper, and mustard.
2. Place the bacon in the air fryer basket. Put the air fryer lid on and air fry in the preheated instant pot at 400ºF (205ºC) for 10 minutes. Flip the bacon when the lid screen indicates TURN FOOD.
3. Assemble the sandwiches with the bacon, lettuce, and tomato.
4. Bon appétit!

Pork Belly with Tomato Sauce

Prep time: 10 minutes | Cook time: 17 minutes | Serves 6

1½ pounds (680 g) pork belly, cut into pieces
¼ cup tomato sauce
1 tablespoon tamari sauce
2 tablespoons dark brown sugar
1 teaspoon minced garlic
Sea salt and ground black pepper, to taste

1. Toss all ingredients in the air fryer basket.
2. Put the air fryer lid on and air fry in the preheated instant pot at 400ºF (205ºC) for 17 minutes. Flip the pork belly when the lid screen indicates TURN FOOD.
3. Bon appétit!

Pork Ribs with Garlic

Prep time: 5 minutes | Cook time: 35 minutes | Serves 4

1½ pounds (680 g) St. Louis-style ribs
1 teaspoon hot sauce
1 tablespoon canola oil
Kosher salt and ground black pepper, to taste
2 garlic cloves, minced

1. Toss all ingredients in a lightly greased air fryer basket.
2. Put the air fryer lid on and roast in the preheated instant pot at 350ºF (180ºC) for 35 minutes. Flip the pork ribs when the lid screen indicates TURN FOOD.
3. Bon appétit!

Pork Tacos with Chiles

Prep time: 10 minutes | Cook time: 55 minutes | Serves 4

2 ancho chiles, seeded and minced
2 garlic cloves, chopped
1 tablespoon olive oil
Kosher salt and freshly ground black pepper, to taste
1 teaspoon dried Mexican oregano
1½ pounds (680 g) pork butt
4 corn tortillas, warmed

1. Toss all ingredients, except for the tortillas, in a lightly greased air fryer basket.
2. Put the air fryer lid on and air fry in the preheated instant pot at 360ºF (182ºC) for 55 minutes. Flip the pork butt when the lid screen indicates TURN FOOD.
3. Using two forks, shred the pork and serve in tortillas with toppings of choice. Serve immediately!

Air Fried Sausage with Ginger

Prep time: 5 minutes | Cook time: 15 minutes | Serves 4

1 pound (454 g) Frankfurter sausage
¼ cup ginger ale
2 tablespoons liquid honey
Red pepper flakes, to taste

1. Place all ingredients in a lightly greased air fryer basket.
2. Put the air fryer lid on and air fry in the preheated instant pot at 370ºF (188ºC) for 15 minutes. Flip the sausage when the lid screen indicates TURN FOOD.
3. Bon appétit!

Bacon Squash and Eggplant Kebabs

Prep time: 15 minutes | Cook time: 10 minutes | Serves 3

1 tablespoon freshly squeezed lemon juice
1 teaspoon peeled and finely grated fresh ginger
1 tablespoon maple syrup
½ pound (227 g) bacon
½ pound (227 g) squash, diced
½ pound (227 g) eggplant, diced
1 large onion, cut into wedges

1. Toss all ingredients in a mixing bowl until well coated on all sides.
2. Thread the ingredients onto skewers and place them in the air fryer basket.
3. Put the air fryer lid on and air fry in the preheated instant pot at 400ºF (205ºC) for 10 minutes. Flip the skewers when the lid screen indicates TURN FOOD.
4. Serve warm with sauce on the side, if desired. Bon appétit!

Pork Ribs with Tomato Sauce

Prep time: 5 minutes | Cook time: 35 minutes | Serves 4

1 tablespoon sesame oil
1½ pounds (680 g) back ribs
½ cup tomato sauce
1 tablespoon soy sauce
2 tablespoons agave syrup
2 tablespoons rice wine

1. Toss all ingredients in a lightly greased air fryer basket.
2. Put the air fryer lid on and air fry in the preheated instant pot at 350ºF (180ºC) for 35 minutes. Flip the pork ribs when the lid screen indicates TURN FOOD.
3. Bon appétit!

Pork with BBQ Sauce

Prep time: 5 minutes | Cook time: 55 minutes | Serves 5

2 pounds (907 g) pork butt
1 tablespoon olive oil
Kosher salt and ground black pepper, to taste
1 teaspoon ground cumin
½ cup BBQ sauce

1. Toss all ingredients in a lightly greased air fryer basket.
2. Put the air fryer lid on and air fry in the preheated instant pot at 360ºF (182ºC) for 55 minutes. Flip the pork butt when the lid screen indicates TURN FOOD.
3. Serve warm and enjoy!

Rosemary Pork Shoulder Chops

Prep time: 5 minutes | Cook time: 15 minutes | Serves 4

1½ pounds (680 g) pork shoulder chops
2 tablespoons olive oil
Kosher salt and ground black pepper, to taste
2 sprigs rosemary, leaves picked and chopped
1 teaspoon crushed garlic

1. Toss all ingredients in a lightly greased air fryer basket.
2. Put the air fryer lid on and air fry in the preheated instant pot at 400ºF (205ºC) for 15 minutes. Flip the pork shoulder chops when the lid screen indicates TURN FOOD.
3. Bon appétit!

Pork Gyros

Prep time: 5 minutes | Cook time: 55 minutes | Serves 4

1 pound (454 g) pork shoulder
1 teaspoon smoked paprika
½ teaspoon onion powder
1 teaspoon garlic powder
½ teaspoon ground cumin
½ teaspoon ground bay leaf
Sea salt and ground black pepper, to taste
4 pitta bread, warmed

1. Toss the pork on all sides, top and bottom, with the spices. Place the pork in a lightly greased air fryer basket.
2. Put the air fryer lid on and air fry in the preheated instant pot at 360ºF (182ºC) for 55 minutes. Flip the pork when the lid screen indicates TURN FOOD.
3. Shred the pork with two forks and serve on warmed pitta bread and some extra toppings of choice. Enjoy!

Sausage Sandwich with Mustard

Prep time: 5 minutes | Cook time: 15 minutes | Serves 3

1 pound (454 g) sweet Italian sausage
6 white bread slices
2 teaspoons mustard

1. Place the sausage in a lightly greased air fryer basket.
2. Put the air fryer lid on and air fry in the preheated instant pot at 370ºF (188ºC) for 15 minutes. Flip the sausage when the lid screen indicates TURN FOOD.
3. Assemble the sandwiches with the bread, mustard, and sausage, and serve immediately.
4. Bon appétit!

Pork Loin Chops with Onions

Prep time: 5 minutes | Cook time: 15 minutes | Serves 4

1½ pounds (680 g) pork loin chops, boneless
2 tablespoons olive oil
½ teaspoon cayenne pepper
1 teaspoon garlic powder
Sea salt and ground black pepper, to taste
1 onion, cut into wedges

1. Place all ingredients in a lightly greased air fryer basket.
2. Put the air fryer lid on and air fry in the preheated instant pot at 400ºF (205ºC) for 15 minutes. Flip the pork loin chops when the lid screen indicates TURN FOOD.
3. Bon appétit!

Spareribs with Sriracha Sauce

Prep time: 5 minutes | Cook time: 35 minutes | Serves 5

2 pounds (907 g) spareribs
¼ cup Sriracha sauce
1 teaspoon paprika
Sea salt and ground black pepper, to taste

1. Toss all ingredients in a lightly greased air fryer basket.
2. Put the air fryer lid on and air fry in the preheated instant pot at 350ºF (180ºC) for 35 minutes. Flip the pork ribs when the lid screen indicates TURN FOOD.
3. Bon appétit!

Fennel and Pork Souvlaki

Prep time: 15 minutes | Cook time: 15 minutes | Serves 4

1 tablespoon olive oil
½ teaspoon sweet paprika
1 pound (454 g) pork tenderloin, cubed
1 small lemon, freshly juiced
1 eggplant, diced
2 bell peppers, diced
½ pound (227 g) fennel, diced

1. Toss all ingredients in a mixing bowl until well coated on all sides.
2. Thread the ingredients onto skewers and place them in the air fryer basket.
3. Put the air fryer lid on and air fry in the preheated instant pot at 400ºF (205ºC) for 15 minutes. Flip the skewers when the lid screen indicates TURN FOOD.
4. Bon appétit!

Pork Loin Roast

Prep time: 5 minutes | Cook time: 55 minutes | Serves 4

1½ pounds (680 g) pork loin roast
2 tablespoons butter, melted
Sea salt and ground black pepper, to taste
1 teaspoon cayenne pepper
1 teaspoon crushed garlic
1 teaspoon dried rosemary

1. Toss all ingredients in a lightly greased air fryer basket.
2. Put the air fryer lid on and air fry in the preheated instant pot at 360ºF (182ºC) for 55 minutes. Flip the pork when the lid screen indicates TURN FOOD.
3. Serve warm and enjoy!

Basil Pork Butt

Prep time: 5 minutes | Cook time: 55 minutes | Serves 4

1½ pounds (680 g) pork butt
1 teaspoon olive oil
1 teaspoon dried rosemary
1 teaspoon dried thyme
1 teaspoon dried oregano
1 teaspoon dried basil
1 teaspoon cayenne pepper
Sea salt and ground black pepper, to taste

1. Toss all ingredients in a lightly greased air fryer basket.
2. Put the air fryer lid on and air fry in the preheated instant pot at 360ºF (182ºC) for 55 minutes. Flip the pork when the lid screen indicates TURN FOOD.
3. Serve warm and enjoy!

Beer Pork Loin

Prep time: 5 minutes | Cook time: 55 minutes | Serves 5

4 tablespoons beer
1 tablespoon crushed garlic
1 teaspoon paprika
Sea salt and ground black pepper, to taste
2 pounds (907 g) pork loin

1. Toss all ingredients in a lightly greased air fryer basket.
2. Put the air fryer lid on and air fry in the preheated instant pot at 360ºF (182ºC) for 55 minutes. Flip the pork when the lid screen indicates TURN FOOD.
3. Serve warm and enjoy!

Bacon and Potato

Prep time: 10 minutes | Cook time: 12 minutes | Serves 4

1 pound (454 g) red-skinned potatoes, cut into 1-inch chunks
Kosher salt and ground black pepper, to taste
1 pound (454 g) bacon, cut into thick slices
1 tablespoon chopped fresh chives
2 cloves garlic, minced

1. Toss all ingredients in the air fryer basket.
2. Put the air fryer lid on and air fry in the preheated instant pot at 400ºF (205ºC) for 12 minutes. Flip the bacon and potatoes when the lid screen indicates TURN FOOD.
3. Serve immediately. Bon appétit!

Rosemary Pork Belly

Prep time: 5 minutes | Cook time: 45 minutes | Serves 5

1 pound (454 g) pork belly
1 tablespoon tomato sauce
2 tablespoons rice vinegar
1 teaspoon dried thyme
1 teaspoon dried rosemary

1. Toss all ingredients in a lightly greased baking dish.
2. Place the baking dish in the air fryer basket. Put the air fryer lid on and bake in the preheated instant pot at 320ºF (160ºC) for 45 minutes. Flip the pork belly when the lid screen indicates TURN FOOD.
3. Serve warm and enjoy!

Pork Rolls with Fish Sauce

Prep time: 5 minutes | Cook time: 55 minutes | Serves 4

1 pound (454 g) pork shoulder
1 tablespoon olive oil
2 cloves garlic, minced
1 teaspoon cayenne pepper
1 tablespoon chopped fresh sage
1 tablespoon chopped fresh thyme
1 tablespoon brown sugar
2 tablespoons fish sauce
Kosher salt and freshly ground pepper, to taste
8 dinner rolls

1. Toss all ingredients, except for the dinner rolls, in a lightly greased air fryer basket.
2. Put the air fryer lid on and air fry in the preheated instant pot at 360ºF (182ºC) for 55 minutes. Flip the pork when the lid screen indicates TURN FOOD.
3. Serve on dinner rolls and enjoy!

Rosemary Pork Butt

Prep time: 5 minutes | Cook time: 55 minutes | Serves 4

1½ pounds (680 g) pork butt
1 teaspoon butter, melted
2 garlic cloves, pressed
2 tablespoons chopped fresh rosemary
Coarse sea salt and freshly ground black pepper, to taste

1. Toss all ingredients in a lightly greased air fryer basket.
2. Put the air fryer lid on and roast in the preheated instant pot at 360ºF (182ºC) for 55 minutes. Flip the pork when the lid screen indicates TURN FOOD.
3. Serve warm and enjoy!

Sausage with Onion Rings

Prep time: 5 minutes | Cook time: 15 minutes | Serves 4

1 pound (454 g) pork sausage, smoked
4 ounces (113 g) onion rings

1. Place the sausage in a lightly greased air fryer basket.
2. Put the air fryer lid on and air fry in the preheated instant pot at 370ºF (188ºC) for 7 minutes. Flip the sausage when the lid screen indicates TURN FOOD.
3. Add in the onion rings and continue to cook for 8 minutes more. Bon appétit!

Pork Chops with Bell Peppers

Prep time: 8 minutes | Cook time: 15 minutes | Serves 4

1½ pounds (680 g) center-cut rib chops
2 bell peppers, seeded and sliced
2 tablespoons olive oil
½ teaspoon mustard powder
Kosher salt and freshly ground black pepper, to taste
1 teaspoon chopped fresh rosemary
1 teaspoon chopped fresh basil

1. Toss all ingredients in a lightly greased air fryer basket.
2. Put the air fryer lid on and air fry in the preheated instant pot at 400ºF (205ºC) for 15 minutes. Flip the pork chops when the lid screen indicates TURN FOOD.
3. Bon appétit!

Pork with Shaoxing Wine

Prep time: 10 minutes | Cook time: 15 minutes | Serves 4

1½ pounds (680 g) pork loin porterhouse, cut into 4 slices
1½ tablespoons sesame oil
½ teaspoon five-spice powder
2 garlic cloves, crushed
1 tablespoon soy sauce
1 tablespoon hoisin sauce
2 tablespoons Shaoxing wine

1. Place all ingredients in a lightly greased air fryer basket.
2. Put the air fryer lid on and air fry in the preheated instant pot at 400ºF (205ºC) for 15 minutes. Flip the pork loin chops when the lid screen indicates TURN FOOD.
3. Bon appétit!

Rib Roast with Tamari Sauce

Prep time: 5 minutes | Cook time: 55 minutes | Serves 4

1½ pounds (680 g) pork center cut rib roast
2 teaspoons butter, melted
1 teaspoon red chili powder
1 teaspoon paprika
1 teaspoon garlic powder
½ teaspoon onion powder
Sea salt and ground black pepper, to taste
2 tablespoons tamari sauce

1. Toss all ingredients in a lightly greased air fryer basket.
2. Put the air fryer lid on and roast in the preheated instant pot at 360ºF (182ºC) for 55 minutes. Flip the pork when the lid screen indicates TURN FOOD.
3. Serve warm and enjoy!

Pork Ribs with Paprika

Prep time: 5 minutes | Cook time: 35 minutes | Serves 5

2 pounds (907 g) Country-style ribs
Coarse sea salt and ground black pepper, to taste
1 teaspoon smoked paprika
1 teaspoon mustard powder
1 tablespoon butter, melted
1 teaspoon chili sauce
4 tablespoons dry red wine

1. Toss all ingredients in a lightly greased air fryer basket.
2. Put the air fryer lid on and air fry in the preheated instant pot at 350ºF (180ºC) for 35 minutes. Flip the pork ribs when the lid screen indicates TURN FOOD.
3. Bon appétit!

Pork Ribs with Thyme

Prep time: 5 minutes | Cook time: 35 minutes | Serves 4

1½ pounds (680 g) baby back ribs
2 tablespoons olive oil
1 teaspoon smoked paprika
1 teaspoon garlic powder
1 teaspoon onion powder
½ teaspoon ground cumin
1 teaspoon mustard powder
1 teaspoon dried thyme
Coarse sea salt and freshly cracked black pepper, to taste

1. Toss all ingredients in a lightly greased air fryer basket.
2. Put the air fryer lid on and air fry in the preheated instant pot at 350ºF (180ºC) for 35 minutes. Flip the pork ribs when the lid screen indicates TURN FOOD.
3. Bon appétit!

Air Fried Sausage Patties

Prep time: 5 minutes | Cook time: 15 minutes | Serves 4

1 pound (454 g) sausage patties
1 tablespoon mustard
1 teaspoon cayenne pepper
1 teaspoon minced jalapeño pepper

1. Place all ingredients in a lightly greased air fryer basket.
2. Put the air fryer lid on and air fry in the preheated instant pot at 370ºF (188ºC) for 15 minutes. Flip the sausage when the lid screen indicates TURN FOOD.
3. Bon appétit!

Pork with Herb

Prep time: 5 minutes | Cook time: 55 minutes | Serves 5

2 pounds (907 g) pork center cut
2 tablespoons olive oil
1 tablespoon Italian herb mix
1 teaspoon crushed red pepper flakes
Sea salt and freshly ground black pepper, to taste

1. Toss all ingredients in a lightly greased air fryer basket.
2. Put the air fryer lid on and air fry in the preheated instant pot at 360ºF (182ºC) for 55 minutes. Flip the pork when the lid screen indicates TURN FOOD.
3. Serve warm and enjoy!

Pork Belly

Prep time: 10 minutes | Cook time: 17 minutes | Serves 5

1 pound (454 g) pork belly, cut into cubes
1 teaspoon coarse sea salt
Freshly ground black pepper, to taste
1 tablespoon granulated sugar
1 teaspoon onion powder
½ teaspoon garlic powder

1. Toss all ingredients in the air fryer basket.
2. Put the air fryer lid on and air fry in the preheated instant pot at 400ºF (205ºC) for 17 minutes. Flip the pork belly when the lid screen indicates TURN FOOD.
3. Bon appétit!

Eggplant and Pork Skewers

Prep time: 15 minutes | Cook time: 15 minutes | Serves 4

1 pound (454 g) pork tenderloin, cubed
1 pound (454 g) bell peppers, diced
1 pound (454 g) eggplant, diced
1 tablespoon olive oil
1 tablespoon chopped parsley
1 tablespoon chopped cilantro
Sea salt and ground black pepper, to taste

1. Toss all ingredients in a mixing bowl until well coated on all sides.
2. Thread the ingredients onto skewers and place them in the air fryer basket.
3. Put the air fryer lid on and air fry in the preheated instant pot at 400ºF (205ºC) for 15 minutes. Flip the skewers when the lid screen indicates TURN FOOD.
4. Bon appétit!

Pork Sausage with Fennel

Prep time: 5 minutes | Cook time: 15 minutes | Serves 4

1 pound (454 g) pork sausage
1 pound (454 g) fennel, quartered
1 teaspoon garlic powder
½ teaspoon onion powder
2 teaspoons mustard

1. Place all ingredients in a lightly greased air fryer basket.
2. Put the air fryer lid on and air fry in the preheated instant pot at 370ºF (188ºC) for 15 minutes. Flip the sausage when the lid screen indicates TURN FOOD.
3. Bon appétit!

Pork Cutlets

Prep time: 5 minutes | Cook time: 15 minutes | Serves 4

1½ pounds (680 g) pork cutlets
Seasoned salt and ground black pepper, to taste
1 cup crushed tortilla chips
½ teaspoon cayenne pepper
2 tablespoons olive oil

1. Toss the pork cutlets with the remaining ingredients; place them in a lightly oiled air fryer basket.
2. Put the air fryer lid on and air fry in the preheated instant pot at 400ºF (205ºC) for 15 minutes. Flip the pork cutlets when the lid screen indicates TURN FOOD.
3. Bon appétit!

Bratwurst with Brussels Sprouts

Prep time: 5 minutes | Cook time: 15 minutes | Serves 4

1 pound (454 g) bratwurst
1 pound (454 g) Brussels sprouts
1 large onion, cut into wedges
1 teaspoon minced garlic
1 tablespoon mustard
2 tablespoons honey

1. Toss all ingredients in a lightly greased air fryer basket.
2. Put the air fryer lid on and air fry in the preheated instant pot at 380ºF (193ºC) for 15 minutes. Flip the sausage when the lid screen indicates TURN FOOD.
3. Bon appétit!

Mustard Pork Top Loin

Prep time: 5 minutes | Cook time: 55 minutes | Serves 4

1½ pounds (680 g) pork top loin
1 tablespoon olive oil
1 tablespoon Dijon mustard
2 cloves garlic, crushed
1 tablespoon parsley
1 tablespoon coriander
½ teaspoon crushed red pepper flakes
Kosher salt and ground black pepper, to taste

1. Toss all ingredients in a lightly greased air fryer basket.
2. Put the air fryer lid on and air fry in the preheated instant pot at 360ºF (182ºC) for 55 minutes. Flip the pork when the lid screen indicates TURN FOOD.
3. Serve warm and enjoy!

Pork Chops with Butter

Prep time: 10 minutes | Cook time: 15 minutes | Serves 3

1 pound (454 g) rib pork chops
1½ tablespoons butter, melted
2 tablespoons freshly squeezed orange juice
1 teaspoon chopped rosemary
Sea salt and cayenne pepper, to taste

1. Toss all ingredients in a lightly greased air fryer basket.
2. Put the air fryer lid on and air fry in the preheated instant pot at 400ºF (205ºC) for 15 minutes. Flip the pork chops when the lid screen indicates TURN FOOD.
3. Bon appétit!

Chapter 5 Rice and Grains

Cheesy Cauliflower Risotto

Prep time: 10 minutes | Cook time: 10 minutes | Serves 4

2 cups rice, cooked
2 tablespoons olive oil
½ cup chopped cauliflower
½ cup vegetable broth
4 tablespoons shredded Mozzarella cheese

1. Thoroughly combine all ingredients in a lightly greased baking dish.
2. Place the baking dish in the air fryer basket. Put the air fryer lid on and bake in the preheated instant pot at 360ºF (182ºC) for 10 minutes or until cooked through.
3. Bon appétit!

Creamy Raisins Bread Pudding

Prep time: 6 minutes | Cook time: 20 minutes | Serves 5

1½ cups cubed ciabatta bread
2 eggs, whisked
½ cup double cream
½ cup milk
½ teaspoon vanilla extract
1 tablespoon bourbon
¼ cup honey
½ cup golden raisins

1. Place the ciabatta bread in a lightly greased baking dish.
2. In a mixing bowl, thoroughly combine the eggs, double cream, milk, vanilla, bourbon, and honey.
3. Pour the egg mixture over the bread cubes. Fold in the raisins and set aside for 15 minutes to soak.
4. Place the baking dish in the air fryer basket. Put the air fryer lid on and bake in the preheated instant pot at 350ºF (180ºC) for 20 minutes or until the custard is set but still a little wobbly.
5. Serve at room temperature. Bon appétit!

Syrupy Apple Oatmeal

Prep time: 5 minutes | Cook time: 12 minutes | Serves 4

1 cup old-fashioned oats
¼ cup agave syrup
1 cup milk
1 egg, whisked
1 cup chopped apple
½ teaspoon baking powder
½ teaspoon ground cinnamon
A pinch of grated nutmeg
A pinch of salt

1. Thoroughly combine all ingredients in a mixing bowl. Spoon the mixture into four lightly greased ramekins.
2. Place the ramekins in the baking dish.
3. Place the baking dish in the air fryer basket. Put the air fryer lid on and bake in the preheated instant pot at 380ºF (193ºC) for 12 minutes.
4. Bon appétit!

Quinoa Cheese Patties

Prep time: 10 minutes | Cook time: 15 minutes | Serves 4

1½ cups quinoa, cooked
½ cup bread crumbs
½ cup grated Pecorino cheese
2 eggs, beaten
2 garlic cloves, minced
½ small onion, chopped
1 small bell pepper, seeded and chopped
1 tablespoon olive oil
2 tablespoons finely chopped fresh Mediterranean herbs
Sea salt and ground black pepper, to taste

1. Mix all ingredients until everything is well combined. Form the mixture into patties. Transfer to the air fryer basket.
2. Put the air fryer lid on and air fry in the preheated instant pot at 380ºF (193ºC) for 15 minutes. Flip the patties when the lid screen indicates TURN FOOD.
3. Bon appétit!

Buttery Banana Muffins

Prep time: 10 minutes | Cook time: 15 minutes | Serves 4

1 large egg, whisked
1 ripe banana, peeled and mashed
¼ cup butter, melted
¼ cup agave nectar
½ cup all-purpose flour
¼ almond flour
1 teaspoon baking powder
¼ cup brown sugar
½ teaspoon vanilla essence
1 teaspoon cinnamon powder
¼ teaspoon ground cloves

1. Mix all ingredients in a bowl.
2. Scrape the batter into silicone baking molds; place them in the baking dish.
3. Place the baking dish in the air fryer basket. Put the air fryer lid on and bake in the preheated instant pot at 320ºF (160ºC) for 15 minutes or until a tester comes out dry and clean.
4. Allow the muffins to cool before unmolding and serving.

Baked Cornbread Bites

Prep time: 5 minutes | Cook time: 22 minutes | Serves 6

½ cup all-purpose flour
½ cup yellow cornmeal
1½ teaspoons baking powder
4 tablespoons honey
A pinch of sea salt
A pinch of grated nutmeg
4 tablespoons coconut oil, room temperature
2 eggs, whisked
½ cup milk

1. Mix all ingredients until everything is well incorporated. Scrape the batter into baking molds and place them in the baking dish.
2. Place the baking dish in the air fryer basket. Put the air fryer lid on and bake in the preheated instant pot at 360ºF (182ºC) for 22 minutes or until a tester comes out dry and clean.
3. Allow the mini cornbread to cool before unmolding and serving. Bon appétit!

Polenta Rounds

Prep time: 5 minutes | Cook time: 15 minutes | Serves 4

1 cup polenta
Sea salt, to taste
1 teaspoon dried oregano
2 tablespoons olive oil

1. Cook the polenta according to the package directions. Season with the salt and oregano to taste.
2. Pour the polenta into a large baking sheet. Let it cool and firm up; cut the polenta into rounds. Drizzle the olive oil over them.
3. Place the baking dish in the air fryer basket. Put the air fryer lid on and bake in the preheated instant pot at 350ºF (180ºC) for 15 minutes. Flip the polenta rounds when the lid screen indicates TURN FOOD.
4. Bon appétit!

Corn Kernels Koftas

Prep time: 10 minutes | Cook time: 15 minutes | Serves 5

6 ounces (170 g) canned corn kernels
½ small-sized onion, peeled and chopped
2 cloves garlic, minced
2 tablespoons chopped fresh parsley
2 tablespoons chopped fresh mint
2 tablespoons butter, melted
2 eggs, beaten
½ cup rice flour
1 teaspoon baking powder
Sea salt and ground black pepper, to taste
1 teaspoon turmeric powder

1. Mix all ingredients until everything is well combined. Form the mixture into balls. Transfer to the air fryer basket.
2. Put the air fryer lid on and air fry in the preheated instant pot at 380ºF (193ºC) for 15 minutes or until cooked through. Flip the balls when the lid screen indicates TURN FOOD.
3. Bon appétit!

Mixed Berry Muffins

Prep time: 5 minutes | Cook time: 15 minutes | Serves 6

¾ cup all-purpose flour
¼ cup honey
½ teaspoon ground cinnamon
¼ teaspoon ground cloves
¼ cup buttermilk
1 egg
4 tablespoons olive oil
1 teaspoon vanilla extract
½ cup fresh mixed berries

1. Mix all ingredients in a bowl. Scrape the batter into silicone baking molds; place them in the baking dish.
2. Place the baking dish in the air fryer basket. Put the air fryer lid on and bake in the preheated instant pot at 320ºF (160ºC) for 15 minutes or until a tester comes out dry and clean.
3. Allow the muffins to cool before unmolding and serving. Bon appétit!

Figs Bread Pudding

Prep time: 10 minutes | Cook time: 20 minutes | Serves 5

8 slices bread, cubed
1 cup milk
2 eggs, beaten
¼ cup brown sugar
2 ounces (57 g) dried figs, chopped
A pinch of sea salt
½ teaspoon ground cinnamon
½ teaspoon vanilla extract

1. Place the bread in a lightly greased baking dish.
2. In a mixing bowl, thoroughly combine the remaining ingredients.
3. Pour the milk mixture over the bread cubes. Set aside for 15 minutes to soak.
4. Place the baking dish in the air fryer basket. Put the air fryer lid on and bake in the preheated instant pot at 350ºF (180ºC) for about 20 minutes or until the custard is set but still a little wobbly.
5. Serve at room temperature. Bon appétit!

Air Fried Millet Patties

Prep time: 10 minutes | Cook time: 15 minutes | Serves 4

2 cups millet, cooked
2 tablespoons olive oil
1 small onion, chopped
2 garlic cloves, minced
1 tablespoon chopped celery leaves
1 tablespoon chopped parsley leaves
Sea salt and ground black pepper, to taste

1. Mix all ingredients until everything is well combined. Form the mixture into patties. Transfer to the air fryer basket.
2. Put the air fryer lid on and air fry in the preheated instant pot at 380ºF (193ºC) for 15 minutes. Flip the patties when the lid screen indicates TURN FOOD.
3. Bon appétit!

Honey Prunes Bread Pudding

Prep time: 10 minutes | Cook time: 20 minutes | Serves 5

8 slices bread, cubed
1 cup coconut milk
¼ cup coconut oil
1 egg, beaten
¼ cup honey
½ teaspoon ground cinnamon
¼ teaspoon ground cloves
A pinch of kosher salt
½ cup pitted and chopped prunes

1. Place the bread cubes in a lightly greased baking dish.
2. In a mixing bowl, thoroughly combine the milk, coconut oil, egg, honey, cinnamon, cloves, and salt.
3. Pour the custard mixture over the bread cubes. Fold in the prunes and set aside for 15 minutes to soak.
4. Preheat the air fryer to .
5. Place the baking dish in the air fryer basket. Put the air fryer lid on and bake in the preheated instant pot at 350ºF (180ºC) for 20 minutes or until the custard is set but still a little wobbly.
6. Bon appétit!

Cherry Cranberry Bread Pudding

Prep time: 5 minutes | Cook time: 20 minutes | Serves 6

2 cups cubed sweet raisin bread
2 eggs, whisked
1 cup milk
½ teaspoon vanilla extract
¼ cup agave syrup
¼ cup dried cherries
¼ cup dried cranberries

1. Place the bread cubes in a lightly greased baking dish.
2. In a mixing bowl, thoroughly combine the remaining ingredients.
3. Pour the egg mixture over the bread cubes; set aside for 15 minutes to soak.
4. Place the baking dish in the air fryer basket. Put the air fryer lid on and bake in the preheated instant pot at 350ºF (180ºC) for 20 minutes or until the custard is set but still a little wobbly.
5. Serve at room temperature. Bon appétit!

Cheesy Macaroni

Prep time: 5 minutes | Cook time: 15 minutes | Serves 4

2 cups macaroni
1 cup milk
2 cups grated Mozzarella cheese
½ teaspoon Italian seasoning
Sea salt and ground black pepper, to taste
½ teaspoon garlic powder
1 teaspoon dry mustard

1. Cook the macaroni according to the package directions.
2. Drain the macaroni and place them in a lightly greased baking dish.
3. Fold in the remaining ingredients and stir to combine.
4. Place the baking dish in the air fryer basket. Put the air fryer lid on and bake in the preheated instant pot at 360ºF (182ºC) for 15 minutes.
5. Serve garnished with fresh Italian herbs, if desired.
6. Bon appétit!

Mushroom and Rice Bake

Prep time: 10 minutes | Cook time: 10 minutes | Serves 4

1 pound (454 g) brown mushrooms, chopped
1 small onion, peeled and chopped
2 tablespoons butter, room temperature
2 garlic cloves, minced
Sea salt and ground black pepper, to taste
1 cup vegetable broth
1½ cups brown rice, cooked

1. Thoroughly combine all ingredients in a lightly greased baking dish.
2. Place the baking dish in the air fryer basket. Put the air fryer lid on and bake in the preheated instant pot at 360ºF (182ºC) for 10 minutes or until cooked through.
3. Bon appétit!

Doughnut Bread Pudding

Prep time: 8 minutes | Cook time: 20 minutes | Serves 6

2 cups diced doughnuts
2 eggs, whisked
1 cup milk
1 cup half-and-half
4 tablespoons honey
1 teaspoon vanilla extract
A pinch of salt
A pinch of grated nutmeg

1. Place the doughnuts in a lightly greased baking dish.
2. In a mixing bowl, thoroughly combine the remaining ingredients.
3. Pour the custard mixture over the doughnuts. Set aside for 15 minutes to soak.
4. Place the baking dish in the air fryer basket. Put the air fryer lid on and bake in the preheated instant pot at 350ºF (180ºC) for about 20 minutes or until the custard is set but still a little wobbly.
5. Serve at room temperature. Bon appétit!

Raisins Buttermilk Scones

Prep time: 15 minutes | Cook time: 17 minutes | Serves 6

1 cup all-purpose flour
1 teaspoon baking powder
¼ teaspoon salt
¼ teaspoon grated nutmeg
½ cup brown sugar
2 egg, beaten
¼ cup buttermilk
½ teaspoon vanilla extract
6 tablespoons raisins, soaked for 15 minutes

1. Mix all ingredients until everything is well incorporated. Spoon the batter into baking cups; lower the cups into the baking dish.
2. Place the baking dish in the air fryer basket. Put the air fryer lid on and bake in the preheated instant pot at 360ºF (182ºC) for 17 minutes or until a tester comes out dry and clean.
3. Bon appétit!

Mini Cornbread Loaves

Prep time: 5 minutes | Cook time: 22 minutes | Serves 6

½ cup all-purpose flour
½ cup yellow cornmeal
1½ teaspoons baking powder
A pinch of kosher salt
A pinch of grated nutmeg
4 tablespoons butter, melted
½ cup milk
2 eggs, whisked
2 tablespoons agave syrup

1. Mix all ingredients until everything is well incorporated. Scrape the batter into baking molds and place them in the baking dish.
2. Place the baking dish in the air fryer basket. Put the air fryer lid on and bake in the preheated instant pot at 360ºF (182ºC) for 22 minutes or until a tester comes out dry and clean.
3. Allow the mini cornbread loaves to cool before unmolding and serving. Bon appétit!

Banana Oatmeal

Prep time: 5 minutes | Cook time: 12 minutes | Serves 4

1 cup old-fashioned oats
1 cup coconut milk
1 cup water
1 banana, mashed
½ teaspoon vanilla extract
½ teaspoon ground cinnamon
A pinch of grated nutmeg
A pinch of sea salt

1. Thoroughly combine all ingredients in a mixing bowl. Spoon the mixture into lightly greased mugs. Place the mugs in the baking dish.
2. Place the baking dish in the air fryer basket. Put the air fryer lid on and bake in the preheated instant pot at 380ºF (193ºC) for 12 minutes.
3. Bon appétit!

Cranberry Granola

Prep time: 10 minutes | Cook time: 15 minutes | Serves 6

½ cup rolled oats
¼ cup toasted wheat germ
½ cup dried cranberries
¼ cup pumpkin seeds
¼ cup sunflower seeds
¼ cup chopped pecans
¼ cup chopped walnuts
½ teaspoon vanilla extract
¼ cup agave syrup
4 tablespoons coconut oil
1 teaspoon pumpkin pie spice mix

1. Thoroughly combine all ingredients in a lightly greased baking dish.
2. Place the baking dish in the air fryer basket. Put the air fryer lid on and bake in the preheated instant pot at 350ºF (180ºC) for 15 minutes, stirring every 5 minutes.
3. Store at room temperature in an airtight container for up to three weeks.
4. Bon appétit!

Apple Oat Muffins

Prep time: 8 minutes | Cook time: 15 minutes | Serves 6

½ cups self-rising flour
½ cup rolled oats
½ cup agave syrup
¼ teaspoon grated nutmeg
½ teaspoon cinnamon powder
A pinch of coarse salt
½ cup milk
¼ cup coconut oil, room temperature
2 eggs
1 teaspoon coconut extract
1 cup cored and chopped apples

1. Mix all ingredients in a bowl.
2. Scrape the batter into silicone baking molds; place them in the baking dish.
3. Place the baking dish in the air fryer basket. Put the air fryer lid on and bake in the preheated instant pot at 320ºF (160ºC) for 15 minutes or until a tester comes out dry and clean.
4. Allow the muffins to cool before unmolding and serving.

Almond Honey Bread Pudding

Prep time: 10 minutes | Cook time: 20 minutes | Serves 6

2 cups cubed brioche bread
1 cup almond milk
2 eggs, whisked
¼ teaspoon ground cinnamon
¼ teaspoon ground cardamom
½ teaspoon vanilla extract
¼ cup honey
½ cup chopped almonds

1. Place the bread cubes in a lightly greased baking dish.
2. In a mixing bowl, thoroughly combine the remaining ingredients.
3. Pour the custard mixture over the bread cubes; set aside for 15 minutes to soak.
4. Place the baking dish in the air fryer basket. Put the air fryer lid on and bake in the preheated instant pot at 350ºF (180ºC) for 20 minutes or until the custard is set but still a little wobbly.
5. Serve at room temperature. Bon appétit!

Scallion Rice Pilaf

Prep time: 10 minutes | Cook time: 10 minutes | Serves 4

1½ cups cooked multigrain rice
1 cup vegetable broth
½ cup thinly sliced scallions
1 tablespoon chopped fresh parsley
1 tablespoon chopped fresh cilantro
2 tablespoons olive oil
Sea salt and cayenne pepper, to taste
1 teaspoon garlic powder

1. Thoroughly combine all ingredients in a lightly greased baking dish.
2. Place the baking dish in the air fryer basket. Put the air fryer lid on and bake in the preheated instant pot at 360ºF (182ºC) for 10 minutes or until cooked through.
3. Bon appétit!

Quinoa and Broccoli Cheese Patties

Prep time: 15 minutes | Cook time: 15 minutes | Serves 4

2 cups quinoa, cooked
2 eggs, whisked
1 small onion, chopped
2 garlic cloves, minced
1 cup chopped broccoli
½ cup bread crumbs
½ cup grated Parmesan cheese
1 tablespoon chopped fresh Italian herbs
Sea salt and ground black pepper, to taste

1. Mix all ingredients until everything is well combined. Form the mixture into patties. Transfer to the air fryer basket.
2. Put the air fryer lid on and air fry in the preheated instant pot at 380ºF (193ºC) for 15 minutes. Flip the patties when the lid screen indicates TURN FOOD.
3. Bon appétit!

Chocolate Chips Honey Muffins

Prep time: 5 minutes | Cook time: 15 minutes | Serves 6

½ cup all-purpose flour
⅓ cup almond flour
1 teaspoon baking powder
A pinch of sea salt
A pinch of grated nutmeg
1 egg
¼ cup honey
¼ cup milk
1 teaspoon vanilla extract
4 tablespoons coconut oil
½ cup dark chocolate chips

1. Mix all ingredients in a bowl. Scrape the batter into silicone baking molds; place them in the baking dish.
2. Place the baking dish in the air fryer basket. Put the air fryer lid on and bake in the preheated instant pot at 320ºF (160ºC) for 15 minutes or until a tester comes out dry and clean.
3. Allow the muffins to cool before unmolding and serving. Bon appétit!

Chocolate Chips Granola

Prep time: 10 minutes | Cook time: 15 minutes | Serves 8

½ cup old-fashioned oats
¼ cup unsweetened coconut flakes
¼ cup quinoa flakes
¼ cup slivered almonds
¼ cup chopped hazelnuts
¼ cup chia seeds
1 teaspoon ground cinnamon
A pinch of grated nutmeg
A pinch of sea salt
2 tablespoons coconut oil
¼ cup maple syrup
1 teaspoon vanilla extract
½ cup chocolate chips

1. Thoroughly combine all ingredients in a lightly greased baking dish.
2. Place the baking dish in the air fryer basket. Put the air fryer lid on and bake in the preheated instant pot at 350ºF (180ºC) for 15 minutes, stirring every 5 minutes.
3. Store at room temperature in an airtight container for up to three weeks.
4. Bon appétit!

Curry Basmati Rice

Prep time: 10 minutes | Cook time: 10 minutes | Serves 4

3 tablespoons olive oil
3 cloves garlic, chopped
1 large onion, peeled and chopped
1 sprigs fresh curry leaves, chopped
2 cups basmati rice, cooked
1 teaspoon cayenne pepper
Kosher salt and ground black pepper, to taste

1. Thoroughly combine all ingredients in a lightly greased baking dish. Pour 1 cup of boiling water over the rice.
2. Place the baking dish in the air fryer basket. Put the air fryer lid on and bake in the preheated instant pot at 360ºF (182ºC) for 10 minutes or until cooked through.
3. Bon appétit!

Cheesy Butter Macaroni

Prep time: 5 minutes | Cook time: 15 minutes | Serves 4

1 cups macaroni
1 cup cream of onion soup
2 tablespoons butter
4 ounces (113 g) Ricotta cheese
6 ounces (170 g) Mozzarella cheese, crumbled
Kosher salt and ground white pepper, to taste
½ teaspoon ground cumin
1 teaspoon dry mustard
1 teaspoon red chili powder

1. Cook the macaroni according to the package directions.
2. Drain the macaroni and place them in a lightly greased baking dish.
3. Fold in the remaining ingredients and stir to combine.
4. Place the baking dish in the air fryer basket. Put the air fryer lid on and bake in the preheated instant pot at 360ºF (182ºC) for 15 minutes.
5. Serve garnished with fresh Italian herbs, if desired.
6. Bon appétit!

Blueberry Cheese Rolls

Prep time: 5 minutes | Cook time: 10 minutes | Serves 6

1 (8-ounce / 227-g) can refrigerated crescent dinner rolls
6 ounces (170 g) cream cheese, room temperature
4 tablespoons granulated sugar
1 teaspoon grated lemon zest
1 cup fresh blueberries
1 cup powdered sugar
¼ teaspoon ground cinnamon

1. Separate the dough into rectangles. Mix the remaining ingredients until well combined.
2. Spread each rectangle with the cheese mixture; roll them up tightly.
3. Place the rolls in the baking dish.
4. Place the baking dish in the air fryer basket. Put the air fryer lid on and bake in the preheated instant pot at 300ºF (150ºC) for 10 minutes. Flip the rolls when the lid screen indicates TURN FOOD.
5. Bon appétit!

Juicy Quinoa Porridge

Prep time: 10 minutes | Cook time: 12 minutes | Serves 4

½ cup old-fashioned oats
½ cup quinoa flakes
¼ cup chopped almonds
¼ cup chopped pecans
2 cups orange juice
4 tablespoons honey
2 tablespoons coconut oil
4 tablespoons chopped dried apricots

1. Thoroughly combine all ingredients in a mixing bowl. Spoon the mixture into lightly greased mugs.
2. Then, place the mugs in the baking dish.
3. Place the baking dish in the air fryer basket. Put the air fryer lid on and bake in the preheated instant pot at 380ºF (193ºC) for 12 minutes.
4. Serve immediately. Bon appétit!

Cocoa Muffins

Prep time: 5 minutes | Cook time: 15 minutes | Serves 6

½ cup coconut flour
½ cup all-purpose flour
½ cup cocoa powder
½ cup brown sugar
½ teaspoon baking powder
A pinch of sea salt
A pinch of grated nutmeg
1 tablespoon instant coffee granules
½ cup milk
2 eggs, whisked
½ teaspoon vanilla extract

1. Mix all ingredients until well combined; then, divide the batter evenly between silicone baking molds; place them in the baking dish.
2. Place the baking dish in the air fryer basket. Put the air fryer lid on and bake in the preheated instant pot at 330ºF (166ºC) for 15 minutes or until a tester comes out dry and clean.
3. Allow the muffins to cool before unmolding and serving. Bon appétit!

Pecans Oatmeal Cups

Prep time: 6 minutes | Cook time: 12 minutes | Serves 4

1 cup full-fat milk
1 cup unsweetened applesauce
1 egg, beaten
½ cup pure maple syrup
1 cup old-fashioned oats
1 teaspoon baking powder
1 teaspoon pure vanilla extract
½ teaspoon ground cinnamon
¼ teaspoon freshly grated nutmeg
A pinch of kosher salt
½ cup chopped pecans

1. Thoroughly combine all ingredients in a mixing bowl. Spoon the mixture into lightly greased mugs.
2. Then, place the mugs in the baking dish.
3. Place the baking dish in the air fryer basket. Put the air fryer lid on and bake in the preheated instant pot at 380ºF (193ºC) for 12 minutes.
4. Bon appétit!

Almonds Oatmeal

Prep time: 5 minutes | Cook time: 12 minutes | Serves 4

1 cup rolled oats
1 cup water
1 cup milk
1 teaspoon vanilla paste
A pinch of kosher salt
½ teaspoon ground cloves
4 tablespoons honey
½ cup slivered almonds

1. Thoroughly combine all ingredients in a mixing bowl. Spoon the mixture into lightly greased ramekins.
2. Then, place the ramekins in the baking dish.
3. Place the baking dish in the air fryer basket. Put the air fryer lid on and bake in the preheated instant pot at 380ºF (193ºC) for 12 minutes.
4. Serve warm or at room temperature.
5. Bon appétit!

Creamy Cornbread Casserole

Prep time: 5 minutes | Cook time: 12 minutes | Serves 6

3 eggs
2 tablespoons coconut oil, room temperature
½ cup heavy cream
1 teaspoon vanilla
½ cup brown sugar
½ teaspoon ground cinnamon
A pinch of grated nutmeg
A pinch of salt
6 slices sweet cornbread

1. In a mixing bowl, thoroughly combine the eggs, coconut oil, heavy cream, vanilla, sugar, cinnamon, nutmeg, and salt.
2. Then, place the cornbread slices in a lightly greased baking dish. Pour the custard mixture over the cornbread slices.
3. Place the baking dish in the air fryer basket. Put the air fryer lid on and bake in the preheated instant pot at 330ºF (166ºC) for 12 minutes.
4. Enjoy!

French Toast

Prep time: 5 minutes | Cook time: 8 minutes | Serves 4

2 eggs, beaten
¼ cup milk
2 tablespoons coconut oil, room temperature
½ teaspoon bourbon vanilla extract
½ teaspoon ground cinnamon
4 slices bread

1. In a mixing bowl, thoroughly combine the eggs, milk, coconut oil, vanilla, and cinnamon.
2. Then dip each piece of bread into the egg mixture; place the bread slices in a lightly greased baking dish.
3. Place the baking dish in the air fryer basket. Put the air fryer lid on and bake in the preheated instant pot at 330ºF (166ºC) for 8 minutes. Flip the bread slices when the lid screen indicates TURN FOOD.
4. Enjoy!

Rice Cheese Casserole

Prep time: 10 minutes | Cook time: 10 minutes | Serves 4

1 small shallot, minced
2 garlic cloves, minced
2 tablespoons olive oil
½ teaspoon paprika
2 eggs, whisked
1 cup half-and-half
1 cup shredded Cheddar cheese
2 cups cooked brown rice
1 tablespoon chopped Italian parsley leaves
1 cup cream of celery soup
Sea salt and freshly ground black pepper, to taste

1. Thoroughly combine all ingredients in a lightly greased baking dish.
2. Place the baking dish in the air fryer basket. Put the air fryer lid on and bake in the preheated instant pot at 360ºF (182ºC) for 10 minutes or until cooked through.
3. Bon appétit!

Apple Pie Cheese Rolls

Prep time: 5 minutes | Cook time: 10 minutes | Serves 5

1 (8-ounce / 227-g) can crescent rolls
1 teaspoon ground cinnamon
4 ounces (113 g) cream cheese, room temperature
¼ cup sugar
2 tablespoons full-fat milk
½ cup canned apple pie filling

1. Separate the dough into rectangles. Mix the remaining ingredients until well combined.
2. Spread each rectangle with the cinnamon mixture; roll them up tightly.
3. Place the rolls in the baking dish.
4. Place the baking dish in the air fryer basket. Put the air fryer lid on and bake in the preheated instant pot at 300ºF (150ºC) for 10 minutes. Flip the rolls when the lid screen indicates TURN FOOD.
5. Bon appétit!

Cabbage Butter Bhajji

Prep time: 10 minutes | Cook time: 15 minutes | Serves 4

1 cup rice flour
4 tablespoons chickpea flour
½ teaspoon sweet paprika
1 teaspoon chili powder
Sea salt and ground black pepper, to taste
½ cup shredded green cabbage
1 teaspoon onion powder
1 teaspoon garlic powder
2 tablespoons butter
½ cup vegetable broth

1. Mix all ingredients until everything is well combined. Form the mixture into patties. Transfer to the air fryer basket.
2. Put the air fryer lid on and air fry in the preheated instant pot at 380ºF (193ºC) for 15 minutes. Flip the patties when the lid screen indicates TURN FOOD.
3. Bon appétit!

Carrot and Green Peas Rice

Prep time: 5 minutes | Cook time: 10 minutes | Serves 4

2 cups multigrain rice, cooked
1 small onion, finely chopped
1 teaspoon minced garlic
2 tablespoons sesame oil
1 egg, whisked
2 tablespoons soy sauce
1 carrot, chopped
1 cup green peas
Sea salt and red chili flakes, to taste

1. Thoroughly combine all ingredients in a lightly greased baking dish.
2. Place the baking dish in the air fryer basket. Put the air fryer lid on and bake in the preheated instant pot at 360ºF (182ºC) for 10 minutes or until cooked through.
3. Bon appétit!

Almonds Bread Pudding

Prep time: 8 minutes | Cook time: 20 minutes | Serves 6

2 cups cubed Brioche bread
½ teaspoon cinnamon powder
4 tablespoons brown sugar
2 eggs, whisked
2 tablespoons coconut oil
1 cup eggnog
½ cup chopped almonds

1. Place the bread cubes in a lightly greased baking dish.
2. In a mixing bowl, thoroughly combine the remaining ingredients.
3. Pour the custard mixture over the bread cubes. Set aside for 15 minutes to soak.
4. Place the baking dish in the air fryer basket. Put the air fryer lid on and bake in the preheated instant pot at 350ºF (180ºC) for 20 minutes or until the custard is set but still a little wobbly.
5. Bon appétit!

Creamy Butter Corn Fritters

Prep time: 5 minutes | Cook time: 15 minutes | Serves 4

1 cup canned and creamed corn kernels
1 cup whole-wheat flour
1 teaspoon baking powder
2 eggs, whisked
½ cup heavy cream
2 tablespoons butter

1. Mix all ingredients until everything is well combined. Form the mixture into patties. Transfer to the air fryer basket.
2. Put the air fryer lid on and air fry in the preheated instant pot at 380°F (193°C) for 15 minutes. Flip the fritters when the lid screen indicates TURN FOOD.
3. Bon appétit!

Baked Rolls with Cheese

Prep time: 5 minutes | Cook time: 10 minutes | Serves 4

1 (8-ounce / 227-g) can refrigerated crescent rolls
4 ounces (113 g) cream cheese, room temperature

1. Separate the dough into rectangles. Spread each rectangle with cream cheese and roll them up.
2. Place the rolls in the baking dish.
3. Place the baking dish in the air fryer basket. Put the air fryer lid on and bake in the preheated instant pot at 300°F (150°C) for 10 minutes. Flip the rolls when the lid screen indicates TURN FOOD.
4. Bon appétit!

Air Fried Butter Toast

Prep time: 5 minutes | Cook time: 8 minutes | Serves 3

2 eggs
½ cup milk
2 tablespoons butter, room temperature
1 teaspoon vanilla extract
¼ teaspoon grated nutmeg
½ teaspoon cinnamon powder
3 slices challah bread

1. In a mixing bowl, thoroughly combine the eggs, milk, butter, vanilla, nutmeg, and cinnamon.
2. Then dip each piece of bread into the egg mixture; place the bread slices in a lightly greased air fryer basket.
3. Put the air fryer lid on and air fry in the preheated instant pot at 330°F (166°C) for 8 minutes. Flip the bread slices when the lid screen indicates TURN FOOD.
4. Enjoy!

Methi and Ragi Fritters

Prep time: 8 minutes | Cook time: 15 minutes | Serves 4

½ cup rice flour
½ cup Ragi
½ teaspoon baking powder
1 cup chopped methi
1 green chilli, finely chopped
1 teaspoon ginger-garlic paste
2 tablespoons sesame oil
Sea salt and ground black pepper, to taste

1. Mix all ingredients until everything is well combined. Form the mixture into patties. Transfer to the air fryer basket.
2. Put the air fryer lid on and air fry in the preheated instant pot at 380°F (193°C) for 15 minutes. Flip the patties when the lid screen indicates TURN FOOD.
3. Bon appétit!

Rye and Quinoa Porridge

Prep time: 5 minutes | Cook time: 12 minutes | Serves 5

½ cup rolled oats
½ cup quinoa flakes
½ cup rye flakes
1 cup coconut milk
1 cup orange juice
2 eggs, whisked
4 tablespoons honey
½ teaspoon ground cinnamon

1. Thoroughly combine all ingredients in a mixing bowl. Spoon the mixture into a lightly greased baking dish.
2. Place the baking dish in the air fryer basket. Put the air fryer lid on and bake in the preheated instant pot at 380°F (193°C) for 12 minutes.
3. Serve immediately. Bon appétit!

Rice with Scallions

Prep time: 5 minutes | Cook time: 10 minutes | Serves 4

2 cups jasmine rice, cooked
1 cup vegetable broth
1 teaspoon garlic powder
½ cup chopped scallions
2 tablespoons butter, room temperature
Kosher salt and red pepper, to taste

1. Thoroughly combine all ingredients in a lightly greased baking dish.
2. Place the baking dish in the air fryer basket. Put the air fryer lid on and bake in the preheated instant pot at 360ºF (182ºC) for 10 minutes or until cooked through.
3. Bon appétit!

Pumpkin Porridge with Chocolate

Prep time: 5 minutes | Cook time: 12 minutes | Serves 5

½ cup old-fashioned oats
½ cup quinoa flakes
¼ cup chopped pecans
2 tablespoons ground chia seeds
2 tablespoons ground flax seeds
1 teaspoon vanilla essence
2 ounces (57 g) dark chocolate chips
½ cup canned pumpkin
½ cup almond milk

1. Thoroughly combine all ingredients in a mixing bowl. Spoon the mixture into a lightly greased baking dish.
2. Place the baking dish in the air fryer basket. Put the air fryer lid on and bake in the preheated instant pot at 380ºF (193ºC) for 12 minutes.
3. Serve immediately. Bon appétit!

Chawal ke Pakore with Cheese

Prep time: 5 minutes | Cook time: 15 minutes | Serves 4

1 cup rice flour
½ onion, chopped
2 garlic cloves, minced
2 tablespoons butter, room temperature
1 teaspoon paprika
1 teaspoon cumin powder
½ cup crumbled Paneer cheese

1. Mix all ingredients until everything is well combined. Form the mixture into patties. Transfer to the air fryer basket.
2. Put the air fryer lid on and air fry in the preheated instant pot at 380ºF (193ºC) for 15 minutes. Flip the patties when the lid screen indicates TURN FOOD.
3. Bon appétit!

Cheesy Cornbread Muffins

Prep time: 5 minutes | Cook time: 22 minutes | Serves 4

1 cup self-rising cornmeal
4 ounces (113 g) canned creamed corn
½ cup shredded Colby cheese
¼ cup milk
¼ cup butter, room temperature

1. Mix all ingredients until everything is well incorporated. Scrape the batter into baking molds and place them in the baking dish.
2. Place the baking dish in the air fryer basket. Put the air fryer lid on and bake in the preheated instant pot at 360ºF (182ºC) for about 22 minutes or until a tester comes out dry and clean.
3. Allow the cornbread muffins to cool before unmolding and serving. Bon appétit!

Biryani with Butter

Prep time: 5 minutes | Cook time: 10 minutes | Serves 4

2 cups jasmine rice, cooked
1 cup water
1 teaspoon ginger-garlic paste
2 tablespoons chopped shallots
½ teaspoon ground cinnamon
2 tablespoons butter
½ teaspoon cumin seeds
1 teaspoon garam masala
½ teaspoon turmeric powder

1. Thoroughly combine all ingredients in a lightly greased baking dish.
2. Place the baking dish in the air fryer basket. Put the air fryer lid on and bake in the preheated instant pot at 360ºF (182ºC) for 10 minutes or until cooked through.
3. Bon appétit!

Millet Porridge with Sultanas

Prep time: 5 minutes | Cook time: 12 minutes | Serves 5

½ cup old-fashioned oats
½ cup millet, rinsed and drained
2 tablespoons ground flax seeds
½ cup Sultanas
2 cups coconut milk
2 tablespoons coconut oil
A pinch of salt
A pinch of ground cloves

1. Thoroughly combine all ingredients in a mixing bowl. Spoon the mixture into a lightly greased baking dish.
2. Place the baking dish in the air fryer basket. Put the air fryer lid on and bake in the preheated instant pot at 380ºF (193ºC) for 12 minutes.
3. Serve immediately. Bon appétit!

Juicy Milk Oatmeal

Prep time: 5 minutes | Cook time: 12 minutes | Serves 4

1 cup old-fashioned oats
1 teaspoon baking powder
½ teaspoon cinnamon
A pinch of sea salt
A pinch of grated nutmeg
1 cup coconut milk
1 cup pineapple juice
¼ cup agave syrup
2 tablespoons ground chia seeds
1 teaspoon vanilla extract

1. Thoroughly combine all ingredients in a mixing bowl. Spoon the mixture into lightly greased mugs. Then, place the mugs in the baking dish.
2. Place the baking dish in the air fryer basket. Put the air fryer lid on and bake in the preheated instant pot at 380ºF (193ºC) for 12 minutes.
3. Bon appétit!

Cheesy Carbonara with Pancetta

Prep time: 10 minutes | Cook time: 10 minutes | Serves 4

2 cups Arborio rice, cooked
2 tablespoons sesame oil
1 shallot, chopped
½ cup white Italian wine
½ cup heavy cream
Coarse sea salt and freshly ground black pepper, to taste
4 tablespoons chopped pancetta
1 cup grated Parmesan cheese
1 tablespoon chopped fresh Italian parsley

1. Thoroughly combine all ingredients in a lightly greased baking dish.
2. Place the baking dish in the air fryer basket. Put the air fryer lid on and bake in the preheated instant pot at 360ºF (182ºC) for 10 minutes or until cooked through.
3. Bon appétit!

Sour Cream Biscuits

Prep time: 5 minutes | Cook time: 15 minutes | Serves 6

1 cup all-purpose flour
1 teaspoon baking powder
4 tablespoons olive oil
½ cup sour cream
A pinch of sea salt
1 teaspoon Mediterranean seasoning mix

1. Mix all ingredients until well combined. Use a 2-inch biscuit cutter and cut out biscuits. Place the biscuits in a lightly greased baking dish.
2. Place the baking dish in the air fryer basket. Put the air fryer lid on and bake in the preheated instant pot at 360ºF (182ºC) for 15 minutes or until a tester comes out dry and clean.
3. Bon appétit!

Chapter 6 Fish and Seafood

Garlicky Calamari

Prep time: 10 minutes | Cook time: 5 minutes | Serves 4

1 pound (454 g) calamari, sliced into rings
2 tablespoons butter, melted
4 garlic cloves, smashed
2 tablespoons sherry wine
2 tablespoons fresh lemon juice
Coarse sea salt and ground black pepper, to taste
1 teaspoon paprika
1 teaspoon dried oregano

1. Toss all ingredients in a lightly greased air fryer basket.
2. Put the air fryer lid on and air fry in the preheated instant pot at 400ºF (205ºC) for 5 minutes. Flip the calamari when the lid screen indicates TURN FOOD.
3. Bon appétit!

Shrimp and Broccoli

Prep time: 10 minutes | Cook time: 6 minutes | Serves 4

1 pound (454 g) raw shrimp, peeled and deveined
½ pound (227 g) broccoli florets
1 tablespoon olive oil
1 garlic clove, minced
2 tablespoons freshly squeezed lemon juice
Coarse sea salt and ground black pepper, to taste
1 teaspoon paprika

1. Toss all ingredients in a lightly greased air fryer basket.
2. Put the air fryer lid on and air fry in the preheated instant pot at 400ºF (205ºC) for 6 minutes. Flip the shrimp and broccoli when the lid screen indicates TURN FOOD.
3. Bon appétit!

Codfish Tacos with Avocado

Prep time: 10 minutes | Cook time: 14 minutes | Serves 4

1 pound (454 g) codfish fillets
1 tablespoon olive oil
1 avocado, pitted, peeled, and mashed
4 tablespoons mayonnaise
1 teaspoon mustard
1 shallot, chopped
1 habanero pepper, chopped
8 small corn tortillas

1. Toss the fish fillets with the olive oil; place them in a lightly oiled air fryer basket.
2. Put the air fryer lid on and air fry in the preheated instant pot at 400ºF (205ºC) for 14 minutes. Flip the fish fillets when the lid screen indicates TURN FOOD.
3. Assemble the tacos with the chopped fish and remaining ingredients and serve warm. Bon appétit!

Butter Mahi-Mahi Fillets

Prep time: 5 minutes | Cook time: 14 minutes | Serves 4

1 pound (454 g) mahi-mahi fillets
2 tablespoons butter, room temperature
2 tablespoons fresh lemon juice
Kosher salt and freshly ground black pepper, to taste
1 teaspoon smoked paprika
1 teaspoon minced garlic
1 teaspoon dried basil
1 teaspoon dried oregano

1. Toss the fish fillets with the remaining ingredients and place them in a lightly oiled air fryer basket.
2. Put the air fryer lid on and air fry in the preheated instant pot at 400ºF (205ºC) for 14 minutes. Flip the fish fillets when the lid screen indicates TURN FOOD.
3. Bon appétit!

Prawn Salad with Mayo

Prep time: 10 minutes | Cook time: 6 minutes | Serves 4

1½ pounds (680 g) king prawns, peeled and deveined
Coarse sea salt and ground black pepper, to taste
1 tablespoon fresh lemon juice
1 cup mayonnaise
1 teaspoon Dijon mustard
1 tablespoon roughly chopped fresh parsley
1 teaspoon minced fresh dill
1 shallot, chopped

1. Toss the prawns with the salt and black pepper in a lightly greased air fryer basket.
2. Put the air fryer lid on and air fry in the preheated instant pot at 400ºF (205ºC) for 6 minutes. Flip the prawns when the lid screen indicates TURN FOOD.
3. Add the prawns to a salad bowl; add in the remaining ingredients and stir to combine well.
4. Bon appétit!

Calamari Rings

Prep time: 10 minutes | Cook time: 5 minutes | Serves 4

1 cup all-purpose flour
½ cup crushed tortilla chips
1 teaspoon mustard powder
1 tablespoon dried parsley
Sea salt and freshly ground black pepper, to taste
1 teaspoon cayenne pepper
2 tablespoons olive oil
1 pound (454 g) calamari, sliced into rings

1. In a mixing bowl, thoroughly combine the flour, tortilla chips, spices, and olive oil. Mix to combine well.
2. Now, dip the calamari into the flour mixture to coat. Place the calamari in the air fryer basket.
3. Put the air fryer lid on and air fry in the preheated instant pot at 400ºF (205ºC) for 5 minutes. Flip the calamari when the lid screen indicates TURN FOOD.
4. Bon appétit!

Breaded Fish Fillets

Prep time: 10 minutes | Cook time: 10 minutes | Serves 4

2 eggs
¼ cup all-purpose flour
Sea salt and ground black pepper, to taste
½ teaspoon onion powder
¼ teaspoon garlic powder
¼ cup plain bread crumbs
1½ tablespoons olive oil
1 pound (454 g) cod fish fillets, sliced into pieces

1. In a mixing bowl, thoroughly combine the eggs, flour, and spices. In a separate bowl, thoroughly combine the bread crumbs and olive oil.
2. Dip the fish pieces into the flour mixture to coat; roll the fish pieces over the bread crumb mixture until they are well coated on all sides.
3. Arrange the fish in the air fryer basket.
4. Put the air fryer lid on and air fry in the preheated instant pot at 400ºF (205ºC) for 10 minutes. Flip the fish fingers when the lid screen indicates TURN FOOD.
5. Bon appétit!

Prawns with Lemon Juice

Prep time: 15 minutes | Cook time: 9 minutes | Serves 4

1½ pounds (680 g) prawns, peeled and deveined
2 garlic cloves, minced
2 tablespoons chopped fresh chives
½ cup whole-wheat flour
½ teaspoon sweet paprika
1 teaspoon hot paprika
Salt and freshly ground black pepper, to taste
2 tablespoons coconut oil
2 tablespoons lemon juice

1. Toss all ingredients in a lightly greased air fryer basket.
2. Put the air fryer lid on and air fry in the preheated instant pot at 400ºF (205ºC) for 9 minutes. Flip the prawns when the lid screen indicates TURN FOOD.
3. Bon appétit!

Buttermilk Tuna Muffins

Prep time: 10 minutes | Cook time: 14 minutes | Serves 4

1 pound (454 g) tuna, boneless and chopped
½ cup all-purpose flour
½ cup bread crumbs
2 tablespoons buttermilk
2 eggs, whisked
Kosher salt and ground black pepper, to taste
½ teaspoon cayenne pepper
1 tablespoon olive oil
4 Mozzarella cheese slices
4 English muffins

1. Mix all ingredients, except for the cheese and English muffins, in a bowl. Shape the mixture into four patties and place them in a lightly oiled air fryer basket.
2. Put the air fryer lid on and air fry in the preheated instant pot at 400ºF (205ºC) for 14 minutes. Flip the fish patties when the lid screen indicates TURN FOOD.
3. Place the cheese slices on the warm patties and serve on hamburger buns and enjoy!

Lemony Squid

Prep time: 15 minutes | Cook time: 5 minutes | Serves 5

1½ pounds (680 g) squid, cut into pieces
1 chili pepper, chopped
1 small lemon, squeezed
2 tablespoons olive oil
1 tablespoon capers, drained
2 garlic cloves, minced
1 tablespoon chopped coriander
2 tablespoons chopped parsley
1 teaspoon sweet paprika
Sea salt and ground black pepper, to taste

1. Toss all ingredients in a lightly greased air fryer basket.
2. Put the air fryer lid on and air fry in the preheated instant pot at 400ºF (205ºC) for 5 minutes. Flip the squid when the lid screen indicates TURN FOOD.
3. Bon appétit!

Swordfish Steaks with Garlic

Prep time: 5 minutes | Cook time: 10 minutes | Serves 4

1 pound (454 g) swordfish steaks
4 garlic cloves, peeled
4 tablespoons olive oil
2 tablespoons fresh lemon juice
1 tablespoon roughly chopped fresh cilantro
1 teaspoon Spanish paprika
Sea salt and ground black pepper, to taste

1. Toss the swordfish steaks with the remaining ingredients and place them in a lightly oiled air fryer basket.
2. Put the air fryer lid on and air fry in the preheated instant pot at 400ºF (205ºC) for 10 minutes. Flip the swordfish steaks when the lid screen indicates TURN FOOD.
3. Bon appétit!

Lemon Salmon Salad

Prep time: 10 minutes | Cook time: 12 minutes | Serves 4

1 pound (454 g) salmon fillets
Sea salt and ground black pepper, to taste
2 tablespoons olive oil
2 garlic cloves, minced
1 bell pepper, sliced
1 shallot, chopped
½ cup pitted and sliced Kalamata olives
½ lemon, juiced
1 teaspoon minced Aleppo pepper

1. Toss the salmon fillets with the salt, black pepper, and olive oil; place them in a lightly oiled air fryer basket.
2. Put the air fryer lid on and roast in the preheated instant pot at 380ºF (193ºC) for 12 minutes. Flip the salmon fillets when the lid screen indicates TURN FOOD.
3. Chop the salmon fillets using two forks and add them to a salad bowl; add in the remaining ingredients and toss to combine.
4. Bon appétit!

Monkfish Pitas with Avocado

Prep time: 10 minutes | Cook time: 14 minutes | Serves 4

1 pound (454 g) monkfish fillets
1 tablespoon olive oil
Sea salt and ground black pepper, to taste
1 teaspoon cayenne pepper
4 tablespoons coleslaw
1 avocado, pitted, peeled, and diced
1 tablespoon chopped fresh parsley
4 (6-inch) Greek pitas, warmed

1. Toss the fish fillets with the olive oil; place them in a lightly oiled air fryer basket.
2. Put the air fryer lid on and air fry in the preheated instant pot at 400ºF (205ºC) for 14 minutes. Flip the fish fillets when the lid screen indicates TURN FOOD.
3. Assemble the pitas with the chopped fish and remaining ingredients and serve warm. Bon appétit!

Tilapia Nuggets with Thyme

Prep time: 10 minutes | Cook time: 10 minutes | Serves 4

1½ pounds (680 g) tilapia fillets, cut into 1½-inch pieces
1 tablespoon dried thyme
1 tablespoon dried oregano
1 tablespoon Dijon mustard
2 tablespoons olive oil
1½ cups all-purpose flour
Sea salt and ground black pepper, to taste
½ teaspoon baking powder

1. Pat the fish dry with kitchen towels.
2. In a mixing bowl, thoroughly combine all remaining ingredients until well mixed. Now, dip the fish pieces into the batter to coat.
3. Arrange the fish in the air fryer basket.
4. Put the air fryer lid on and air fry in the preheated instant pot at 400ºF (205ºC) for 10 minutes. Flip the fish nuggets when the lid screen indicates TURN FOOD.
5. Bon appétit!

Breaded Shrimp

Prep time: 10 minutes | Cook time: 10 minutes | Serves 4

½ cup flour
Sea salt and lemon pepper, to taste
2 large eggs
1 cup seasoned bread crumbs
2 tablespoons olive oil
1 pound (454 g) shrimp, peeled and deveined

1. In a shallow bowl, mix the flour, salt, and lemon pepper. Beat the eggs in a second bowl, and place the bread crumbs in a third bowl.
2. Dip the shrimp in the flour mixture, then in the whisked eggs; finally, roll the shrimp over the bread crumbs until they are well coated on all sides.
3. Arrange the shrimp in the air fryer basket. Drizzle the olive oil over the shrimp.
4. Put the air fryer lid on and air fry in the preheated instant pot at 400ºF (205ºC) for 10 minutes. Flip the shrimp when the lid screen indicates TURN FOOD.
5. Bon appétit!

Swordfish Steaks with Rosemary

Prep time: 5 minutes | Cook time: 10 minutes | Serves 4

1 pound (454 g) swordfish steaks
2 tablespoons olive oil
2 teaspoons tamari sauce
Salt and freshly ground pepper, to taste
¼ cup dry red wine
2 sprigs rosemary
1 sprig thyme
1 tablespoon grated lemon rind

1. Toss the swordfish steaks with the remaining ingredients in a ceramic dish; cover and let it marinate in the refrigerator for about 2 hours.
2. Then, discard the marinade and place the fish in a lightly oiled air fryer basket.
3. Put the air fryer lid on and air fry in the preheated instant pot at 400ºF (205ºC) for 10 minutes. Flip the swordfish steaks when the lid screen indicates TURN FOOD.
4. Bon appétit!

Coconut Sea Bass with Tomato

Prep time: 10 minutes | Cook time: 16 minutes | Serves 4

1½ pounds (680 g) sea bass fillet
2 tablespoons lemon juice
2 garlic cloves, minced
½ cup shredded coconut
½ cup all-purpose flour
Coarse sea salt and ground black pepper, to taste
2 tomatoes, sliced

1. Toss the fish fillets with the lemon juice, garlic, coconut, flour, salt, and black pepper; place them in a lightly oiled air fryer basket.
2. Put the air fryer lid on and air fry in the preheated instant pot at 400ºF (205ºC) for 16 minutes. Flip the fish fillets and top with the tomatoes when the lid screen indicates TURN FOOD.
3. Bon appétit!

Panko Salmon Strips

Prep time: 5 minutes | Cook time: 10 minutes | Serves 4

1 egg, beaten
½ cup all-purpose flour
Sea salt and ground black pepper, to taste
1 teaspoon hot paprika
½ cup seasoned bread crumbs
1 tablespoon olive oil
1 pound (454 g) salmon strips

1. In a mixing bowl, thoroughly combine the egg, flour, and spices. In a separate bowl, thoroughly combine the bread crumbs and olive oil.
2. Now, dip the salmon strips into the flour mixture to coat; roll the fish pieces over the bread crumb mixture until they are well coated on all sides.
3. Arrange the salmon strips in the air fryer basket.
4. Put the air fryer lid on and air fry in the preheated instant pot at 400ºF (205ºC) for 10 minutes. Flip the salmon strips when the lid screen indicates TURN FOOD.
5. Bon appétit!

Mackerel Fillets with Lime

Prep time: 5 minutes | Cook time: 14 minutes | Serves 4

1 tablespoon olive oil
1½ pounds (680 g) mackerel fillets
Sea salt and ground black pepper, to taste
2 tablespoons parsley
2 garlic cloves, minced
2 tablespoons fresh lime juice

1. Toss the fish fillets with the remaining ingredients and place them in a lightly oiled air fryer basket.
2. Put the air fryer lid on and air fry in the preheated instant pot at 400ºF (205ºC) for 14 minutes. Flip the fish fillets when the lid screen indicates TURN FOOD.
3. Bon appétit!

Cheesy Shrimp

Prep time: 10 minutes | Cook time: 10 minutes | Serves 4

1½ pounds (680 g) shrimp, cleaned and deveined
½ cup all-purpose flour
½ teaspoon shallot powder
½ teaspoon garlic powder
1 teaspoon crushed red pepper flakes
Sea salt and ground black pepper, to taste
2 large eggs
1 cup crushed crackers
½ cup grated Parmesan cheese

1. In a shallow bowl, mix the flour and spices. Beat the eggs in the second bowl, and mix the crackers and cheese in the third bowl.
2. Dip the shrimp in the flour mixture, then in the whisked eggs; finally, roll the shrimp over the cracker and cheese mixture until they are well coated on all sides.
3. Arrange the shrimp in a greased air fryer basket.
4. Put the air fryer lid on and air fry in the preheated instant pot at 400ºF (205ºC) for 10 minutes. Flip the shrimp when the lid screen indicates TURN FOOD.
5. Bon appétit!

Buttery Halibut Steaks

Prep time: 5 minutes | Cook time: 12 minutes | Serves 4

1 pound (454 g) halibut steaks
¼ cup butter
Sea salt, to taste
2 tablespoons chopped fresh chives
1 teaspoon minced garlic
1 teaspoon ground mixed peppercorns

1. Toss the halibut steaks with the rest of the ingredients and place them in a lightly oiled air fryer basket.
2. Put the air fryer lid on and air fry in the preheated instant pot at 400ºF (205ºC) for 12 minutes. Flip the halibut steaks when the lid screen indicates TURN FOOD.
3. Bon appétit!

Tilapia Fillets

Prep time: 10 minutes | Cook time: 10 minutes | Serves 4

½ cup all-purpose flour
1 large egg
2 tablespoons buttermilk
½ cup crushed crackers
1 teaspoon garlic powder
Sea salt and ground black pepper, to taste
½ teaspoon cayenne pepper
1 pound (454 g) tilapia fillets, cut into strips

1. In a shallow bowl, place the flour. Whisk the egg and buttermilk in a second bowl, and mix the crushed crackers and spices in a third bowl.
2. Dip the fish strips in the flour mixture, then in the whisked eggs; finally, roll the fish strips over the cracker mixture until they are well coated on all sides.
3. Arrange the fish sticks in the air fryer basket.
4. Put the air fryer lid on and air fry in the preheated instant pot at 400ºF (205ºC) for 10 minutes. Flip the fish sticks when the lid screen indicates TURN FOOD.
5. Bon appétit!

Orange Roughy Fillets

Prep time: 5 minutes | Cook time: 10 minutes | Serves 4

1 pound (454 g) orange roughy fillets
2 tablespoons butter
2 cloves garlic, minced
Sea salt and red pepper flakes, to taste

1. Toss the fish fillets with the remaining ingredients and place them in a lightly oiled air fryer basket.
2. Put the air fryer lid on and air fry in the preheated instant pot at 400ºF (205ºC) for 10 minutes. Flip the fish fillets when the lid screen indicates TURN FOOD.
3. Bon appétit!

Shrimp Salad with Cucumber

Prep time: 15 minutes | Cook time: 6 minutes | Serves 4

1 pound (454 g) shrimp, peeled and chilled
1 teaspoon olive oil
1 stalks celery, sliced
1 English cucumber, sliced
1 shallot, sliced
1 tablespoon roughly chopped fresh dill
1 tablespoon roughly chopped fresh parsley
1 tablespoon fresh lime juice
1 tablespoon apple cider vinegar
½ cup mayonnaise
1 teaspoon Creole seasoning mix
1½ teaspoons Dijon mustard
Coarse sea salt and lemon pepper, to taste
4 hoagie rolls

1. Toss the shrimp and olive oil in the air fryer basket.
2. Put the air fryer lid on and air fry in the preheated instant pot at 400ºF (205ºC) for 6 minutes. Flip the shrimp when the lid screen indicates TURN FOOD.
3. Place the shrimp in a mixing bowl along with the remaining ingredients; toss to combine and serve on the prepared hoagie rolls.
4. Bon appétit!

Squid Tubes with Cheese

Prep time: 6 minutes | Cook time: 5 minutes | Serves 4

1½ pounds (680 g) small squid tubes
2 tablespoons butter, melted
1 chili pepper, chopped
2 garlic cloves, minced
1 teaspoon red pepper flakes
Sea salt and ground black pepper, to taste
¼ cup dry white wine
2 tablespoons fresh lemon juice
1 teaspoon Mediterranean herb mix
2 tablespoons grated Parmigiano-Reggiano cheese

1. Toss all ingredients , except for the Parmigiano-Reggiano cheese, in a lightly greased air fryer basket.
2. Put the air fryer lid on and air fry in the preheated instant pot at 400ºF (205ºC) for 5 minutes. Flip the squid when the lid screen indicates TURN FOOD.
3. Top the warm squid with the cheese. Bon appétit!

Cod Fish Patties

Prep time: 10 minutes | Cook time: 14 minutes | Serves 4

1 pound (454 g) boneless cod fish, chopped
½ cup bread crumbs
2 medium eggs
1 teaspoon Dijon mustard
2 garlic cloves, minced
Sea salt and ground black pepper, to taste
½ teaspoon onion powder
1 teaspoon hot paprika
1 tablespoon olive oil
4 hamburger buns

1. Mix all ingredients , except for the hamburger buns, in a bowl. Shape the mixture into four patties and place them in a lightly oiled air fryer basket.
2. Put the air fryer lid on and air fry in the preheated instant pot at 400ºF (205ºC) for 14 minutes. Flip the fish patties when the lid screen indicates TURN FOOD.
3. Serve on hamburger buns and enjoy!

Lemony Salmon Fillets

Prep time: 6 minutes | Cook time: 12 minutes | Serves 4

1½ pounds (680 g) salmon fillets
2 sprigs fresh rosemary
1 tablespoon fresh basil
1 tablespoon fresh thyme
1 tablespoon fresh dill
1 small lemon, juiced
2 tablespoons olive oil
Sea salt and ground black pepper, to taste
1 teaspoon stone-ground mustard
2 cloves garlic, chopped

1. Toss the salmon with the remaining ingredients; place them in a lightly oiled air fryer basket.
2. Put the air fryer lid on and roast in the preheated instant pot at 380ºF (193ºC) for 12 minutes. Flip the salmon fillets when the lid screen indicates TURN FOOD.
3. Serve immediately and enjoy!

Shrimp Salad with Mayo

Prep time: 15 minutes | Cook time: 6 minutes | Serves 4

1½ pounds (680 g) shrimp, peeled and deveined
1 tablespoon olive oil
Sea salt and freshly ground black pepper, to taste
1 teaspoon chopped fresh dill
1 teaspoon chopped fresh basil
1 tablespoon chopped fresh parsley
2 tablespoons chopped chives
1 bell pepper, seeded and chopped
1 celery stalk, trimmed and chopped
½ cup mayonnaise
1 teaspoon stone-ground mustard
1 tablespoon fresh lime juice

1. Toss the shrimp and olive oil in the air fryer basket.
2. Put the air fryer lid on and air fry in the preheated instant pot at 400ºF (205ºC) for 6 minutes. Flip the shrimp when the lid screen indicates TURN FOOD.
3. Place the shrimp in a salad bowl; add in the remaining ingredients and gently stir to combine. Serve chilled.

Mackerel Patties Muffins

Prep time: 10 minutes | Cook time: 14 minutes | Serves 4

1 pound (454 g) mackerel fillet, boneless and chopped
1 tablespoon olive oil
½ onion, chopped
2 garlic cloves, crushed
1 teaspoon hot paprika
1 tablespoon chopped fresh cilantro
2 tablespoons chopped fresh parsley
Sea salt and ground black pepper, to taste
4 English muffins, toasted

1. Mix all ingredients , except for the English muffins, in a bowl. Shape the mixture into four patties and place them in a lightly oiled air fryer basket.
2. Put the air fryer lid on and air fry in the preheated instant pot at 400ºF (205ºC) for 14 minutes. Flip the fish patties when the lid screen indicates TURN FOOD.
3. Serve on English muffins and enjoy!

Calamari with Lemon

Prep time: 15 minutes | Cook time: 5 minutes | Serves 4

1 pound (454 g) calamari, sliced into rings
2 garlic cloves, minced
1 teaspoon red pepper flakes
2 tablespoons dry white wine
2 tablespoons olive oil
2 tablespoons fresh lemon juice
1 teaspoon chopped basil
1 teaspoon chopped dill
1 teaspoon chopped parsley
Coarse sea salt and freshly cracked black pepper, to taste

1. Toss all ingredients in a lightly greased air fryer basket.
2. Put the air fryer lid on and air fry in the preheated instant pot at 400ºF (205ºC) for 5 minutes. Flip the calamari when the lid screen indicates TURN FOOD.
3. Bon appétit!

Rosemary Sea Scallops

Prep time: 5 minutes | Cook time: 7 minutes | Serves 4

1½ pounds (680 g) sea scallops
4 tablespoons butter, melted
1 tablespoon minced garlic
Sea salt and ground black pepper, to taste
2 rosemary sprigs, leaves picked and chopped
4 tablespoons dry white wine

1. Toss all ingredients in a lightly greased air fryer basket.
2. Put the air fryer lid on and air fry in the preheated instant pot at 400ºF (205ºC) for 7 minutes. Flip the scallops when the lid screen indicates TURN FOOD.
3. Bon appétit!

Sausage-Stuffed Squid Tubes

Prep time: 10 minutes | Cook time: 5 minutes | Serves 4

2 tablespoons olive oil, divided, plus more as needed
1 small onion, chopped
2 cloves garlic, minced
1 tablespoon chopped fresh parsley
1 small Italian pepper, chopped
Sea salt and ground black pepper, to taste
4 ounces (113 g) beef sausage, crumbled
1 pound (454 g) squid tubes, cleaned

1. In a mixing bowl, thoroughly combine the olive oil, onion, garlic, parsley, Italian pepper, salt, black pepper, and sausage.
2. Stuff the squid tubes with the sausage filling and secure them with toothpicks. Place them in a lightly oiled air fryer basket.
3. Put the air fryer lid on and air fry in the preheated instant pot at 400ºF (205ºC) for 5 minutes. Flip the stuffed squid tubes when the lid screen indicates TURN FOOD.
4. Bon appétit!

Calamari Rings with Lemon

Prep time: 10 minutes | Cook time: 5 minutes | Serves 4

1 pound (454 g) calamari, sliced into rings
Sea salt and ground black pepper, to taste
1 teaspoon cayenne pepper
1 teaspoon garlic powder
2 tablespoons lemon juice
2 tablespoons olive oil

1. Toss all ingredients in a lightly greased air fryer basket.
2. Put the air fryer lid on and air fry in the preheated instant pot at 400ºF (205ºC) for 5 minutes. Flip the calamari when the lid screen indicates TURN FOOD.
3. Bon appétit!

Sea Scallop Salad

Prep time: 8 minutes | Cook time: 7 minutes | Serves 4

1½ pounds (680 g) sea scallops
Sea salt and ground black pepper, to taste
2 tablespoons olive oil
1 tablespoon balsamic vinegar
2 garlic cloves, minced
2 teaspoons minced fresh tarragon
1 teaspoon Dijon mustard
1 cup mixed baby greens
1 small tomato, diced

1. Toss the scallops, salt, and black pepper in a lightly greased air fryer basket.
2. Put the air fryer lid on and air fry in the preheated instant pot at400ºF (205ºC) scallops for 7 minutes. Flip the when the lid screen indicates TURN FOOD.
3. Toss the scallops with the remaining ingredients and serve at room temperature or chilled.
4. Bon appétit!

Halibut Burgers with Nutmeg

Prep time: 10 minutes | Cook time: 14 minutes | Serves 4

1 pound (454 g) halibut, chopped
2 garlic cloves, crushed
4 tablespoons chopped scallions
Sea salt and ground black pepper, to taste
1 teaspoon smoked paprika
A pinch of grated nutmeg
1 tablespoon olive oil
4 hamburger buns

1. Mix all ingredients , except for the hamburger buns, in a bowl. Shape the mixture into four patties and place them in a lightly oiled air fryer basket.
2. Put the air fryer lid on and air fry in the preheated instant pot at 400ºF (205ºC) for 14 minutes. Flip the fish patties when the lid screen indicates TURN FOOD.
3. Serve on hamburger buns and enjoy!

Coconut Shrimp

Prep time: 10 minutes | Cook time: 9 minutes | Serves 4

½ cup whole wheat flour
1 cup shredded coconut
¼ cup buttermilk
2 tablespoons olive oil
2 garlic cloves, crushed
1 tablespoon fresh lemon juice
Sea salt and red pepper flakes, to taste
1½ pounds (680 g) shrimp, peeled and deveined

1. Mix the flour, coconut, buttermilk, olive oil, garlic, lemon juice, salt, and red pepper in a mixing bowl.
2. Dip the shrimp in the batter and place them in a greased air fryer basket.
3. Put the air fryer lid on and air fry in the preheated instant pot at 400ºF (205ºC) for 9 minutes. Flip the shrimp when the lid screen indicates TURN FOOD.
4. Bon appétit!

Tuna Salad with Spinach

Prep time: 10 minutes | Cook time: 10 minutes | Serves 4

1 pound (454 g) fresh tuna steak
Sea salt and ground black pepper, to taste
2 tablespoons fresh lemon juice
1 small onion, thinly sliced
1 carrot, julienned
2 cups baby spinach
2 tablespoons roughly chopped parsley

1. Toss the fish with the salt and black pepper; place the tuna in a lightly oiled air fryer basket.
2. Put the air fryer lid on and air fry in the preheated instant pot at 400ºF (205ºC) for 10 minutes. Flip the tuna when the lid screen indicates TURN FOOD.
3. Chop the tuna with two forks and add in the remaining ingredients; stir to combine and serve well chilled.
4. Bon appétit!

Sea Scallops

Prep time: 5 minutes | Cook time: 7 minutes | Serves 4

1 pound (454 g) sea scallops
2 tablespoons butter, room temperature
2 tablespoons lemon juice
2 garlic cloves, crushed
Salt and fresh ground black pepper, to taste
¼ cup dry white wine

1. Toss all ingredients in a lightly greased air fryer basket.
2. Put the air fryer lid on and air fry in the preheated instant pot at 400ºF (205ºC) for 7 minutes. Flip the scallops when the lid screen indicates TURN FOOD.
3. Bon appétit!

Lobster Tails with Butter

Prep time: 5 minutes | Cook time: 8 minutes | Serves 4

1 pound (454 g) lobster tails
4 tablespoons butter, room temperature
2 garlic cloves, minced
Coarse sea salt and freshly cracked black pepper, to taste
4 tablespoons spring onions
1 tablespoon fresh lime juice

1. Butterfly the lobster tails by cutting through the shell and place them in a lightly oiled air fryer basket.
2. In a mixing bowl, thoroughly combine the remaining ingredients.
3. Now, spread ½ of the butter mixture over the top of the lobster meat.
4. Put the air fryer lid on and air fry in the preheated instant pot at 380ºF (193ºC) for 4 minutes.
5. After that, spread another ½ of the butter mixture on top; continue to cook for a further 4 minutes.
6. Bon appétit!

Butter Calamari Rings

Prep time: 10 minutes | Cook time: 5 minutes | Serves 4

1 pound (454 g) calamari, sliced into rings
2 tablespoons butter
2 tablespoons chopped parsley
2 garlic cloves, minced
1 teaspoon cayenne pepper
Sea salt and freshly ground black pepper, to taste

1. Toss all ingredients in a lightly greased air fryer basket.
2. Put the air fryer lid on and air fry in the preheated instant pot at 400ºF (205ºC) for 5 minutes. Flip the calamari when the lid screen indicates TURN FOOD.
3. Bon appétit!

Mustard Calamari

Prep time: 10 minutes | Cook time: 5 minutes | Serves 4

2 cups flour
Sea salt and ground black pepper, to taste
1 teaspoon minced garlic
1 tablespoon mustard
2 tablespoons olive oil
1 pound (454 g) calamari, sliced into rings

1. In a mixing bowl, thoroughly combine the flour, salt, black pepper, garlic, mustard, and, and olive oil. Mix to combine well.
2. Now, dip the calamari into the flour mixture to coat. Place the calamari in the air fryer basket.
3. Put the air fryer lid on and air fry in the preheated instant pot at 400ºF (205ºC) for 5 minutes. Flip the calamari when the lid screen indicates TURN FOOD.
4. Bon appétit!

Cheesy Monkfish Strips

Prep time: 10 minutes | Cook time: 10 minutes | Serves 4

½ cup all-purpose flour
Sea salt and ground black pepper, to taste
1 teaspoon cayenne pepper
½ teaspoon onion powder
1 tablespoon chopped Italian parsley
1 teaspoon garlic powder
1 egg, whisked
½ cup grated Pecorino Romano cheese
1 pound (454 g) monkfish, sliced into strips

1. In a shallow bowl, mix the flour, spices, egg, and cheese. Dip the fish strips in the batter until they are well coated on all sides.
2. Arrange the fish strips in the air fryer basket.
3. Put the air fryer lid on and air fry in the preheated instant pot at 400ºF (205ºC) for 10 minutes. Flip the fish strips when the lid screen indicates TURN FOOD.
4. Bon appétit!

Monkfish Fillets with Cheese

Prep time: 5 minutes | Cook time: 14 minutes | Serves 4

1 pound (454 g) monkfish fillets
Coarse sea salt and ground black pepper, to taste
2 tablespoons butter
2 tablespoons lemon juice
4 tablespoon grated Parmesan cheese

1. Toss the fish fillets with the remaining ingredients, except for the Parmesan cheese; place them in a lightly oiled air fryer basket.
2. Put the air fryer lid on and air fry in the preheated instant pot at 400ºF (205ºC) for 14 minutes. Flip the fish fillets when the lid screen indicates TURN FOOD.
3. Top the fish fillets with the grated Parmesan cheese and serve immediately. Bon appétit!

Chili Calamari

Prep time: 10 minutes | Cook time: 5 minutes | Serves 4

½ cup milk
1 cup all-purpose flour
2 tablespoons olive oil
1 teaspoon turmeric powder
Sea salt flakes and ground black, to taste
1 teaspoon paprika
1 red chili, minced
1 pound (454 g) calamari, cut into rings

1. In a mixing bowl, thoroughly combine the milk, flour, olive oil, turmeric powder, salt, black pepper, paprika, and red chili. Mix to combine well.
2. Now, dip the calamari into the flour mixture to coat. Place the calamari in the air fryer basket.
3. Put the air fryer lid on and air fry in the preheated instant pot at 400ºF (205ºC) for 5 minutes. Flip the calamari when the lid screen indicates TURN FOOD.
4. Bon appétit!

Beer Calamari Rings

Prep time: 5 minutes | Cook time: 5 minutes | Serves 4

2 cups all-purpose flour
1 cup beer
Sea salt and ground black pepper, to taste
2 teaspoons garlic powder
1 teaspoon dried parsley flakes
1 tablespoon olive oil
1 pound (454 g) calamari rings

1. In a mixing bowl, thoroughly combine the flour, beer, spices, and olive oil. Mix to combine well.
2. Now, dip the calamari into the flour mixture to coat. Place the calamari in the air fryer basket.
3. Put the air fryer lid on and air fry in the preheated instant pot at 400ºF (205ºC) for 5 minutes. Flip the calamari when the lid screen indicates TURN FOOD.
4. Bon appétit!

Buttermilk Shrimp

Prep time: 10 minutes | Cook time: 10 minutes | Serves 4

1 cup all-purpose flour
1 teaspoon Old Bay seasoning
Sea salt and lemon pepper, to taste
½ cup buttermilk
1 cup seasoned bread crumbs
1½ pounds (680 g) shrimp, peeled and deveined

1. In a shallow bowl, mix the flour, spices, and buttermilk. Place the seasoned bread crumbs in the second bowl.
2. Dip the shrimp in the flour mixture, then in the bread crumbs until they are well coated on all sides.
3. Arrange the shrimp in a greased air fryer basket.
4. Put the air fryer lid on and air fry in the preheated instant pot at 400ºF (205ºC) for 10 minutes. Flip the shrimp when the lid screen indicates TURN FOOD.
5. Bon appétit!

Barramundi Fillets with Mustard

Prep time: 5 minutes | Cook time: 12 minutes | Serves 4

1 pound (454 g) Barramundi fillets
Sea salt and ground Szechuan pepper, to taste
1 tablespoon sesame oil
2 tablespoons rice wine vinegar
½ cup seasoned bread crumbs
1 tablespoon grain mustard

1. Toss the fish with the remaining ingredients; place them in a lightly oiled air fryer basket.
2. Put the air fryer lid on and air fry in the preheated instant pot at 400ºF (205ºC) for 12 minutes. Flip the fish when the lid screen indicates TURN FOOD.
3. Bon appétit!

Sea Bass with Butter

Prep time: 5 minutes | Cook time: 10 minutes | Serves 3

2 tablespoons butter, room temperature
1 pound (454 g) sea bass
¼ cup dry white wine
¼ cup all-purpose flour
Sea salt and ground black pepper, to taste
1 teaspoon mustard seeds
1 teaspoon fennel seeds
2 cloves garlic, minced

1. Toss the fish with the remaining ingredients; place them in a lightly oiled air fryer basket.
2. Put the air fryer lid on and air fry in the preheated instant pot at 400ºF (205ºC) for 10 minutes. Flip the fish when the lid screen indicates TURN FOOD.
3. Bon appétit!

Prawns with Sherry Wine

Prep time: 10 minutes | Cook time: 9 minutes | Serves 4

1½ pounds (680 g) tiger prawns, peeled and deveined
1 tablespoon coconut oil
1 teaspoon crushed garlic
1 teaspoon Old Bay seasoning
Coarse sea salt and ground black pepper, to taste
¼ cup sherry wine
1 teaspoon Dijon mustard

1. Toss all ingredients in a lightly greased air fryer basket.
2. Put the air fryer lid on and air fry in the preheated instant pot at 400ºF (205ºC) for 9 minutes. Flip the prawns when the lid screen indicates TURN FOOD.
3. Bon appétit!

Swordfish Steaks with Lemon

Prep time: 5 minutes | Cook time: 10 minutes | Serves 4

1 pound (454 g) swordfish steaks
2 tablespoons olive oil
2 tablespoons chopped fresh mint leaves
3 tablespoons fresh lemon juice
1 teaspoon garlic powder
½ teaspoon shallot powder
Sea salt and freshly ground black pepper, to taste

1. Toss the swordfish steaks with the remaining ingredients and place them in a lightly oiled air fryer basket.
2. Put the air fryer lid on and air fry in the preheated instant pot at 400ºF (205ºC) for 10 minutes. Flip the swordfish steaks when the lid screen indicates TURN FOOD.
3. Bon appétit!

Pollock Fishcakes

Prep time: 8 minutes | Cook time: 14 minutes | Serves 4

1 pound (454 g) pollock, chopped
1 teaspoon chili sauce
Sea salt and ground black pepper, to taste
4 tablespoons all-purpose flour
1 teaspoon smoked paprika
2 tablespoons olive oil
4 ciabatta buns

1. Mix all ingredients , except for the ciabatta buns, in a bowl. Shape the mixture into four patties and place them in a lightly oiled air fryer basket.
2. Put the air fryer lid on and air fry in the preheated instant pot at 400ºF (205ºC) for 14 minutes. Flip the fish patties when the lid screen indicates TURN FOOD.
3. Serve on hamburger buns and enjoy!

Tilapia Cheese Rolls

Prep time: 10 minutes | Cook time: 14 minutes | Serves 4

1 pound (454 g) tilapia fish fillets, chopped
½ cup bread crumbs
4 tablespoons chopped shallots
2 garlic cloves, minced
1 tablespoon olive oil
8 dinner rolls
8 slices Provolone cheese

1. Mix all ingredients , except for the dinner rolls and cheese, in a bowl. Shape the mixture into four patties and place them in a lightly oiled air fryer basket.
2. Put the air fryer lid on and air fry in the preheated instant pot at 400ºF (205ºC) for 14 minutes. Flip the fish patties when the lid screen indicates TURN FOOD.
3. Serve with the cheese and dinner rolls. Enjoy!

Catfish Croquettes

Prep time: 10 minutes | Cook time: 14 minutes | Serves 4

1 pound (454 g) catfish, skinless, boneless, and chopped
2 tablespoons olive oil
2 cloves garlic, minced
1 small onion, minced
¼ cup all-purpose flour
Sea salt and ground black pepper, to taste
½ cup bread crumbs

1. Mix all ingredients in a bowl. Shape the mixture into bite-sized balls and place them in a lightly oiled air fryer basket.
2. Put the air fryer lid on and air fry in the preheated instant pot at 400ºF (205ºC) for 14 minutes. Flip the fish croquettes when the lid screen indicates TURN FOOD.
3. Bon appétit!

Mackerel Pitas with Cheese

Prep time: 5 minutes | Cook time: 14 minutes | Serves 4

1 pound (454 g) mackerel fish fillets
2 tablespoons olive oil
1 tablespoon Mediterranean seasoning mix
½ teaspoon chili powder
Sea salt and freshly ground black pepper, to taste
2 ounces (57 g) feta cheese, crumbled
4 tortillas

1. Toss the fish fillets with the olive oil; place them in a lightly oiled air fryer basket.
2. Put the air fryer lid on and air fry in the preheated instant pot at 400ºF (205ºC) for 14 minutes. Flip the fish fillets when the lid screen indicates TURN FOOD.
3. Assemble the pitas with the chopped fish and remaining ingredients and serve warm. Bon appétit!

Jumbo Shrimp with Butter

Prep time: 6 minutes | Cook time: 8 minutes | Serves 4

1 pound (454 g) jumbo shrimp
2 tablespoons butter, room temperature
Coarse sea salt and lemon pepper, to taste
2 tablespoons chopped fresh cilantro
2 tablespoons chopped fresh chives
2 garlic cloves, crushed

1. Toss all ingredients in a lightly greased air fryer basket.
2. Put the air fryer lid on and air fry in the preheated instant pot at 400ºF (205ºC) for 8 minutes. Flip the shrimp when the lid screen indicates TURN FOOD.
3. Bon appétit!

Squid Tubes with Parsley

Prep time: 5 minutes | Cook time: 5 minutes | Serves 4

1½ pounds (680 g) small squid tubes
Sea salt and ground black pepper, to taste
1 teaspoon paprika
½ cup minced parsley
2 cloves garlic, minced
¼ cup olive oil

1. Toss the squid, salt, black pepper, and paprika in a lightly greased air fryer basket.
2. Put the air fryer lid on and air fry in the preheated instant pot at 400ºF (205ºC) for 5 minutes. Flip the squid when the lid screen indicates TURN FOOD.
3. Bon appétit!

Shrimp with Cayenne Pepper

Prep time: 10 minutes | Cook time: 6 minutes | Serves 4

1½ pounds (680 g) raw shrimp, peeled and deveined
1 tablespoon olive oil
1 teaspoon minced garlic
1 teaspoon cayenne pepper
½ teaspoon lemon pepper
Sea salt, to taste

1. Toss all ingredients in a lightly greased air fryer basket.
2. Put the air fryer lid on and air fry in the preheated instant pot at 400ºF (205ºC) for 6 minutes. Flip the shrimp when the lid screen indicates TURN FOOD.
3. Bon appétit!

Trout with Honey

Prep time: 10 minutes | Cook time: 12 minutes | Serves 4

1 pound (454 g) trout, cut into sticks
1 tablespoon olive oil
2 tablespoons honey
2 teaspoons apple cider vinegar
2 cloves garlic, minced
Sea salt and ground black pepper, to taste
½ teaspoon cayenne pepper

1. Toss all ingredients in a lightly greased air fryer basket.
2. Put the air fryer lid on and air fry in the preheated instant pot at 390ºF (199ºC) for 12 minutes. Flip the fish when the lid screen indicates TURN FOOD.
3. Bon appétit!

Haddock Cheese Fishcakes

Prep time: 5 minutes | Cook time: 14 minutes | Serves 4

1 pound (454 g) haddock, boneless and chopped
¼ cup all-purpose flour
2 eggs
½ cup grated Parmesan cheese
½ cup bread crumbs
4 brioche buns

1. Mix all ingredients, except for the brioche buns, in a bowl. Shape the mixture into four patties and place them in a lightly oiled air fryer basket.
2. Put the air fryer lid on and air fry in the preheated instant pot at 400ºF (205ºC) for 14 minutes. Flip the fish patties when the lid screen indicates TURN FOOD.
3. Serve on hamburger buns and enjoy!

Sea Bass with Garlic

Prep time: 5 minutes | Cook time: 10 minutes | Serves 4

1 pound (454 g) sea bass
2 garlic cloves, minced
2 tablespoons olive oil
1 tablespoon Italian seasoning mix
Sea salt and ground black pepper, to taste
¼ cup dry white wine

1. Toss the fish with the remaining ingredients; place them in a lightly oiled air fryer basket.
2. Put the air fryer lid on and air fry in the preheated instant pot at 400ºF (205ºC) for 10 minutes. Flip the fish when the lid screen indicates TURN FOOD.
3. Bon appétit!

Chapter 7 Snacks and Appetizers

Sweet Potato Chips

Prep time: 10 minutes | Cook time: 14 minutes | Serves 3

2 large-sized sweet potatoes, peeled and cut into thin slices
2 teaspoons butter, melted
Sea salt and ground black pepper, to taste
½ teaspoon dried oregano
½ teaspoon dried basil
½ teaspoon dried rosemary

1. Toss the sweet potato with the remaining ingredients and place them in the air fryer basket.
2. Put the air fryer lid on and air fry in the preheated instant pot at 360ºF (182ºC) for 14 minutes. Flip the sweet potato chips when the lid screen indicates TURN FOOD. Work in batches.
3. Enjoy!

Cheese Stuffed Mushrooms

Prep time: 10 minutes | Cook time: 7 minutes | Serves 4

1 tablespoon butter
6 ounces (170 g) Pecorino Romano cheese, grated
2 tablespoons chopped chives
1 tablespoon minced garlic
½ teaspoon cayenne pepper
Sea salt and ground black pepper, to taste
1 pound (454 g) button mushrooms, stems removed

1. In a mixing bowl, thoroughly combine the butter, cheese, chives, garlic, cayenne pepper, salt, and black pepper.
2. Divide the filling between the mushrooms. Arrange the mushrooms in the air fryer basket.
3. Put the air fryer lid on and air fry in the preheated instant pot at 400ºF (205ºC) for 7 minutes. Flip the mushrooms when the lid screen indicates TURN FOOD.
4. Bon appétit!

Golden Onion Rings

Prep time: 5 minutes | Cook time: 8 minutes | Serves 4

1 cup all-purpose flour
Sea salt and black pepper, to taste
1 teaspoon crushed red pepper flakes
½ teaspoon cumin powder
1 egg
1 cup bread crumbs
1 medium yellow onion, sliced

1. In a shallow bowl, mix the flour, salt, black pepper, red pepper flakes, and cumin powder.
2. Whisk the egg in another shallow bowl. Place the bread crumbs in a separate bowl.
3. Dip the onion rings in the flour, then in the eggs, then in the bread crumbs. Place the onion rings in the air fryer basket.
4. Put the air fryer lid on and air fry in the preheated instant pot at 380ºF (193ºC) for 8 minutes or until golden brown and cooked through. Flip the onion rings when the lid screen indicates TURN FOOD.
5. Bon appétit!

Tortilla Chips with Paprika

Prep time: 8 minutes | Cook time: 5 minutes | Serves 4

9 corn tortillas, cut into wedges
1 tablespoon olive oil
1 teaspoon hot paprika
Sea salt and ground black pepper, to taste

1. Toss the tortilla wedges with the remaining ingredients. Transfer to the air fryer basket.
2. Put the air fryer lid on and air fry in the preheated instant pot at 360ºF (182ºC) for 5 minutes. Flip the tortilla chips when the lid screen indicates TURN FOOD. Work in batches.
3. Enjoy!

Jalapeño Poppers with Bacon

Prep time: 5 minutes | Cook time: 7 minutes | Serves 4

4 ounces (113 g) Cottage cheese, crumbled
4 ounces (113 g) Cheddar cheese, shredded
1 teaspoon mustard seeds
8 jalapeños, seeded and sliced in half lengthwise
8 slices bacon, sliced in half lengthwise

1. Thoroughly combine the cheese and mustard seeds. Spoon the mixture into the jalapeño halves.
2. Wrap each jalapeño with half a slice of bacon and secure with toothpicks. Transfer to the air fryer basket.
3. Put the air fryer lid on and air fry in the preheated instant pot at 370ºF (188ºC) for 7 minutes or until golden brown.
4. Bon appétit!

Tomato Chips with Basil

Prep time: 6 minutes | Cook time: 15 minutes | Serves 2

1 beefsteak tomato, thinly sliced
2 tablespoons extra-virgin olive oil
Coarse sea salt and freshly ground pepper, to taste
1 teaspoon dried basil
1 teaspoon dried thyme
1 teaspoon dried rosemary

1. Toss the tomato slices with the remaining ingredients until they are well coated on all sides.
2. Arrange the tomato slices in the air fryer basket.
3. Put the air fryer lid on and air fry in the preheated instant pot at 360ºF (182ºC) for 10 minutes. Flip the tomato slices when the lid screen indicates TURN FOOD.
4. Reduce the temperature to 330ºF (166ºC) and continue to cook for a further 5 minutes.
5. Bon appétit!

Chicken Wings with Mustard

Prep time: 5 minutes | Cook time: 18 minutes | Serves 3

¾ pound (340 g) chicken wings
1 tablespoon olive oil
1 teaspoon mustard seeds
1 teaspoon cayenne pepper
1 teaspoon garlic powder
Sea salt and ground black pepper, to taste

1. Toss the chicken wings with the remaining ingredients. Transfer to the air fryer basket.
2. Put the air fryer lid on and roast in the preheated instant pot at 380ºF (193ºC) for 18 minutes. Flip the chicken wings when the lid screen indicates TURN FOOD.
3. Bon appétit!

Green Tomato with Cayenne

Prep time: 6 minutes | Cook time: 15 minutes | Serves 4

½ cup all-purpose flour
Sea salt and ground black pepper, to taste
1 teaspoon garlic powder
1 teaspoon cayenne pepper
2 eggs
½ cup milk
2 tablespoons olive oil
1 cup bread crumbs
1 pound (454 g) green tomatoes, sliced

1. In a shallow bowl, mix the flour, salt, black pepper, garlic powder, and cayenne pepper.
2. Whisk the egg and milk in another shallow bowl. Mix the olive oil and bread crumbs in a separate bowl.
3. Dip the green tomatoes in the flour, then in the eggs, then in the bread crumbs. Place the green tomatoes in the air fryer basket.
4. Put the air fryer lid on and air fry in the preheated instant pot at 390ºF (199ºC) for 15 minutes or until golden brown and cooked through.
5. Serve with toothpicks. Bon appétit!

Chili Cauliflower Florets

Prep time: 5 minutes | Cook time: 15 minutes | Serves 4

2 eggs, whisked
1 cup bread crumbs
Sea salt and ground black pepper, to taste
1 teaspoon cayenne pepper
1 teaspoon chili powder
½ teaspoon onion powder
½ teaspoon cumin powder
½ teaspoon garlic powder
1 pound (454 g) cauliflower florets

1. Mix the eggs, bread crumbs, and spices until well combined. Dip the cauliflower florets in the batter. Transfer to the air fryer basket.
2. Put the air fryer lid on and air fry in the preheated instant pot at 350ºF (180ºC) for 15 minutes. Flip the cauliflower florets when the lid screen indicates TURN FOOD.
3. Bon appétit!

Green Beans with Cheese

Prep time: 5 minutes | Cook time: 6 minutes | Serves 4

1 pound (454 g) green beans
4 tablespoons all-purpose flour
2 eggs, whisked
½ cup bread crumbs
½ cup grated Parmesan cheese
1 teaspoon cayenne pepper
½ teaspoon mustard seeds
1 teaspoon garlic powder
Sea salt and ground black pepper, to taste

1. In a shallow bowl, thoroughly combine the flour and eggs; mix to combine well.
2. Then, in another bowl, mix the remaining ingredients.
3. Dip the green beans in the egg mixture, then, in the bread crumb mixture. Transfer to the air fryer basket.
4. Put the air fryer lid on and air fry in the preheated instant pot at 390ºF (199ºC) for 6 minutes. Flip the green beans when the lid screen indicates TURN FOOD.
5. Enjoy!

Brussels Sprouts with Syrup

Prep time: 6 minutes | Cook time: 10 minutes | Serves 4

1 pound Brussels sprouts, trimmed
2 tablespoons sesame oil
2 tablespoons agave syrup
2 tablespoons rice wine
1 teaspoon chili flakes
1 teaspoon garlic powder
½ teaspoon paprika
Sea salt and ground black pepper, to taste

1. Toss the Brussels sprouts with the remaining ingredients; then, arrange the Brussels sprouts in the air fryer basket.
2. Put the air fryer lid on and air fry in the preheated instant pot at 380ºF (193ºC) for 10 minutes. Flip the Brussels sprouts when the lid screen indicates TURN FOOD.
3. Serve warm and enjoy!

Cauliflower with Cheese

Prep time: 5 minutes | Cook time: 15 minutes | Serves 4

½ cup milk
1 cup all-purpose flour
1 teaspoon garlic powder
1 teaspoon onion powder
1 teaspoon hot paprika
Sea salt and ground black pepper, to taste
2 tablespoons olive oil
1 pound (454 g) cauliflower florets
4 ounces (113 g) Parmesan cheese, preferably freshly grated

1. In a mixing bowl, thoroughly combine the milk, flour, spices, and olive oil.
2. Dip the cauliflower florets in the flour mixture. Transfer to the air fryer basket.
3. Put the air fryer lid on and air fry in the preheated instant pot at 350ºF (180ºC) for 10 minutes. Flip the cauliflower florets when the lid screen indicates TURN FOOD.
4. Top the cauliflower florets with cheese and continue to cook an additional 5 minutes.
5. Bon appétit!

Pork Ribs with Honey and Butter

Prep time: 5 minutes | Cook time: 35 minutes | Serves 4

2 pounds (907 g) pork ribs
2 tablespoons honey
2 tablespoons butter
1 teaspoon sweet paprika
1 teaspoon hot paprika
1 teaspoon granulated garlic
Sea salt and ground black pepper, to taste
1 teaspoon brown mustard
1 teaspoon ground cumin

1. Toss all ingredients in a lightly greased air fryer basket.
2. Put the air fryer lid on and air fry in the preheated instant pot at 350°F (180°C) for 35 minutes. Flip the pork ribs when the lid screen indicates TURN FOOD.
3. Bon appétit!

Lemon Eggplant Chips

Prep time: 10 minutes | Cook time: 15 minutes | Serves 4

1 pound (454 g) eggplant, sliced
2 tablespoons olive oil
1 teaspoon minced garlic
Sea salt and ground black pepper, to taste
2 tablespoons freshly squeezed lemon juice

1. Toss the eggplant pieces with the remaining ingredients until they are well coated on all sides.
2. Arrange the eggplant in the air fryer basket.
3. Put the air fryer lid on and air fry in the preheated instant pot at 400°F (205°C) for 15 minutes. Flip the eggplant when the lid screen indicates TURN FOOD.
4. Bon appétit!

Cheese Stuffed Mushrooms

Prep time: 10 minutes | Cook time: 7 minutes | Serves 4

2 tablespoons olive oil
½ cup bread crumbs
½ cup grated Parmesan cheese
1 teaspoon minced garlic
1 tablespoon chopped fresh parsley
1 tablespoon chopped fresh chives
Sea salt and freshly ground black pepper, to taste
1 pound (454 g) button mushrooms, stems removed

1. In a mixing bowl, thoroughly combine the olive oil, bread crumbs, Parmesan cheese, garlic, parsley, chives, salt, and black pepper.
2. Divide the filling between the mushrooms. Arrange the mushrooms in the air fryer basket.
3. Put the air fryer lid on and air fry in the preheated instant pot at 400°F (205°C) for 7 minutes. Flip the mushrooms when the lid screen indicates TURN FOOD.
4. Bon appétit!

Beer Onion Rings

Prep time: 5 minutes | Cook time: 8 minutes | Serves 4

½ cup beer
1 cup plain flour
1 teaspoon baking powder
1 teaspoon cayenne pepper
Sea salt and ground black pepper, to taste
2 eggs, whisked
1 cup crushed tortilla chips
2 sweet onions

1. In a shallow bowl, mix the beer, flour, baking powder, cayenne pepper, salt, and black pepper.
2. Whisk the egg in another shallow bowl. Place the crushed tortilla chips in a separate bowl.
3. Dip the onion rings in the flour mixture, then in the eggs, then in the tortilla chips. Place the onion rings in the air fryer basket.
4. Put the air fryer lid on and air fry in the preheated instant pot at 380°F (193°C) for 8 minutes or until golden brown and cooked through.
5. Bon appétit!

Chicken Wings with Sriracha Sauce

Prep time: 5 minutes | Cook time: 18 minutes | Serves 4

2 pounds (907 g) chicken wings
1 tablespoon white vinegar
Sea salt and ground black pepper, to taste
1 teaspoon cayenne pepper
1 teaspoon garlic powder
½ teaspoon onion powder
4 tablespoons butter, room temperature
¼ cup Sriracha sauce

1. Toss the chicken wings with the remaining ingredients. Transfer to the air fryer basket.
2. Put the air fryer lid on and roast in the preheated instant pot at 380ºF (193ºC) for 18 minutes. Flip the chicken wings when the lid screen indicates TURN FOOD.
3. Bon appétit!

Apple Cheese Rolls

Prep time: 10 minutes | Cook time: 10 minutes | Serves 4

6 ounces (170 g) refrigerated crescent rolls
1 apple, peeled, cored, and grated
6 ounces (170 g) cream cheese, crumbled
¼ cup brown sugar
1 teaspoon apple pie spice

1. Separate the dough into rectangles. Mix the remaining ingredients until well combined.
2. Spread each rectangle with the cheese mixture; roll them up tightly. Place the rolls in the baking dish.
3. Place the baking dish in the air fryer basket. Put the air fryer lid on and bake in the preheated instant pot at 320ºF (160ºC) for 10 minutes. Flip the rolls when the lid screen indicates TURN FOOD.
4. Bon appétit!

Butter Cheese Cauliflower Bites

Prep time: 10 minutes | Cook time: 13 minutes | Serves 4

1 pound (454 g) cauliflower, grated
½ cup shredded Cheddar cheese
1 ounce (28 g) butter, room temperature
Sea salt and ground black pepper, to taste
½ cup crushed tortilla chips
2 eggs, whisked

1. Thoroughly combine all the ingredients in a mixing bowl. Shape the mixture into bite-sized balls. Transfer to the air fryer basket.
2. Put the air fryer lid on and air fry in the preheated instant pot at 350ºF (180ºC) for 13 minutes. Flip the cauliflower balls when the lid screen indicates TURN FOOD.
3. Bon appétit!

Bacon-Wrapped Sausages

Prep time: 8 minutes | Cook time: 15 minutes | Serves 4

1 pound (454 g) mini sausages
2 tablespoons tamari sauce
2 tablespoons maple syrup
1 teaspoon chili powder
Ground black pepper, to taste
4 ounces (113 g) bacon, thinly sliced

1. Toss the mini sausages with the tamari sauce, maple syrup, chili powder, and black pepper.
2. Wrap the mini sausages with the bacon.
3. Place the sausages in a lightly oiled air fryer basket.
4. Put the air fryer lid on and air fry in the preheated instant pot at 380ºF (193ºC) for 15 minutes. Flip the sausages when the lid screen indicates TURN FOOD.
5. Serve warm and enjoy!

Paprika Beet Chips

Prep time: 10 minutes | Cook time: 30 minutes | Serves 2

½ pound (227 g) golden beets, peeled and thinly sliced
Kosher salt and ground black pepper, to taste
1 teaspoon paprika
2 tablespoons olive oil
½ teaspoon garlic powder
1 teaspoon ground turmeric

1. Toss the beets with the remaining ingredients and place them in the air fryer basket.
2. Put the air fryer lid on and air fry in the preheated instant pot at 330ºF (166ºC) for 30 minutes. Flip the chips when the lid screen indicates TURN FOOD. Work in batches.
3. Enjoy!

Wax Beans with Cumin

Prep time: 6 minutes | Cook time: 6 minutes | Serves 4

1 pound (454 g) fresh wax beans, trimmed
2 teaspoons olive oil
½ teaspoon onion powder
1 teaspoon garlic powder
½ teaspoon cumin powder
Sea salt and ground black pepper, to taste

1. Toss the wax beans with the remaining ingredients. Transfer to the air fryer basket.
2. Put the air fryer lid on and air fry in the preheated instant pot at 390ºF (199ºC) for 6 minutes. Flip the wax beans when the lid screen indicates TURN FOOD.
3. Enjoy!

Kale Chips with Garlic

Prep time: 6 minutes | Cook time: 8 minutes | Serves 4

4 cups kale, torn into pieces
1 tablespoon sesame oil
1 teaspoon garlic powder
Sea salt and ground black pepper, to taste

1. Start by preheating the air fryer to 360ºF (182ºC).
2. Toss the kale leaves with the remaining ingredients and place them in the air fryer basket.
3. Put the air fryer lid on and air fry in the preheated instant pot at for minutes. Flip the when the lid screen indicates TURN FOOD. the chips for 8 minutes, shaking the air fryer basket occasionally and working in batches.
4. Enjoy!

Paprika Carrot Bites

Prep time: 10 minutes | Cook time: 15 minutes | Serves 4

1 pound (454 g) carrots, cut into slices
2 tablespoons coconut oil
1 teaspoon paprika
½ teaspoon garlic powder
½ teaspoon dried oregano
½ teaspoon dried parsley flakes
Sea salt and ground black pepper, to taste

1. Toss the carrots with the remaining ingredients; then, arrange the carrots in the air fryer basket.
2. Put the air fryer lid on and air fry in the preheated instant pot at 380ºF (193ºC) for 15 minutes. Flip the carrots when the lid screen indicates TURN FOOD.
3. Bon appétit!

Hot Dogs Rolls

Prep time: 5 minutes | Cook time: 8 minutes | Serves 6

6 ounces (170 g) refrigerated crescent rolls
1 tablespoon mustard
10 ounces (283 g) mini hot dogs

1. Separate the dough into triangles. Cut them lengthwise into 3 small triangles. Spread each triangle with mustard.
2. Place a mini hot dog on the shortest side of each triangle and roll it up.
3. Place the rolls in the baking dish.
4. Place the baking dish in the air fryer basket. Put the air fryer lid on and bake in the preheated instant pot at 320ºF (160ºC) for 8 minutes. Flip the rolls when the lid screen indicates TURN FOOD.
5. Bon appétit!

Honey Chicken Wings

Prep time: 5 minutes | Cook time: 18 minutes | Serves 4

2 pounds (907 g) chicken wings
¼ cup honey
2 tablespoons fish sauce
2 garlic cloves, crushed
1 teaspoon peeled and grated ginger
2 tablespoons butter, melted
Sea salt and ground black pepper, to taste

1. Toss the chicken wings with the remaining ingredients. Transfer to the air fryer basket.
2. Put the air fryer lid on and roast in the preheated instant pot at 380ºF (193ºC) for 18 minutes. Flip the chicken wings when the lid screen indicates TURN FOOD.
3. Bon appétit!

Potato Wedges with Paprika

Prep time: 10 minutes | Cook time: 35 minutes | Serves 4

1 pound (454 g) potatoes, cut into wedges
2 tablespoons olive oil
Sea salt and ground black pepper, to taste
1 teaspoon paprika
1 teaspoon dried parsley flakes
1 teaspoon Greek seasoning mix

1. Toss the potatoes with the remaining ingredients and place them in the air fryer basket.
2. Put the air fryer lid on and air fry in the preheated instant pot at 400ºF (205ºC) for 35 minutes. Flip the potato wedges when the lid screen indicates TURN FOOD.
3. Enjoy!

Potato Chips with Peppercorns

Prep time: 10 minutes | Cook time: 16 minutes | Serves 3

2 large-sized potatoes, peeled and thinly sliced
2 tablespoons olive oil
1 teaspoon Sichuan peppercorns
1 teaspoon garlic powder
½ teaspoon Chinese five-spice powder
Sea salt, to taste

1. Toss the potatoes with the remaining ingredients and place them in the air fryer basket.
2. Put the air fryer lid on and air fry in the preheated instant pot at 360ºF (182ºC) for 16 minutes. Flip the potato chips when the lid screen indicates TURN FOOD. Work in batches.
3. Enjoy!

Tomato Chips with Cheese

Prep time: 5 minutes | Cook time: 15 minutes | Serves 3

1 large-sized beefsteak tomatoes
2 tablespoons olive oil
½ teaspoon paprika
Sea salt, to taste
1 teaspoon garlic powder
1 tablespoon chopped fresh cilantro
4 tablespoons grated Pecorino cheese

1. Toss the tomato slices with the olive oil and spices until they are well coated on all sides.
2. Arrange the tomato slices in the air fryer basket.
3. Put the air fryer lid on and air fry in the preheated instant pot at 360ºF (182ºC) for 10 minutes.
4. Reduce the temperature to 330ºF (166ºC). Top the tomato slices with the cheese and continue to cook for a further 5 minutes.
5. Bon appétit!

Panko Cheese Green Beans

Prep time: 5 minutes | Cook time: 6 minutes | Serves 4

½ cup flour
2 eggs, beaten
½ cup bread crumbs
½ cup grated Parmesan cheese
½ teaspoon onion powder
¼ teaspoon cumin powder
½ teaspoon garlic powder
1 pound (454 g) fresh green beans

1. In a shallow bowl, thoroughly combine the flour and eggs; mix to combine well.
2. Then, in another bowl, mix the remaining ingredients.
3. Dip the green beans in the egg mixture, then, in the bread crumb mixture. Transfer to the air fryer basket.
4. Put the air fryer lid on and air fry in the preheated instant pot at 390ºF (199ºC) for 6 minutes. Flip the green beans when the lid screen indicates TURN FOOD.
5. Enjoy!

Potato Chips with Paprika

Prep time: 10 minutes | Cook time: 16 minutes | Serves 3

1 pound (454 g) potatoes, thinly sliced
2 tablespoons olive oil
1 teaspoon paprika
Coarse salt and cayenne pepper, to taste

1. Toss the potatoes with the remaining ingredients and place them in the air fryer basket.
2. Put the air fryer lid on and air fry in the preheated instant pot at 360ºF (182ºC) for 16 minutes. Flip the potato chips when the lid screen indicates TURN FOOD. Work in batches.
3. Enjoy!

Air Fried Mixed Nuts

Prep time: 2 minutes | Cook time: 6 minutes | Serves 4

¼ cup almonds
½ cup hazelnuts
¼ cup peanuts

1. Place the nuts in the air fryer basket.
2. Put the air fryer lid on and air fry in the preheated instant pot at 330ºF (166ºC) for 6 minutes. Flip the nuts when the lid screen indicates TURN FOOD. Work in batches.
3. Enjoy!

Ham and Cheese Stuffed Peppers

Prep time: 5 minutes | Cook time: 7 minutes | Serves 4

8 Serrano peppers
4 ounces (113 g) ham cubes
4 ounces (113 g) goat cheese, crumbled

1. Stuff the peppers with ham and cheese; transfer them to a lightly oiled air fryer basket.
2. Put the air fryer lid on and air fry in the preheated instant pot at 370ºF (188ºC) for 7 minutes or until golden brown.
3. Bon appétit!

Tortilla Chips with Lime

Prep time: 8 minutes | Cook time: 5 minutes | Serves 4

4 corn tortillas, cut into wedges
1 tablespoon olive oil
1 tablespoon Mexican oregano
2 tablespoons lime juice
1 teaspoon chili powder
1 teaspoon ground cumin
Sea salt, to taste

1. Toss the tortilla wedges with the remaining ingredients. Transfer to the air fryer basket.
2. Put the air fryer lid on and air fry in the preheated instant pot at 360ºF (182ºC) for 5 minutes or until crispy, working in batches.
3. Enjoy!

Bacon and Cheese Stuffed Peppers

Prep time: 10 minutes | Cook time: 7 minutes | Serves 4

8 poblano peppers, seeded and halved
4 ounces (113 g) Gruyere cheese
4 ounces (113 g) bacon, chopped

1. Stuff the peppers with the cheese and bacon; transfer them to a lightly oiled air fryer basket.
2. Put the air fryer lid on and air fry in the preheated instant pot at 370ºF (188ºC) for 7 minutes or until golden brown.
3. Bon appétit!

Red Beet Chips with Cayenne

Prep time: 10 minutes | Cook time: 30 minutes | Serves 4

1 pound (454 g) red beets, peeled and cut into ⅛-inch slices
1 tablespoon olive oil
1 teaspoon cayenne pepper
Sea salt and ground black pepper, to taste

1. Toss the beets with the remaining ingredients and place them in the air fryer basket.
2. Put the air fryer lid on and air fry in the preheated instant pot at 330ºF (166ºC) for 30 minutes. Flip the chips when the lid screen indicates TURN FOOD. Work in batches.
3. Enjoy!

Zucchini with Cheese

Prep time: 10 minutes | Cook time: 10 minutes | Serves 4

1 pound (454 g) zucchini, cut into sticks
½ cup Parmesan cheese
½ cup almond flour
1 egg, whisked
2 tablespoons olive oil
1 teaspoon hot paprika
Sea salt and ground black pepper, to taste

1. Toss the zucchini sticks with the remaining ingredients and arrange them in a single layer in the air fryer basket.
2. Put the air fryer lid on and air fry in the preheated instant pot at 390ºF (199ºC) for 10 minutes. Flip the zucchini sticks when the lid screen indicates TURN FOOD. Work in batches.
3. Bon appétit!

Vinegary Chicken Drumettes

Prep time: 5 minutes | Cook time: 18 minutes | Serves 4

1 pound (454 g) chicken drumettes
4 tablespoons soy sauce
¼ cup rice vinegar
4 tablespoons honey
2 tablespoons sesame oil
1 teaspoon Gochugaru, Korean chili powder
2 tablespoons chopped scallions
2 garlic cloves, minced

1. Toss the chicken drumettes with the remaining ingredients. Transfer to the air fryer basket.
2. Put the air fryer lid on and roast in the preheated instant pot at 380ºF (193ºC) for 18 minutes. Flip the chicken drumettes when the lid screen indicates TURN FOOD.
3. Bon appétit!

Air Fried Potato Chips

Prep time: 10 minutes | Cook time: 16 minutes | Serves 3

2 large-sized potatoes, thinly sliced
2 tablespoons olive oil
1 teaspoon Mediterranean herb mix
1 teaspoon cayenne pepper
Coarse sea salt and ground black pepper, to taste

1. Toss the potatoes with the remaining ingredients and place them in the air fryer basket.
2. Put the air fryer lid on and air fry in the preheated instant pot at 360ºF (182ºC) for 16 minutes. Flip the potato chips when the lid screen indicates TURN FOOD. Work in batches.
3. Enjoy!

Chile Pork Ribs

Prep time: 5 minutes | Cook time: 35 minutes | Serves 4

1½ pounds (680 g) spare ribs
Kosher salt and ground black pepper, to taste
2 teaspoons brown sugar
1 teaspoon paprika
1 teaspoon chile powder
1 teaspoon garlic powder

1. Toss all the ingredients in a lightly greased air fryer basket.
2. Put the air fryer lid on and air fry in the preheated instant pot at 350ºF (180ºC) for 35 minutes. Flip the pork ribs when the lid screen indicates TURN FOOD.
3. Bon appétit!

Carrot with Butter

Prep time: 5 minutes | Cook time: 15 minutes | Serves 4

1 pound (454 g) baby carrots
2 tablespoons butter
Kosher salt and ground white pepper, to taste
1 teaspoon paprika
1 teaspoon dried oregano

1. Toss the carrots with the remaining ingredients; then, arrange the carrots in the air fryer basket.
2. Put the air fryer lid on and air fry in the preheated instant pot at 380ºF (193ºC) for 15 minutes. Flip the carrots when the lid screen indicates TURN FOOD.
3. Bon appétit!

Air Fried Yam Sticks

Prep time: 10 minutes | Cook time: 15 minutes | Serves 2

1 large-sized yam, peeled and cut into ¼-inch sticks
1 tablespoon olive oil
Kosher salt and red pepper, to taste

1. Toss the yam with the remaining ingredients and place them in the air fryer basket.
2. Put the air fryer lid on and air fry in the preheated instant pot at 360ºF (182ºC) for 15 minutes. Flip the yam sticks when the lid screen indicates TURN FOOD. Work in batches.
3. Enjoy!

Chile Chicken Drumettes

Prep time: 5 minutes | Cook time: 18 minutes | Serves 5

2 pounds (907 g) chicken drumettes
1 teaspoon ancho chile pepper
1 teaspoon smoked paprika
1 teaspoon onion powder
1 teaspoon garlic powder
Kosher salt and ground black pepper, to taste
¼ tsp black pepper
2 tablespoons olive oil

1. Toss the chicken drumettes with the remaining ingredients. Transfer to the air fryer basket.
2. Put the air fryer lid on and roast in the preheated instant pot at 380ºF (193ºC) for 18 minutes. Flip the chicken drumettes when the lid screen indicates TURN FOOD.
3. Bon appétit!

Glazed Pork Ribs

Prep time: 5 minutes | Cook time: 35 minutes | Serves 4

2 pounds (907 g) spare ribs
¼ cup soy sauce
¼ cup rice vinegar
¼ cup sesame oil
2 garlic cloves, minced

1. Toss all ingredients in a lightly greased baking dish.
2. Place the baking dish in the air fryer basket. Put the air fryer lid on and bake in the preheated instant pot at 350ºF (180ºC) for 35 minutes. Flip the ribs when the lid screen indicates TURN FOOD.
3. Bon appétit!

Apple Chips with Cinnamon

Prep time: 10 minutes | Cook time: 9 minutes | Serves 4

2 large sweet, crisp apples, cored and sliced
1 teaspoon ground cinnamon
½ teaspoon grated nutmeg
A pinch of salt

1. Toss the apple slices with the remaining ingredients and arrange them in a single layer in the air fryer basket.
2. Put the air fryer lid on and air fry in the preheated instant pot at 390ºF (199ºC) for 9 minutes. Flip the apple chips when the lid screen indicates TURN FOOD. Work in batches.
3. Bon appétit!

Eggplant with Paprika

Prep time: 5 minutes | Cook time: 15 minutes | Serves 3

¾ pound (340 g) eggplant
Sea salt and ground black pepper, to taste
½ teaspoon paprika
2 tablespoons olive oil
2 tablespoons balsamic vinegar

1. Toss the eggplant pieces with the remaining ingredients until they are well coated on all sides.
2. Arrange the eggplant in the air fryer basket.
3. Put the air fryer lid on and air fry in the preheated instant pot at 400ºF (205ºC) for 15 minutes. Flip the eggplant when the lid screen indicates TURN FOOD.
4. Bon appétit!

Cinnamon Mixed Nuts

Prep time: 5 minutes | Cook time: 6 minutes | Serves 4

1 egg white, lightly beaten
½ cup pecan halves
½ cup almonds
½ cup walnuts
Sea salt and cayenne pepper, to taste
1 teaspoon chili powder
½ teaspoon ground cinnamon
½ teaspoon ground allspice

1. Mix the nuts with the rest of the ingredients and place them in the air fryer basket.
2. Put the air fryer lid on and air fry in the preheated instant pot at 330ºF (166ºC) for 6 minutes. Flip the nuts when the lid screen indicates TURN FOOD. Work in batches.
3. Enjoy!

Zucchini with Cheese

Prep time: 10 minutes | Cook time: 10 minutes | Serves 4

1 pound (454 g) zucchini, cut into sticks
1 egg, whisked
¼ cup grated Parmesan cheese
½ cup bread crumbs
1 teaspoon garlic powder
½ teaspoon onion powder
Sea salt and ground black pepper, to taste

1. Toss the zucchini sticks with the remaining ingredients and arrange them in a single layer in the air fryer basket.
2. Put the air fryer lid on and air fry in the preheated instant pot at 390ºF (199ºC) for 10 minutes. Flip the zucchini sticks when the lid screen indicates TURN FOOD. Work in batches.
3. Bon appétit!

Pancetta-Wrapped Shrimp

Prep time: 12 minutes | Cook time: 6 minutes | Serves 4

12 shrimp, peeled and deveined
3 slices pancetta, cut into strips
2 tablespoons maple syrup
1 tablespoon Dijon mustard

1. Wrap the shrimp in the pancetta strips and toss them with the maple syrup and mustard.
2. Place the shrimp in a lightly greased air fryer basket.
3. Put the air fryer lid on and air fry in the preheated instant pot at 400ºF (205ºC) for 6 minutes. Flip the shrimp when the lid screen indicates TURN FOOD.
4. Bon appétit!

Cheesy Broccoli Bites

Prep time: 5 minutes | Cook time: 10 minutes | Serves 4

1 pound (454 g) broccoli florets
1 teaspoon granulated garlic
1 tablespoon dried onion flakes
1 teaspoon crushed red pepper flakes
2 tablespoons olive oil
½ cup grated Pecorino Romano cheese

1. Toss all ingredients in a lightly oiled air fryer basket.
2. Put the air fryer lid on and air fry in the preheated instant pot at 370ºF (188ºC) for 10 minutes. Flip the broccoli florets when the lid screen indicates TURN FOOD.
3. Enjoy!

Garlicky Kale Crisps

Prep time: 8 minutes | Cook time: 8 minutes | Serves 4

5 cups kale leaves, torn into pieces and stems removed
1 tablespoon olive oil
1 teaspoon chili powder
Sea salt and ground black pepper, to taste
2 garlic cloves, minced

1. Toss the kale leaves with the remaining ingredients and place them in the air fryer basket.
2. Put the air fryer lid on and air fry in the preheated instant pot at 360ºF (182ºC) for 8 minutes. Flip the kale crisps when the lid screen indicates TURN FOOD. Work in batches.
3. Enjoy!

Beet Chips with Rosemary

Prep time: 10 minutes | Cook time: 30 minutes | Serves 4

1 pound (454 g) red and yellow beets, peeled and sliced
1 tablespoon olive oil
Coarse sea salt and ground black pepper, to taste
1 teaspoon dried rosemary
1 teaspoon dried parsley flakes
1 teaspoon garlic
2 tablespoons chopped scallions

1. Toss the beets with the remaining ingredients and place them in the air fryer basket.
2. Put the air fryer lid on and air fry in the preheated instant pot at 330ºF (166ºC) for 30 minutes. Flip the chips when the lid screen indicates TURN FOOD. Work in batches.
3. Enjoy!

Eggplant Cheese Chips

Prep time: 10 minutes | Cook time: 15 minutes | Serves 4

1 pound (454 g) eggplant, cut into slices
2 tablespoons butter, melted
½ teaspoon smoked paprika
1 teaspoon Italian seasoning
Sea salt and ground black pepper, to taste
1 cup shredded Mozzarella cheese

1. Toss the eggplant with the butter and spices. Arrange the eggplant slices in the air fryer basket.
2. Put the air fryer lid on and air fry in the preheated instant pot at 400ºF (205ºC) for 15 minutes. Flip the eggplant when the lid screen indicates TURN FOOD.
3. Bon appétit!

Carrot with Honey

Prep time: 8 minutes | Cook time: 15 minutes | Serves 3

¾ pound (340 g) baby carrots, halved lengthwise
2 tablespoons coconut oil
½ teaspoon cumin powder
2 tablespoons honey
2 tablespoons white wine

1. Toss the carrots with the remaining ingredients; then, arrange the carrots in the air fryer basket.
2. Put the air fryer lid on and air fry in the preheated instant pot at 380ºF (193ºC) for 15 minutes. Flip the carrots when the lid screen indicates TURN FOOD.
3. Bon appétit!

Cheesy Zucchini Chips

Prep time: 10 minutes | Cook time: 10 minutes | Serves 4

1 pound (454 g) zucchini, sliced
1 cup grated Pecorino Romano cheese
Sea salt and cayenne pepper, to taste

1. Toss the zucchini slices with the remaining ingredients and arrange them in a single layer in the air fryer basket.
2. Put the air fryer lid on and air fry in the preheated instant pot at 390ºF (199ºC) for 10 minutes. Flip the zucchini slices when the lid screen indicates TURN FOOD. Work in batches.
3. Bon appétit!

Brussels Sprouts with Cheese

Prep time: 10 minutes | Cook time: 10 minutes | Serves 4

1 pound (454 g) Brussels sprouts, trimmed
2 tablespoons butter, melted
Sea salt and freshly ground black pepper, to taste
1 teaspoon minced garlic
2 tablespoons red wine vinegar
2 ounces (57 g) Cheddar cheese, shredded

1. Toss the Brussels sprouts with the remaining ingredients; then, arrange the Brussels sprouts in the air fryer basket.
2. Put the air fryer lid on and air fry in the preheated instant pot at 380ºF (193ºC) for 10 minutes. Flip the Brussels sprouts when the lid screen indicates TURN FOOD.
3. Serve warm and enjoy!

Broccoli Florets with Butter

Prep time: 5 minutes | Cook time: 10 minutes | Serves 4

1 pound (454 g) broccoli florets
2 tablespoons butter, room temperature
¼ teaspoon mustard seeds
1 tablespoon soy sauce
Sea salt and freshly ground black pepper, to taste

1. Toss all the ingredients in a lightly oiled air fryer basket.
2. Put the air fryer lid on and air fry in the preheated instant pot at 370ºF (188ºC) for 10 minutes. Flip the broccoli florets when the lid screen indicates TURN FOOD.
3. Bon appétit!

Sweet Potato with Herb

Prep time: 10 minutes | Cook time: 15 minutes | Serves 3

2 large-sized sweet potatoes, peeled and cut into ¼-inch sticks
2 teaspoons olive oil
1 teaspoon garlic powder
1 tablespoon Mediterranean herb mix
Kosher salt and freshly ground black pepper, to taste

1. Toss the sweet potato with the remaining ingredients and place them in the air fryer basket.
2. Put the air fryer lid on and air fry in the preheated instant pot at 360ºF (182ºC) for 15 minutes. Flip the sweet potato sticks when the lid screen indicates TURN FOOD. Work in batches.
3. Enjoy!

Chapter 8 Vegan

Chickpeas Falafel

Prep time: 5 minutes | Cook time: 15 minutes | Serves 4

1 (15-ounce / 425-g) cans chickpeas, rinsed and drained
¼ cup chopped fresh cilantro
2 cloves garlic, minced
1 onion, minced
2 tablespoons tahini
1 teaspoon smoked paprika
2 tablespoons fresh lemon juice
Sea salt and ground black pepper, to taste
2 tablespoons olive oil

1. Pulse all the ingredients in the food processor until everything is well incorporated.
2. Shape the mixture into balls and place them in a lightly greased air fryer basket.
3. Put the air fryer lid on and air fry in the preheated instant pot at 380ºF (193ºC) for 15 minutes. Flip the falafel when the lid screen indicates TURN FOOD.
4. Serve in pita bread with toppings of the choice. Enjoy!

Cornmeal Cucumber

Prep time: 10 minutes | Cook time: 15 minutes | Serves 4

2 cucumbers, sliced
2 tablespoons olive oil
½ cup cornmeal
Sea salt and ground black pepper, to taste

1. Toss the cucumbers with the remaining ingredients; place them in the air fryer basket.
2. Put the air fryer lid on and air fry in the preheated instant pot at 400ºF (205ºC) for 15 minutes. Flip the cucumbers when the lid screen indicates TURN FOOD.
3. Serve warm and enjoy!

Zucchini Slices with Cayenne

Prep time: 8 minutes | Cook time: 10 minutes | Serves 4

1 pound (454 g) zucchini, sliced
1 tablespoon ground chia seeds
½ cup crushed crackers
2 tablespoons olive oil
1 teaspoon cayenne pepper
Kosher salt and ground black pepper, to taste

1. Mix the remaining ingredients; dip the zucchini slices in the batter mixture, then, arrange them in a single layer in the air fryer basket.
2. Put the air fryer lid on and air fry in the preheated instant pot at 390ºF (199ºC) for 10 minutes. Flip the zucchini slices when the lid screen indicates TURN FOOD. Work in batches.
3. Bon appétit!

Lentil Stuffed Eggplant

Prep time: 10 minutes | Cook time: 15 minutes | Serves 2

1 medium eggplant, halved
2 tablespoons olive oil
1 onion, minced
2 garlic cloves, minced
2 tablespoons tomato paste
6 ounces (170 g) canned red lentils, drained
Sea salt and ground black pepper, to taste

1. Toss the eggplant with the oil; place them in the air fryer basket.
2. Mix the remaining ingredients to make the filling. Spoon the filling into the eggplant halves.
3. Put the air fryer lid on and air fry in the preheated instant pot at 400ºF (205ºC) for 15 minutes.
4. Serve warm and enjoy!

Potato with Thyme

Prep time: 5 minutes | Cook time: 20 minutes | Serves 3

1 pound (454 g) baby potatoes
2 tablespoons olive oil
1 teaspoon dried thyme
1 teaspoon dried rosemary
1 teaspoon dried basil
1 teaspoon dried oregano
1 teaspoon dried parsley flakes
1 teaspoon minced garlic
Sea salt and ground black pepper, to taste
1 teaspoon cayenne pepper

1. Toss the potatoes with the remaining ingredients until well coated on all sides.
2. Arrange the potatoes in the air fryer basket.
3. Put the air fryer lid on and air fry in the preheated instant pot at 400ºF (205ºC) for 20 minutes. Flip the potatoes when the lid screen indicates TURN FOOD.
4. Bon appétit!

Chickpeas Burgers with Flaxseeds

Prep time: 8 minutes | Cook time: 15 minutes | Serves 4

16 ounces (454 g) canned chickpeas, drained and rinsed
¼ cup ground flaxseeds
2 garlic cloves, minced
1 medium-sized onion, chopped
2 tablespoons fresh lemon juice
2 tablespoons olive oil
½ teaspoon ground cumin
¼ teaspoon ground allspice
Sea salt and ground black pepper, to taste

1. Pulse all ingredients in the food processor until everything is well incorporated.
2. Toss the beets with the remaining ingredients and place them in the air fryer basket.
3. Put the air fryer lid on and air fry in the preheated instant pot at 380ºF (193ºC) for 15 minutes. Flip the burgers when the lid screen indicates TURN FOOD.
4. Bon appétit!

Mushrooms with Parsley

Prep time: 8 minutes | Cook time: 10 minutes | Serves 4

¼ cup crumbled crackers
1 clove garlic, minced
3 tablespoons olive oil
2 tablespoons chopped fresh parsley
Sea salt and freshly ground black pepper, to taste
1 pound (454 g) button mushrooms, stemmed

1. Toss the mushrooms with the remaining ingredients. Arrange them in a lightly greased air fryer basket.
2. Put the air fryer lid on and air fry in the preheated instant pot at 375ºF (190ºC) for 10 minutes. Flip the mushrooms when the lid screen indicates TURN FOOD.
3. Enjoy!

Red Wine Tofu Cubes

Prep time: 8 minutes | Cook time: 22 minutes | Serves 4

14 ounces (397 g) extra-firm tofu, pressed and cubed
2 tablespoons soy sauce
1 tablespoon Dijon mustard
¼ cup red wine
2 teaspoons sesame oil
1 teaspoon minced garlic
1 chili pepper, seeded and minced
4 tablespoons corn flour
Sea salt and ground black pepper, to taste

1. Toss the tofu with the soy sauce, mustard, red wine, sesame oil, garlic, and chili pepper. Let it marinate for 30 minutes.
2. Toss the tofu cubes with the corn flour, salt, and black pepper; place them in the air fryer basket, discarding the marinade.
3. Put the air fryer lid on and air fry in the preheated instant pot at 360ºF (182ºC) for 22 minutes. Flip the tofu cubes when the lid screen indicates TURN FOOD.
4. Bon appétit!

Chickpeas Falafel with Scallions

Prep time: 10 minutes | Cook time: 15 minutes | Serves 4

12 ounces (340 g) canned chickpeas, rinsed and drained
1 bell pepper, seeded and minced
1 small onion, quartered
2 cloves garlic, roughly chopped
¼ cup roughly chopped fresh parsley
¼ cup chopped fresh scallions
½ teaspoon ground cumin
Kosher salt and ground black pepper, to taste
1 teaspoon paprika
1 teaspoon coriander
2 tablespoons plain flour
2 tablespoons olive oil

1. Pulse all ingredients in the food processor until everything is well incorporated.
2. Shape the mixture into balls and place them in a lightly greased air fryer basket.
3. Put the air fryer lid on and air fry in the preheated instant pot at 380ºF (193ºC) for 15 minutes. Flip the falafel when the lid screen indicates TURN FOOD.
4. Serve in pita bread with toppings of the choice. Enjoy!

Lentils and Tomato Stuffed Eggplant

Prep time: 6 minutes | Cook time: 15 minutes | Serves 2

2 small eggplants, halved lengthwise
2 tablespoons olive oil
Sea salt and ground black pepper, to taste
1 cup red lentils, canned, drained, and rinsed
1 tomato, crushed
1 tablespoon Italian seasoning mix
¼ teaspoon grated nutmeg

1. Toss the eggplants with the oil; place them in the air fryer basket.
2. Mix the remaining ingredients to make the filling. Spoon the filling into the eggplant halves.
3. Put the air fryer lid on and air fry in the preheated instant pot at 400ºF (205ºC) for about 15 minutes.
4. Bon appétit!

Sweet Potato with Scallions

Prep time: 10 minutes | Cook time: 35 minutes | Serves 3

1 pound (454 g) sweet potatoes, cubed
2 tablespoons coconut oil
Kosher salt and freshly ground black pepper, to taste
1 teaspoon minced garlic
½ teaspoon ground cumin
2 tablespoons chopped fresh coriander
2 tablespoons chopped fresh parsley
2 tablespoons chopped fresh scallions

1. Toss the sweet potatoes with the remaining ingredients. Transfer to the air fryer basket.
2. Put the air fryer lid on and air fry in the preheated instant pot at 380ºF (193ºC) for 35 minutes. Flip the sweet potatoes when the lid screen indicates TURN FOOD.
3. Taste and adjust the seasonings. Bon appétit!

Soy Sauce Cabbage

Prep time: 5 minutes | Cook time: 7 minutes | Serves 3

1 pound (454 g) Chinese cabbage, cut into wedges
2 tablespoons olive oil
2 tablespoons soy sauce
1 tablespoon rice vinegar
1 teaspoon stoneground mustard
1 teaspoon granulated garlic
Sea salt and cayenne pepper, to taste

1. Toss the cabbage wedges with the remaining ingredients. Transfer to the air fryer basket.
2. Put the air fryer lid on and air fry in the preheated instant pot at 350ºF (180ºC) for 7 minutes. Flip the cabbage wedges when the lid screen indicates TURN FOOD.
3. Taste and adjust the seasonings. Bon appétit!

Tofu and Corn Stuffed Peppers

Prep time: 6 minutes | Cook time: 15 minutes | Serves 2

2 bell peppers, seeded and halved
4 ounces (113 g) firm tofu, crumbled
4 tablespoons canned sweetcorn
1 tomato, crushed
Sea salt and ground black pepper, to taste
1 teaspoon minced garlic
1 teaspoon smoked paprika

1. Arrange the peppers in the air fryer basket.
2. Mix the remaining ingredients until well combined. Dived the filling between the peppers.
3. Put the air fryer lid on and air fry in the preheated instant pot at 400ºF (205ºC) for 15 minutes.
4. Bon appétit!

Potato with Tofu Cheese

Prep time: 10 minutes | Cook time: 20 minutes | Serves 3

1 pound (454 g) French fingerling potatoes, halved lengthwise
2 tablespoons olive oil
2 cloves garlic, pressed
1 tablespoon chopped fresh parsley
1 tablespoon chopped fresh coriander
1 tablespoon chopped fresh chives
Sea salt and ground black pepper, to taste
2 ounces (57 g) tofu cheese, crumbled

1. Toss the potatoes with the remaining ingredients, except for the tofu cheese, until well coated on all sides.
2. Arrange the potatoes in the air fryer basket.
3. Put the air fryer lid on and air fry in the preheated instant pot at 400ºF (205ºC) for 15 minutes. Flip the potatoes when the lid screen indicates TURN FOOD.
4. Top with the tofu cheese and continue cooking for an additional 5 minutes.
5. Bon appétit!

Zucchini with Mushrooms and Chickpeas

Prep time: 10 minutes | Cook time: 13 minutes | Serves 2

2 medium zucchinis, halved
2 tablespoons olive oil
1 teaspoon minced garlic
1 shallot, minced
2 tablespoons marinara sauce
2 ounces (57 g) canned chickpeas, drained and rinsed
2 ounces (57 g) button mushrooms, chopped
Sea salt and ground black pepper, to taste

1. Arrange the zucchini halves in the air fryer basket.
2. Mix the remaining ingredients until well combined. Divided the filling between the zucchini halves.
3. Put the air fryer lid on and air fry in the preheated instant pot at 390ºF (199ºC) for 13 minutes.
4. Bon appétit!

Chickpeas Meatballs

Prep time: 10 minutes | Cook time: 15 minutes | Serves 4

16 ounces (454 g) canned chickpeas, rinsed and drained
1 shallot, chopped
4 cloves garlic, roughly chopped
¼ cup roughly chopped fresh parsley
¼ cup roughly chopped fresh coriander
½ teaspoon stone-ground mustard
½ teaspoon ground cumin
2 tablespoons tahini
Kosher salt and ground black pepper, to taste

1. Pulse all ingredients in the food processor until everything is well incorporated.
2. Form the mixture into balls and place them in a lightly greased air fryer basket.
3. Put the air fryer lid on and air fry in the preheated instant pot at 380ºF (193ºC) for 15 minutes. Flip the meatballs when the lid screen indicates TURN FOOD.
4. Serve in pita bread with toppings of the choice. Enjoy!

Potato with Herb

Prep time: 10 minutes | Cook time: 20 minutes | Serves 4

1 pound (454 g) potatoes, peeled and cut into wedges
2 tablespoons olive oil
1 teaspoon granulated garlic
1 tablespoon Italian herb mix
1 teaspoon cayenne pepper
Kosher salt and freshly ground black pepper, to taste

1. Toss the potatoes with the remaining ingredients until well coated on all sides. Arrange the potatoes in the air fryer basket.
2. Put the air fryer lid on and air fry in the preheated instant pot at 400ºF (205ºC) for 20 minutes. Flip the potatoes when the lid screen indicates TURN FOOD.
3. Bon appétit!

Panko Chickpeas Patties

Prep time: 6 minutes | Cook time: 15 minutes | Serves 4

14 ounces (397 g) canned chickpeas, drained
½ large onion, chopped
1 small onion, chopped
2 garlic cloves, minced
1 teaspoon grated ginger
¼ cup chopped fresh scallions
¼ cup chopped fresh parsley
2 tablespoons olive oil
1 teaspoon ground cumin
Sea salt and ground black pepper, to taste
½ cup panko crumbs
½ teaspoon baking powder

1. Pulse all the ingredients in the food processor until everything is well incorporated.
2. Form the mixture into patties and place them in a lightly greased air fryer basket.
3. Put the air fryer lid on and air fry in the preheated instant pot at 380ºF (193ºC) for 15 minutes. Flip the patties when the lid screen indicates TURN FOOD.
4. Serve with toppings of choice. Enjoy!

Bok Choy with Garlic

Prep time: 5 minutes | Cook time: 6 minutes | Serves 4

1 pound (454 g) baby Bok choy, leaves separated
2 tablespoons sesame oil
2 garlic cloves, minced
1 teaspoon five-spice powder

1. Toss the Bok choy with the remaining ingredients until well coated on all sides. Transfer to the air fryer basket.
2. Put the air fryer lid on and air fry in the preheated instant pot at 350ºF (180ºC) for 6 minutes. Flip the Bok choy when the lid screen indicates TURN FOOD.
3. Bon appétit!

Chickpeas and Carrot Meatballs

Prep time: 12 minutes | Cook time: 15 minutes | Serves 4

16 ounces (454 g) canned chickpeas, rinsed and drained
1 medium onion, chopped
3 cloves garlic, roughly chopped
1 large carrot, peeled and roughly chopped
¼ cup roughly chopped fresh parsley
¼ cup roughly chopped fresh coriander
½ teaspoon peeled and grated ginger
½ teaspoon ground cinnamon
2 tablespoons olive oil
Sea salt and ground black pepper, to taste

1. Pulse all the ingredients in the food processor until everything is well incorporated.
2. Form the mixture into balls and place them in a lightly greased air fryer basket.
3. Put the air fryer lid on and air fry in the preheated instant pot at 380ºF (193ºC) for 15 minutes. Flip the meatballs when the lid screen indicates TURN FOOD.
4. Serve in pita bread with toppings of the choice. Enjoy!

Easy Celery Sticks

Prep time: 10 minutes | Cook time: 15 minutes | Serves 4

4 stalks celery, cleaned and cut into matchsticks
Sea salt and ground black pepper, to taste
1 cup bread crumbs
2 tablespoons avocado oil

1. Toss the celery with the remaining ingredients; place them in the air fryer basket.
2. Put the air fryer lid on and air fry in the preheated instant pot at 400ºF (205ºC) for 15 minutes. Flip the celery sticks when the lid screen indicates TURN FOOD.
3. Serve warm and enjoy!

Chickpeas Falafel with Parsley

Prep time: 6 minutes | Cook time: 15 minutes | Serves 4

1½ cups canned or boiled chickpeas
1 shallot, diced
2 cloves garlic, minced
2 tablespoons olive oil
¼ cup chopped parsley leaves
1 teaspoon red chili powder
½ teaspoon cumin powder
½ teaspoon mustard powder
1 teaspoon cayenne pepper
Sea salt and ground black pepper, to taste

1. Pulse all the ingredients in the food processor until everything is well incorporated.
2. Shape the mixture into balls and place them in a lightly greased air fryer basket.
3. Put the air fryer lid on and air fry in the preheated instant pot at 380ºF (193ºC) for 15 minutes. Flip the falafel when the lid screen indicates TURN FOOD.
4. Serve in pita bread with toppings of the choice. Enjoy!

Cauliflower Bites

Prep time: 5 minutes | Cook time: 15 minutes | Serves 4

1 pound (454 g) cauliflower florets
Sea salt and ground black pepper, to taste
1 teaspoon ground ginger
¼ teaspoon ground cloves
½ teaspoon ground cumin
½ teaspoon coriander
½ teaspoon cayenne pepper
2 tablespoons olive oil
4 tablespoons cornflour

1. Toss the cauliflower florets with the remaining ingredients. Transfer to the air fryer basket.
2. Put the air fryer lid on and air fry in the preheated instant pot at 350ºF (180ºC) for 15 minutes. Flip the cauliflower florets when the lid screen indicates TURN FOOD.
3. Bon appétit!

Cabbage Wedges with Lemon

Prep time: 8 minutes | Cook time: 7 minutes | Serves 4

1 pound (454 g) cabbage, cut into wedges
2 tablespoons olive oil
1 teaspoon minced garlic
Kosher salt and freshly ground black pepper, to taste
¼ teaspoon cumin powder
½ teaspoon crushed bay leaf
2 tablespoons fresh lemon juice
1 teaspoon crushed red pepper flakes

1. Toss the cabbage wedges with the remaining ingredients. Transfer to the air fryer basket.
2. Put the air fryer lid on and air fry in the preheated instant pot at 350ºF (180ºC) for 7 minutes. Flip the cabbage wedges when the lid screen indicates TURN FOOD.
3. Taste and adjust the seasonings. Bon appétit!

Broccoli Florets with Mayo

Prep time: 5 minutes | Cook time: 6 minutes | Serves 4

1 pound (454 g) broccoli florets
½ cup mayonnaise
¼ cup minced parsley leaves
¼ cup minced coriander leaves
4 tablespoons cornstarch
Sea salt and ground black pepper, to taste

1. Toss the broccoli florets with the remaining ingredients until well coated.
2. Arrange the broccoli florets in the air fryer basket.
3. Put the air fryer lid on and air fry in the preheated instant pot at 395ºF (202ºC) for 6 minutes. Flip the broccoli florets when the lid screen indicates TURN FOOD.
4. Bon appétit!

Cauliflower with Turmeric

Prep time: 5 minutes | Cook time: 15 minutes | Serves 3

1 pound (454 g) cauliflower florets
2 teaspoons olive oil
½ teaspoon turmeric powder
½ teaspoon smoked paprika
Sea salt and ground black pepper, to taste

1. Toss the cauliflower florets with the remaining ingredients. Transfer to the air fryer basket.
2. Put the air fryer lid on and air fry in the preheated instant pot at 350ºF (180ºC) for 15 minutes. Flip the cauliflower florets when the lid screen indicates TURN FOOD.
3. Bon appétit!

Carrot with Spice

Prep time: 10 minutes | Cook time: 15 minutes | Serves 3

¾ pound (340 g) carrots, peeled and sliced
2 tablespoons coconut oil
1 tablespoon Moroccan spice mix
Sea salt and ground black pepper, to taste

1. Toss the carrots with the remaining ingredients; then, arrange the carrots in the air fryer basket.
2. Put the air fryer lid on and air fry in the preheated instant pot at 380ºF (193ºC) for 15 minutes. Flip the carrots when the lid screen indicates TURN FOOD.
3. Bon appétit!

Bell Peppers with Garlic

Prep time: 6 minutes | Cook time: 15 minutes | Serves 2

4 bell peppers, seeded and halved lengthwise
2 tablespoons olive oil
1 tablespoon chopped fresh parsley
2 cloves garlic, minced
Sea salt and ground black pepper, to taste

1. Toss the peppers with the remaining ingredients; place them in the air fryer basket.
2. Put the air fryer lid on and air fry in the preheated instant pot at 400ºF (205ºC) for 15 minutes. Flip the peppers when the lid screen indicates TURN FOOD.
3. Taste, adjust the seasonings and serve at room temperature. Bon appétit!

Parsnip with Mayo

Prep time: 10 minutes | Cook time: 15 minutes | Serves 4

1 pound (454 g) parsnip, trimmed and sliced
2 tablespoons vegan mayonnaise
½ teaspoon cayenne pepper
½ teaspoon dried oregano
Kosher salt and ground black pepper, to taste

1. Toss the parsnip with the remaining ingredients; place them in the air fryer basket.
2. Put the air fryer lid on and air fry in the preheated instant pot at 400ºF (205ºC) for 15 minutes. Flip the parsnip slices when the lid screen indicates TURN FOOD.
3. Serve warm and enjoy!

Garlic Cauliflower Florets

Prep time: 5 minutes | Cook time: 15 minutes | Serves 4

1 pound (454 g) cauliflower florets
2 tablespoon olive oil
1 teaspoon minced garlic
½ teaspoon cayenne pepper
Sea salt and ground black pepper, to taste

1. Toss the cauliflower florets with the remaining ingredients. Transfer to the air fryer basket.
2. Put the air fryer lid on and air fry in the preheated instant pot at 350ºF (180ºC) for 15minutes. Flip the cauliflower florets when the lid screen indicates TURN FOOD.
3. Bon appétit!

Polenta Bites with Pepper

Prep time: 5 minutes | Cook time: 15 minutes | Serves 4

1 pound (454 g) prepared polenta
2 tablespoons olive oil
1 bell peppers, seeded and sliced

1. Cut the polenta into pieces. Drizzle the olive oil over them and top each piece with the peppers. Transfer to the baking dish.
2. Place the baking dish in the air fryer basket. Put the air fryer lid on and bake in the preheated instant pot at 350ºF (180ºC) for about 15 minutes.
3. Bon appétit!

Soy Sauce Tofu

Prep time: 6 minutes | Cook time: 22 minutes | Serves 3

12 ounces (340 g) extra-firm tofu, cubed
1 tablespoon soy sauce
1 tablespoon sesame oil
1 teaspoon Sriracha
1 teaspoon shallot powder
1 teaspoon minced garlic

1. Toss the tofu with the remaining ingredients. Let it marinate for 30 minutes.
2. Place the tofu cubes in the air fryer basket, discarding the marinade.
3. Put the air fryer lid on and air fry in the preheated instant pot at 360ºF (182ºC) for 22 minutes. Flip the tofu cubes when the lid screen indicates TURN FOOD.
4. Bon appétit!

Parsnip with Herb

Prep time: 10 minutes | Cook time: 15 minutes | Serves 4

1 pound (454 g) parsnip, trimmed and cut into sticks
1 tablespoon Mediterranean herb mix
1 teaspoon minced garlic
Sea salt and ground black pepper, to taste

1. Toss the parsnip with the remaining ingredients; place them in the air fryer basket.
2. Put the air fryer lid on and air fry in the preheated instant pot at 400ºF (205ºC) for 15 minutes. Flip the parsnip slices when the lid screen indicates TURN FOOD.
3. Serve warm and enjoy!

Air Fried Red Beets

Prep time: 10 minutes | Cook time: 30 minutes | Serves 4

1 pound (454 g) red beets, peeled and diced
2 teaspoons olive oil
Coarse sea salt and ground black pepper, to taste
2 tablespoons agave syrup
2 tablespoons balsamic vinegar

1. Toss the red beets with the remaining ingredients until well coated on all sides. Transfer to the air fryer basket.
2. Put the air fryer lid on and air fry in the preheated instant pot at 390ºF (199ºC) for 30 minutes. Flip the red beets when the lid screen indicates TURN FOOD.
3. Bon appétit!

Chili Potato Wedges

Prep time: 8 minutes | Cook time: 20 minutes | Serves 4

1 pound (454 g) potatoes, peeled and cut into wedges
2 tablespoons olive oil
1 teaspoon red chili powder
1 teaspoon garlic powder
Kosher salt and ground black pepper, to taste

1. Toss the potatoes with the remaining ingredients until well coated on all sides. Arrange the potatoes in the air fryer basket.
2. Put the air fryer lid on and air fry in the preheated instant pot at 400ºF (205ºC) for 20 minutes. Flip the potatoes when the lid screen indicates TURN FOOD.
3. Bon appétit!

Potato with Masala

Prep time: 5 minutes | Cook time: 20 minutes | Serves 4

1 pound (454 g) fingerling potatoes
2 tablespoons olive oil
1 teaspoon garam masala
Sea salt and ground black pepper, to taste

1. Toss the potatoes with the remaining ingredients until well coated on all sides.
2. Arrange the potatoes in the air fryer basket.
3. Put the air fryer lid on and air fry in the preheated instant pot at 400ºF (205ºC) for 20 minutes. Flip the potatoes when the lid screen indicates TURN FOOD.
4. Bon appétit!

Five-Spice Broccoli

Prep time: 5 minutes | Cook time: 6 minutes | Serves 4

½ pound (227 g) broccoli florets
2 tablespoons sesame oil
2 scallions, chopped
1 teaspoon five-spice powder
Sea salt and ground black pepper, to taste

1. Toss the broccoli florets with the remaining ingredients until well coated.
2. Arrange the broccoli florets in the air fryer basket.
3. Put the air fryer lid on and air fry in the preheated instant pot at 395ºF (202ºC) for 6 minutes. Flip the broccoli florets when the lid screen indicates TURN FOOD.
4. Bon appétit!

Homemade Mushrooms

Prep time: 5 minutes | Cook time: 10 minutes | Serves 3

10 ounces (283 g) button mushrooms
2 tablespoons olive oil
1 teaspoon granulated garlic
2 tablespoons rice vinegar
1 tablespoon agave syrup
1 tablespoon soy sauce

1. Toss the mushrooms with the remaining ingredients. Arrange them in a lightly greased air fryer basket.
2. Put the air fryer lid on and air fry in the preheated instant pot at 375ºF (190ºC) for 10 minutes. Flip the mushrooms when the lid screen indicates TURN FOOD.
3. Enjoy!

Green Beans with Mayo

Prep time: 6 minutes | Cook time: 6 minutes | Serves 3

¾ pound (340 g) green beans, trimmed and halved
½ cup vegan mayonnaise
1 teaspoon granulated garlic
1 teaspoon paprika
Kosher salt and ground black pepper, to taste

1. Toss the green beans with the remaining ingredients until well coated on all sides. Transfer to the air fryer basket.
2. Put the air fryer lid on and air fry in the preheated instant pot at 390ºF (199ºC) for 6 minutes. Flip the green beans when the lid screen indicates TURN FOOD.
3. Enjoy!

Sweet Potato with Paprika

Prep time: 10 minutes | Cook time: 35 minutes | Serves 4

1 pound (454 g) sweet potatoes, peeled and cut into cubes
2 tablespoons olive oil, melted
Sea salt and ground black pepper, to taste
1 teaspoon granulated garlic
1 teaspoon ginger powder
½ teaspoon ground chili powder
1 teaspoon paprika
½ teaspoon ground allspice

1. Toss the sweet potatoes with the remaining ingredients. Transfer to the air fryer basket.
2. Put the air fryer lid on and air fry in the preheated instant pot at 380ºF (193ºC) for 35 minutes. Flip the sweet potatoes when the lid screen indicates TURN FOOD.
3. Taste and adjust the seasonings. Bon appétit!

Beer Broccoli Tempura

Prep time: 5 minutes | Cook time: 6 minutes | Serves 4

1 cup all-purpose flour
½ cup beer
2 tablespoons sesame oil
½ teaspoon cayenne pepper
1 teaspoon chili powder
Sea salt and ground black pepper, to taste
1 pound (454 g) broccoli florets

1. In a mixing bowl, thoroughly combine the flour, beer, oil, and spices.
2. Dip the broccoli florets in the tempura mixture and place them in a lightly oiled air fryer basket.
3. Put the air fryer lid on and air fry in the preheated instant pot at 395ºF (202ºC) for 6 minutes. Flip the broccoli florets when the lid screen indicates TURN FOOD.
4. Bon appétit!

Chickpea Burgers

Prep time: 10 minutes | Cook time: 15 minutes | Serves 4

16 ounces (454 g) canned or boiled chickpeas, drained
2 tablespoons all-purpose flour
½ teaspoon baking soda
¼ cup fresh parsley leaves
¼ cup fresh cilantro leaves
1 teaspoon green chili paste
1 onion, quartered
4 garlic cloves, peeled
Sea salt and ground black pepper, to taste
2 tablespoons olive oil

1. Pulse all the ingredients in the food processor until everything is well incorporated.
2. Form the mixture into burgers and place them in a lightly greased air fryer basket.
3. Put the air fryer lid on and air fry in the preheated instant pot at 380ºF (193ºC) for 15 minutes. Flip the burgers when the lid screen indicates TURN FOOD.
4. Serve with burger buns and enjoy!

Polenta with Marinara Sauce

Prep time: 5 minutes | Cook time: 15 minutes | Serves 2

½ pound (227 g) polenta
2 tablespoons olive oil, plus more as needed
1 teaspoon dried basil
1 teaspoon dried oregano
¼ cup marinara sauce

1. Cut the polenta into pieces. Toss each piece with the olive oil, basil, oregano, and marinara sauce. Transfer to the air fryer basket.
2. Put the air fryer lid on and air fry in the preheated instant pot at 350ºF (180ºC) for 15 minutes. Flip the polenta bites when the lid screen indicates TURN FOOD.
3. Enjoy!

Tomato Stuffed Eggplant

Prep time: 8 minutes | Cook time: 15 minutes | Serves 2

2 small eggplants, halved lengthwise
1 tablespoon olive oil
1 small shallot, chopped
2 garlic cloves, minced
1 bell pepper, chopped
1 medium tomato, chopped
2 tablespoons minced fresh parsley
1 tablespoon minced fresh basil
Sea salt and ground black pepper, to taste

1. Toss the eggplants with the oil; place them in the air fryer basket.
2. Mix the remaining ingredients to make the filling. Spoon the filling into the eggplant halves.
3. Put the air fryer lid on and air fry in the preheated instant pot at 400ºF (205ºC) for about 15 minutes.
4. Serve warm and enjoy!

Cabbage with Pepper

Prep time: 5 minutes | Cook time: 7 minutes | Serves 4

1 pound (454 g) cabbage, cut into wedges
1 teaspoon minced garlic
2 tablespoons olive oil
1 teaspoon red pepper flakes
Sea salt and ground black pepper, to taste

1. Toss the cabbage wedges with the remaining ingredients. Transfer to the air fryer basket.
2. Put the air fryer lid on and air fry in the preheated instant pot at 350ºF (180ºC) for 7 minutes. Flip the cabbage wedges when the lid screen indicates TURN FOOD.
3. Taste and adjust the seasonings. Bon appétit!

Red Beets with Tofu Cheese

Prep time: 10 minutes | Cook time: 30 minutes | Serves 2

½ pound (227 g) red beets, peeled and sliced
2 tablespoons mayonnaise
Sea salt and ground black pepper, to taste
½ teaspoon cumin powder
1 tablespoon Dijon mustard
2 ounces (57 g) tofu cheese, crumbled

1. Toss the red beets with the mayo, salt, black pepper, cumin powder, and Dijon mustard until well coated on all sides. Transfer to the air fryer basket.
2. Put the air fryer lid on and air fry in the preheated instant pot at 390ºF (199ºC) for 30 minutes. Flip the red beets when the lid screen indicates TURN FOOD.
3. Top the roasted beets with tofu cheese and enjoy!

White Beans Sausage

Prep time: 5 minutes | Cook time: 15 minutes | Serves 3

1 cup canned white beans, drained and rinsed
1 medium onion, chopped
2 cloves garlic, chopped
2 tablespoons olive oil
1 teaspoon liquid smoke
2 tablespoons buckwheat flour

1. Pulse all the ingredients in the food processor until everything is well incorporated.
2. Shape the mixture into three sausages and place them in a lightly greased air fryer basket.
3. Put the air fryer lid on and air fry in the preheated instant pot at 390ºF (199ºC) for 15 minutes. Flip the sausage when the lid screen indicates TURN FOOD.
4. Bon appétit!

Wheat Gluten Sausage

Prep time: 6 minutes | Cook time: 55 minutes | Serves 4

1 onion, chopped
2 cloves garlic, minced
2 tablespoons olive oil
¼ cup tomato paste
2 tablespoons chopped sun-dried tomatoes
Kosher salt and ground black pepper, to taste
½ teaspoon liquid smoke
1 cup vital wheat gluten

1. Pulse all the ingredients in the food processor until everything is well incorporated.
2. Shape the mixture into three sausages and roll them in a piece of aluminum foil; twist the ends closed. Transfer to the air fryer basket.
3. Put the air fryer lid on and air fry in the preheated instant pot at 390ºF (199ºC) for 15 minutes. Flip the sausage when the lid screen indicates TURN FOOD.
4. Bon appétit!

Zucchini Slices

Prep time: 10 minutes | Cook time: 10 minutes | Serves 4

1 pound (454 g) zucchini, sliced
1 teaspoon granulated garlic
2 tablespoons olive oil
Sea salt and ground black pepper, to taste
1 teaspoon Italian seasoning
2 tablespoons white balsamic vinegar

1. Toss the zucchini slices with the remaining ingredients and place them in the air fryer basket.
2. Put the air fryer lid on and air fry in the preheated instant pot at 390ºF (199ºC) for 10 minutes. Flip the zucchini slices when the lid screen indicates TURN FOOD. Work in batches.
3. Bon appétit!

Carrot Sticks with Syrup

Prep time: 10 minutes | Cook time: 15 minutes | Serves 4

1 pound (454 g) carrots, trimmed and cut into sticks
2 tablespoons agave syrup
½ teaspoon ground cinnamon
Himalayan salt and cayenne pepper, to taste
2 tablespoons avocado oil
1 teaspoon garlic powder
1 teaspoon dried parsley flakes

1. Toss the carrots with the remaining ingredients; then, arrange the carrots in the air fryer basket.
2. Put the air fryer lid on and air fry in the preheated instant pot at 380ºF (193ºC) for 15 minutes. Flip the carrots when the lid screen indicates TURN FOOD.
3. Bon appétit!

Cheese Stuffed Peppers

Prep time: 10 minutes | Cook time: 15 minutes | Serves 3

6 Italian peppers, seeded and stems removed
2 garlic cloves, minced
1 tablespoon taco seasoning mix
½ cup grated vegan Cheddar cheese
Sea salt and red pepper flakes, to taste
2 tablespoons olive oil

1. Arrange the peppers in the air fryer basket.
2. Mix the remaining ingredients until well combined. Dived the filling between the peppers.
3. Put the air fryer lid on and air fry in the preheated instant pot at 400ºF (205ºC) for 15 minutes.
4. Bon appétit!

Tangy Beets

Prep time: 10 minutes | Cook time: 30 minutes | Serves 3

1 pound (454 g) beets, peeled and diced
2 tablespoons olive oil
Sea salt and ground black pepper, to taste
1 tablespoon stone-ground mustard
2 tablespoons balsamic vinegar
¼ cup fresh orange juice
1 tablespoon chopped fresh rosemary

1. Toss the red beets with the remaining ingredients until well coated on all sides. Transfer to the air fryer basket.
2. Put the air fryer lid on and air fry in the preheated instant pot at 390ºF (199ºC) for 30 minutes. Flip the red beets when the lid screen indicates TURN FOOD.
3. Bon appétit!

Peppers with Tofu Cheese

Prep time: 10 minutes | Cook time: 15 minutes | Serves 3

1 red bell pepper, seeded and halved
1 green bell pepper, seeded and halved
1 orange bell pepper, seeded and halved
2 tablespoons olive oil
2 tablespoons balsamic vinegar
Sea salt and red pepper flakes, to taste
3 ounces (85 g) tofu cheese, crumbled

1. Toss the peppers with the olive oil, vinegar, salt, and red pepper; place them in the air fryer basket.
2. Put the air fryer lid on and air fry in the preheated instant pot at 400ºF (205ºC) for 15 minutes. Flip the peppers when the lid screen indicates TURN FOOD.
3. Serve the roasted peppers with tofu cheese. Bon appétit!

Tempeh with Cayenne

Prep time: 5 minutes | Cook time: 22 minutes | Serves 3

10 ounces (283 g) tempeh
2 tablespoons soy sauce
1 tablespoon rice vinegar
1 teaspoon cayenne pepper
Sea salt and ground black pepper, to taste

1. Toss the tempeh with the remaining ingredients. Let it marinate for 30 minutes.
2. Place the tempeh in the air fryer basket, discarding the marinade.
3. Put the air fryer lid on and air fry in the preheated instant pot at 360ºF (182ºC) for 22 minutes. Flip the tempeh when the lid screen indicates TURN FOOD.
4. Bon appétit!

Tomato Stuffed Zucchini

Prep time: 8 minutes | Cook time: 10 minutes | Serves 2

2 medium zucchinis, halved
2 tablespoons olive oil
1 shallot, chopped
2 garlic cloves, minced
1 small tomato, chopped
1 teaspoon hot sauce
1 teaspoon tamari sauce
Sea salt and ground black pepper, to taste

1. Place the zucchini halves in a lightly oiled air fryer basket.
2. Mix the remaining ingredients to make the filling; stuff the zucchini halves with the prepared filling.
3. Put the air fryer lid on and air fry in the preheated instant pot at 390ºF (199ºC) for 10 minutes or until cooked through.
4. Bon appétit!

Chapter 9 Vegetables and Side Dishes

Simple Green Beans

Prep time: 5 minutes | Cook time: 7 minutes | Serves 4

1 pound (454 g) fresh green beans, cleaned and trimmed
½ teaspoon garlic powder
½ teaspoon cumin powder
½ teaspoon onion powder
½ teaspoon dried dill weed
1 teaspoon olive oil
Sea salt and red pepper flakes, to taste

1. Toss the green beans with the remaining ingredients until they are well coated.
2. Arrange the green beans in the air fryer basket.
3. Put the air fryer lid on and air fry in the preheated instant pot at 375ºF (190ºC) for 7 minutes. Flip the green beans when the lid screen indicates TURN FOOD.
4. Taste, adjust the seasonings, and serve warm. Bon appétit!

Butter Brussels Sprouts

Prep time: 5 minutes | Cook time: 14 minutes | Serves 3

¾ pound (340 g) Brussels sprouts
2 tablespoons butter, melted
2 garlic cloves, crushed
Kosher salt and ground black pepper, to taste

1. Toss the Brussels sprouts with the remaining ingredients until well coated.
2. Arrange the Brussels sprouts in the air fryer basket.
3. Put the air fryer lid on and air fry in the preheated instant pot at 380ºF (193ºC) for 14 minutes. Flip the Brussels sprouts when the lid screen indicates TURN FOOD.
4. Bon appétit!

Air Fried Mushrooms

Prep time: 8 minutes | Cook time: 11 minutes | Serves 3

¾ pound (340 g) button mushrooms, cleaned and cut into halves
2 tablespoons olive oil
1 garlic clove, pressed
Sea salt and ground black pepper, to taste
1 tablespoon fresh lemon juice
1 tablespoon chopped fresh cilantro

1. Toss the mushrooms with the olive oil, garlic, salt, and black pepper.
2. Arrange them in a lightly oiled air fryer basket.
3. Put the air fryer lid on and air fry in the preheated instant pot at 375ºF (190ºC) for 11 minutes. Flip the mushrooms when the lid screen indicates TURN FOOD.
4. Drizzle fresh lemon juice over the mushroom and serve with the fresh cilantro. Enjoy!

Broccoli with Garlic

Prep time: 5 minutes | Cook time: 6 minutes | Serves 3

¾ pound (340 g) broccoli florets
1 tablespoon olive oil
1 teaspoon garlic powder
Sea salt and ground black pepper, to taste

1. Toss the broccoli florets with the remaining ingredients until well coated.
2. Arrange the broccoli florets in the air fryer basket.
3. Put the air fryer lid on and air fry in the preheated instant pot at 395ºF (202ºC) for 6 minutes. Flip the broccoli florets when the lid screen indicates TURN FOOD.
4. Bon appétit!

Homemade Potato

Prep time: 5 minutes | Cook time: 20 minutes | Serves 3

¾ pound (340 g) fingerling potatoes
1 tablespoon olive oil
½ teaspoon onion powder
1 teaspoon garlic powder
1 teaspoon chili pepper
Sea salt and ground black pepper, to taste

1. Toss the potatoes with the remaining ingredients until well coated on all sides.
2. Arrange the potatoes in the air fryer basket.
3. Put the air fryer lid on and air fry in the preheated instant pot at 400ºF (205ºC) for 20 minutes. Flip the potatoes when the lid screen indicates TURN FOOD.
4. Garnish with fresh or dried herbs, if desired. Bon appétit!

Creamy Cauliflower Salad with Bacon

Prep time: 5 minutes | Cook time: 12 minutes | Serves 3

¾ pound (340 g) cauliflower florets
2 ounces (57 g) bacon, diced
¼ cup sour cream
¼ cup mayonnaise
1 teaspoon Dijon mustard
1 tablespoon apple cider vinegar
1 garlic clove, minced
1 small red onion, thinly sliced
Kosher salt and freshly ground black pepper, to taste

1. Place the cauliflower florets in a lightly greased air fryer basket.
2. Put the air fryer lid on and air fry in the preheated instant pot at 400ºF (205ºC) for 12 minutes. Flip the cauliflower florets when the lid screen indicates TURN FOOD.
3. Thoroughly combine the cauliflower florets with the remaining ingredients. Serve well chilled and enjoy!

Beet Salad

Prep time: 5 minutes | Cook time: 40 minutes | Serves 4

1 pound (454 g) beets
½ teaspoon cumin seeds
Sea salt and red pepper flakes, to taste
2 tablespoons apple cider vinegar
4 tablespoons olive oil
1 teaspoon crushed garlic

1. Arrange the beets in the air fryer basket.
2. Put the air fryer lid on and air fry in the preheated instant pot at 400ºF (205ºC) for 40 minutes. Flip the beets when the lid screen indicates TURN FOOD. Let them cool completely.
3. Peel the beets and cut them into thin slices; transfer to a salad bowl. Add in the remaining ingredients and stir to combine.
4. Bon appétit!

Easy Eggplant

Prep time: 10 minutes | Cook time: 15 minutes | Serves 3

¾ pound (340 g) eggplant, peeled and diced
2 tablespoons sesame oil
½ teaspoon cumin powder
½ teaspoon onion powder
1 teaspoon granulated garlic

1. Toss the eggplant pieces with the remaining ingredients until they are well coated on all sides.
2. Arrange the eggplant in the air fryer basket.
3. Put the air fryer lid on and air fry in the preheated instant pot at 400ºF (205ºC) for 15 minutes. Flip the eggplant when the lid screen indicates TURN FOOD.
4. Garnish with fresh herbs, if desired. Bon appétit!

Cauliflower with Onion

Prep time: 5 minutes | Cook time: 13 minutes | Serves 3

¾ pound (340 g) cauliflower florets
1 large onion, cut into wedges
2 cloves garlic, pressed
1 tablespoon olive oil
Sea salt and ground black pepper, to taste
1 teaspoon paprika

1. Toss the cauliflower florets and onion with the garlic, olive oil, and spices. Toss until they are well coated on all sides.
2. Arrange the vegetables in the air fryer basket.
3. Put the air fryer lid on and air fry in the preheated instant pot at 400ºF (205ºC) for 13 minutes. Flip the vegetables when the lid screen indicates TURN FOOD.
4. Bon appétit!

Yellow Beans with Tomato

Prep time: 5 minutes | Cook time: 8 minutes | Serves 3

½ pound (227 g) yellow beans, trimmed
2 small tomatoes, sliced
1 tablespoon sesame oil
Sea salt and ground black pepper, to taste

1. Toss the yellow beans and tomatoes with the sesame oil, salt, and black pepper; toss until they are well coated.
2. Arrange the vegetables in the air fryer basket.
3. Put the air fryer lid on and air fry in the preheated instant pot at 390ºF (199ºC) for 8 minutes. Stir the vegetables when the lid screen indicates TURN FOOD.
4. Taste, adjust the seasonings, and serve immediately. Bon appétit!

Coconut-Mushrooms

Prep time: 10 minutes | Cook time: 7 minutes | Serves 4

1 pound (454 g) cremini mushrooms, sliced
2 tablespoons olive oil
½ teaspoon shallot powder
½ teaspoon garlic powder
1 tablespoon coconut aminos
1 tablespoon white wine
Sea salt and ground black pepper, to taste
1 tablespoon chopped fresh parsley

1. Toss the mushrooms with the remaining ingredients. Toss until they are well coated on all sides.
2. Arrange the mushrooms in the air fryer basket.
3. Put the air fryer lid on and roast in the preheated instant pot at 400ºF (205ºC) for 7 minutes. Flip the mushrooms when the lid screen indicates TURN FOOD.
4. Garnish with the fresh herbs, if desired. Bon appétit!

Gold Potato with Paprika

Prep time: 10 minutes | Cook time: 13 minutes | Serves 3

¾ pound (340 g) Yukon Gold potatoes, peeled and cut into 1-inch chunks
1 tablespoon olive oil
Sea salt and ground black pepper, to taste
½ turmeric powder
½ teaspoon garlic powder
½ teaspoon paprika

1. Toss the potatoes with the remaining ingredients until well coated on all sides.
2. Arrange the potatoes in the air fryer basket.
3. Put the air fryer lid on and air fry in the preheated instant pot at 400ºF (205ºC) for 13 minutes. Flip the potatoes when the lid screen indicates TURN FOOD.
4. Bon appétit!

Caponata with Olives and Tomato

Prep time: 5 minutes | Cook time: 15 minutes | Serves 3

3 bell peppers, sliced
1 medium-sized onion, sliced
2 tablespoons olive oil
2 ounces (57 g) olives, pitted and sliced
1 large tomato, sliced
1 teaspoon capers, drained

1. Toss the peppers, onion, and olive oil in the air fryer basket.
2. Put the air fryer lid on and air fry in the preheated instant pot at 400ºF (205ºC) for 10 minutes. Flip the vegetables when the lid screen indicates TURN FOOD.
3. Add in the olives, tomato, and capers. Continue to cook for an additional 5 minutes or until everything is cooked through.
4. Bon appétit!

Cheesy Broccoli Florets

Prep time: 5 minutes | Cook time: 6 minutes | Serves 3

¾ pound (340 g) broccoli florets
1 tablespoon olive oil
½ teaspoon dried dill weed
Coarse sea salt and freshly ground black pepper, to taste
2 ounces (57 g) Parmesan cheese, freshly grated

1. Toss the broccoli florets with the olive oil, dill, salt, and black pepper until well coated.
2. Arrange the broccoli florets in the air fryer basket.
3. Put the air fryer lid on and air fry in the preheated instant pot at 395ºF (202ºC) for 6 minutes. Flip the broccoli florets when the lid screen indicates TURN FOOD.
4. Top with the Parmesan cheese and serve warm. Bon appétit!

Cauliflower Salad with Chickpeas

Prep time: 5 minutes | Cook time: 12 minutes | Serves 4

1 pound (454 g) cauliflower florets
1 cup canned or boiled chickpeas
¼ cup mayonnaise
1 teaspoon Dijon mustard
1 teaspoon ancho chili powder
Sea salt and ground black pepper, to taste
2 tablespoons chopped fresh chives
2 tablespoons apple cider vinegar

1. Arrange the cauliflower florets in a lightly greased air fryer basket.
2. Put the air fryer lid on and air fry in the preheated instant pot at 400ºF (205ºC) for 12 minutes. Flip the cauliflower florets when the lid screen indicates TURN FOOD.
3. Thoroughly combine the cauliflower florets with the remaining ingredients. Serve well chilled and enjoy!

Beets with Cheese

Prep time: 5 minutes | Cook time: 40 minutes | Serves 4

1 pound (454 g) beets
Sea salt and red pepper flakes, to taste
2 tablespoons apple cider vinegar
4 tablespoons olive oil
1 teaspoon garlic powder
4 ounces (113 g) feta cheese, crumbled

1. Arrange the beets in the air fryer basket.
2. Put the air fryer lid on and air fry in the preheated instant pot at 400ºF (205ºC) for 40 minutes. Flip the beets when the lid screen indicates TURN FOOD. Let them cool completely.
3. Peel the beets and cut them into thin slices; transfer to a salad bowl. Add in the remaining ingredients and stir to combine.
4. Bon appétit!

Green Beans with Cheese

Prep time: 5 minutes | Cook time: 7 minutes | Serves 3

¾ pound (340 g) green beans, cleaned and trimmed
1 tablespoon olive oil
1 clove garlic, pressed
Sea salt and ground black pepper, to taste
2 ounces (57 g) feta cheese, crumbled
1 tablespoon chopped pistachio

1. Toss the green beans with the olive oil, garlic, salt, and black pepper until they are well coated.
2. Arrange the green beans in the air fryer basket.
3. Put the air fryer lid on and air fry in the preheated instant pot at 375ºF (190ºC) for 7 minutes. Flip the green beans when the lid screen indicates TURN FOOD.
4. Taste, adjust the seasonings, and serve garnished with cheese and chopped pistachio. Enjoy!

Five-Spice Brussels Sprouts

Prep time: 5 minutes | Cook time: 10 minutes | Serves 2

½ pound (227 g) Brussels sprouts, trimmed
2 tablespoons sesame oil
Sea salt and ground black pepper, to taste
1 teaspoon five-spice powder
1 teaspoon soy sauce
1 teaspoon rice vinegar

1. Toss the Brussels sprouts with the oil until well coated on all sides; then, arrange the Brussels sprouts in the air fryer basket.
2. Put the air fryer lid on and roast in the preheated instant pot at 380ºF (193ºC) for 10 minutes. Flip the Brussels sprouts when the lid screen indicates TURN FOOD.
3. Toss them with the remaining ingredients and continue to cook for 3 to 4 minutes more. Serve warm and enjoy!

Cheesy Eggplant

Prep time: 10 minutes | Cook time: 13 minutes | Serves 4

2 eggs, whisked
½ cup almond flour
½ cup grated Parmesan cheese
1 teaspoon Italian seasoning mix
¾ pound (340 g) eggplant, peeled and sliced

1. In a mixing bowl, thoroughly combine the eggs, almond flour, cheese, and Italian seasoning mix.
2. Dip the eggplant slices in the egg mixture until they are well coated on all sides.
3. Arrange the eggplant in the air fryer basket.
4. Put the air fryer lid on and air fry in the preheated instant pot at 400ºF (205ºC) for 13 minutes. Flip the eggplant when the lid screen indicates TURN FOOD.
5. Bon appétit!

Basil Cauliflower Florets

Prep time: 5 minutes | Cook time: 13 minutes | Serves 3

¾ pound (340 g) cauliflower florets
1 tablespoon olive oil
½ teaspoon dried oregano
1 teaspoon dried basil
1 teaspoon dried rosemary
Sea salt and ground black pepper, to taste

1. Toss the cauliflower florets and onion with the olive oil and spices. Toss until they are well coated on all sides.
2. Arrange the cauliflower florets in the air fryer basket.
3. Put the air fryer lid on and air fry in the preheated instant pot at 400ºF (205ºC) for 13 minutes. Flip the cauliflower florets when the lid screen indicates TURN FOOD.
4. Bon appétit!

Bell Peppers with Chili

Prep time: 5 minutes | Cook time: 15 minutes | Serves 3

1 pound (454 g) bell peppers, seeded and halved
1 chili pepper, seeded
2 tablespoons olive oil
Kosher salt and ground black pepper, to taste
1 teaspoon granulated garlic

1. Toss the peppers with the remaining ingredients; place them in the air fryer basket.
2. Put the air fryer lid on and air fry in the preheated instant pot at 400ºF (205ºC) for 15 minutes. Flip the peppers when the lid screen indicates TURN FOOD.
3. Taste, adjust the seasonings and serve at room temperature. Bon appétit!

Carrot and Parsnip

Prep time: 15 minutes | Cook time: 15 minutes | Serves 4

1 carrot, trimmed and sliced
1 parsnip, trimmed and sliced
1 celery stalk, trimmed and sliced
1 onion, peeled and diced
2 tablespoons olive oil
Sea salt and ground black pepper, to taste
1 teaspoon crushed red pepper flakes

1. Toss all ingredients in the air fryer basket.
2. Put the air fryer lid on and air fry in the preheated instant pot at 380ºF (193ºC) for 15 minutes. Flip the vegetables when the lid screen indicates TURN FOOD.
3. Bon appétit!

Mushrooms with Tamari Sauce

Prep time: 5 minutes | Cook time: 7 minutes | Serves 4

1 pound (454 g) brown mushrooms, quartered
2 tablespoons sesame oil
1 tablespoon tamari sauce
1 garlic clove, pressed
Sea salt and ground black pepper, to taste

1. Toss the mushrooms with the remaining ingredients. Toss until they are well coated on all sides.
2. Arrange the mushrooms in the air fryer basket.
3. Put the air fryer lid on and roast in the preheated instant pot at 400ºF (205ºC) for 7 minutes. Flip the mushrooms when the lid screen indicates TURN FOOD.
4. Bon appétit!

Chili Potato

Prep time: 10 minutes | Cook time: 13 minutes | Serves 4

1 pound (454 g) potatoes, diced into bite-sized chunks
1 tablespoon olive oil
Sea salt and ground black pepper, to taste
1 teaspoon chili powder

1. Toss the potatoes with the remaining ingredients until well coated on all sides.
2. Arrange the potatoes in the air fryer basket.
3. Put the air fryer lid on and air fry in the preheated instant pot at 400ºF (205ºC) for 13 minutes. Flip the potatoes when the lid screen indicates TURN FOOD.
4. Bon appétit!

Broccoli with Pepitas

Prep time: 5 minutes | Cook time: 6 minutes | Serves 3

¾ pound (340 g) broccoli florets
1½ tablespoons olive oil
1 teaspoon garlic powder
½ teaspoon onion powder
½ teaspoon mustard seeds
Sea salt and freshly ground black pepper, to taste
2 tablespoons lightly roasted pepitas

1. Toss the broccoli with the olive oil, garlic powder, onion powder, mustard seeds, salt, and black pepper.
2. Arrange the broccoli in the air fryer basket.
3. Put the air fryer lid on and roast in the preheated instant pot at 395ºF (202ºC) for 6 minutes. Flip the broccoli florets when the lid screen indicates TURN FOOD.
4. Top with roasted pepitas and serve warm. Bon appétit!

Potato with Paprika

Prep time: 10 minutes | Cook time: 35 minutes | Serves 4

1 pound (454 g) sweet potatoes, scrubbed and halved
3 tablespoons olive oil
1 teaspoon paprika
Sea salt and ground black pepper, to taste

1. Toss the sweet potatoes with the olive oil, paprika, salt, and black pepper.
2. Arrange the sweet potatoes in the air fryer basket.
3. Put the air fryer lid on and roast in the preheated instant pot at 380ºF (193ºC) for 35 minutes. Flip the sweet potatoes when the lid screen indicates TURN FOOD.
4. Taste and adjust the seasonings. Bon appétit!

Green Beans and Spinach Salad

Prep time: 10 minutes | Cook time: 7 minutes | Serves 3

¾ pound (340 g) fresh green beans, washed and trimmed
2 tablespoons olive oil
½ cup thinly sliced green onions
2 cups baby spinach
1 tablespoon chopped fresh basil
1 green pepper, sliced
2 tablespoons fresh lemon juice
Sea salt and ground black pepper, to taste

1. Toss the green beans with 1 tablespoon of the olive oil. Arrange the green beans in the air fryer basket.
2. Put the air fryer lid on and air fry in the preheated instant pot at 375ºF (190ºC) for 7 minutes. Flip the green beans when the lid screen indicates TURN FOOD.
3. Add the green beans to a salad bowl; add in the remaining ingredients and stir to combine well. Enjoy!

Corn on the Cob

Prep time: 10 minutes | Cook time: 6 minutes | Serves 2

2 ears of corn, husked and halved
2 tablespoons Chinese chili oil
Sea salt and red pepper, to taste
2 tablespoons chopped fresh cilantro

1. Toss the ears of corn with the oil, salt, and red pepper. Arrange the ears of corn in the air fryer basket.
2. Put the air fryer lid on and air fry in the preheated instant pot at 390ºF (199ºC) for 6 minutes. Flip the ears of corn when the lid screen indicates TURN FOOD.
3. Garnish the ears of corn with the fresh cilantro. Bon appétit!

Buttery Brussels Sprouts

Prep time: 5 minutes | Cook time: 10 minutes | Serves 3

¾ pound (340 g) Brussels sprouts, trimmed
1 tablespoon butter, melted
1 teaspoon crushed red pepper flakes
Kosher salt and ground black pepper, to taste

1. Toss the Brussels sprouts with the butter and spices until they are well coated on all sides; then, arrange the Brussels sprouts in the air fryer basket.
2. Put the air fryer lid on and roast in the preheated instant pot at 380ºF (193ºC) for 10 minutes. Flip the Brussels sprouts when the lid screen indicates TURN FOOD.
3. Serve warm and enjoy!

Breaded Eggplant

Prep time: 5 minutes | Cook time: 13 minutes | Serves 3

Sea salt and freshly ground black pepper, to taste
½ cup all-purpose flour
2 eggs
¾ pound (340 g) eggplant, sliced
½ cup bread crumbs

1. In a shallow bowl, mix the salt, black pepper, and flour. Whisk the eggs in the second bowl, and place the bread crumbs in the third bowl.
2. Dip the eggplant slices in the flour mixture, then in the whisked eggs; finally, roll the eggplant slices over the bread crumbs until they are well coated on all sides.
3. Arrange the eggplant in the air fryer basket.
4. Put the air fryer lid on and air fry in the preheated instant pot at 400ºF (205ºC) for 13 minutes. Flip the eggplant when the lid screen indicates TURN FOOD.
5. Bon appétit!

Parsnips with Herb

Prep time: 5 minutes | Cook time: 10 minutes | Serves 4

1 pound (454 g) parsnips, trimmed
1 tablespoon olive oil
1 teaspoon herbes de Provence
1 teaspoon cayenne pepper
Sea salt and ground black pepper, to taste

1. Toss the parsnip with the olive oil and spices until they are well coated on all sides; then, arrange the parsnip in the air fryer basket.
2. Put the air fryer lid on and air fry in the preheated instant pot at 380ºF (193ºC) for 10 minutes. Flip the parsnip when the lid screen indicates TURN FOOD.
3. Bon appétit!

Breaded Mushrooms

Prep time: 5 minutes | Cook time: 7 minutes | Serves 3

½ cup flour
2 eggs
1 cup seasoned bread crumbs
1 teaspoon smoked paprika
Sea salt and ground black pepper, to taste
¾ pound (340 g) portobello mushrooms, sliced

1. Place the flour in a plate. Whisk the eggs in a shallow bowl. In a third bowl, mix the bread crumbs, paprika, salt, and black pepper.
2. Dip the mushrooms in the flour, then dunk them in the whisked eggs, and finally toss them in the bread crumb mixture. Toss until well coated on all sides. Arrange the mushrooms in the air fryer basket.
3. Put the air fryer lid on and air fry in the preheated instant pot at 400ºF (205ºC) for 7 minutes. Flip the mushrooms when the lid screen indicates TURN FOOD.
4. Bon appétit!

Tomato and Cheese Stuffed Peppers

Prep time: 5 minutes | Cook time: 15 minutes | Serves 3

3 bell peppers, seeded and halved
1 tablespoon olive oil
1 small onion, chopped
2 garlic cloves, minced
Sea salt and ground black pepper, to taste
1 cup tomato sauce
2 ounces (57 g) Cheddar cheese, shredded

1. Toss the peppers with the oil; place them in the air fryer basket.
2. Mix the onion, garlic, salt, black pepper, and tomato sauce. Spoon the sauce into the pepper halves.
3. Put the air fryer lid on and roast in the preheated instant pot at 400ºF (205ºC) for 10 minutes. Flip the peppers when the lid screen indicates TURN FOOD.
4. Top the peppers with the cheese. Continue to cook for 5 minutes more.
5. Bon appétit!

Parsnip Burgers

Prep time: 8 minutes | Cook time: 15 minutes | Serves 3

¾ pound (340 g) peeled parsnips, shredded
¼ cup all-purpose flour
¼ cup cornflour
1 egg, lightly beaten
1 teaspoon cayenne pepper
Sea salt and ground black pepper, to taste

1. Mix all ingredients until everything is well combined. Form the mixture into three patties.
2. Arrange the patties in the air fryer basket.
3. Put the air fryer lid on and air fry in the preheated instant pot at 380ºF (193ºC) for 15 minutes or until cooked through.
4. Bon appétit!

Broccoli Salad with Cranberry

Prep time: 5 minutes | Cook time: 6 minutes | Serves 3

¾ pound (340 g) broccoli florets
¼ cup raw sunflower seeds
1 clove garlic, peeled and minced
1 small red onion, thinly sliced
¼ cup dried cranberries
¼ cup extra-virgin olive oil
2 tablespoons fresh lemon juice
1 tablespoon Dijon mustard
Sea salt and ground black pepper, to taste

1. Place the broccoli florets in a lightly greased air fryer basket.
2. Put the air fryer lid on and air fry in the preheated instant pot at 395ºF (202ºC) for 6 minutes. Flip the broccoli florets when the lid screen indicates TURN FOOD.
3. Toss the broccoli florets with the remaining ingredients. Serve at room temperature.
4. Bon appétit!

Cauliflower with Cheese

Prep time: 5 minutes | Cook time: 13 minutes | Serves 4

1 pound (454 g) cauliflower florets
2 tablespoons olive oil
1 teaspoon smoked paprika
Sea salt and ground black pepper, to taste
4 ounces (113 g) Parmesan cheese, grated

1. Toss the cauliflower florets with the olive oil and spices. Toss until they are well coated on all sides.
2. Arrange the cauliflower florets in the air fryer basket.
3. Put the air fryer lid on and air fry in the preheated instant pot at 400ºF (205ºC) for 13 minutes. Flip the cauliflower florets when the lid screen indicates TURN FOOD.
4. Toss the warm cauliflower florets with cheese. Bon appétit!

Potato with Cheese

Prep time: 10 minutes | Cook time: 15 minutes | Serves 3

¾ pound (340 g) potatoes, diced
1 tablespoon olive oil
1 teaspoon smoked paprika
1 teaspoon crushed red pepper flakes
Sea salt and ground black pepper, to taste
2 ounces (57 g) Parmesan cheese, grated

1. Toss the potatoes with the olive oil and spices until well coated on all sides.
2. Arrange the potatoes in the air fryer basket.
3. Put the air fryer lid on and air fry in the preheated instant pot at 400ºF (205ºC) for 15 minutes. Flip the potatoes when the lid screen indicates TURN FOOD.
4. Top the warm potatoes with cheese and serve immediately. Enjoy!

Green Beans with Sesame Seeds

Prep time: 5 minutes | Cook time: 7 minutes | Serves 4

1 pound (454 g) fresh green beans, trimmed
1 tablespoon sesame oil
½ teaspoon garlic powder
1 tablespoon soy sauce
Sea salt and Szechuan pepper, to taste
2 tablespoons lightly toasted sesame seeds

1. Toss the green beans with the sesame oil and garlic powder; then, arrange them in the air fryer basket.
2. Put the air fryer lid on and air fry in the preheated instant pot at 380ºF (193ºC) for 7 minutes. Flip the green beans when the lid screen indicates TURN FOOD.
3. Toss the green beans with the remaining ingredients and stir to combine well. Enjoy!

Butter Carrot

Prep time: 8 minutes | Cook time: 15 minutes | Serves 3

¾ pound (340 g) carrots, trimmed and cut into sticks
2 tablespoons butter, melted
Coarse sea salt and white pepper, to taste
1 tablespoon lightly toasted sesame seeds

1. Toss the carrots with the butter, salt, and white pepper; then, arrange them in the air fryer basket.
2. Put the air fryer lid on and roast in the preheated instant pot at 380ºF (193ºC) for 15 minutes. Flip the carrots when the lid screen indicates TURN FOOD.
3. Top the carrots with the sesame seeds. Bon appétit!

Brussels Sprout Salad

Prep time: 5 minutes | Cook time: 10 minutes | Serves 3

¾ pound (340 g) Brussels sprouts, trimmed
2 tablespoons olive oil
Sea salt and ground black pepper, to taste
½ teaspoon dried dill weed
1 tablespoon fresh lemon juice
1 tablespoon rice vinegar

1. Toss the Brussels sprouts with the olive oil and spices until they are well coated on all sides; then, arrange the Brussels sprouts in the air fryer basket.
2. Put the air fryer lid on and air fry in the preheated instant pot at 380ºF (193ºC) for 10 minutes. Flip the Brussels sprouts when the lid screen indicates TURN FOOD.
3. Toss the Brussels sprouts with lemon juice and vinegar. Enjoy!

Buttery Sweet Potato

Prep time: 10 minutes | Cook time: 15 minutes | Serves 2

2 sweet potatoes, peeled and halved
1 tablespoon butter, melted
1 teaspoon dried dill weed
Sea salt and red pepper flakes, to taste

1. Toss the sweet potatoes with the remaining ingredients.
2. Place the sweet potatoes in the air fryer basket.
3. Put the air fryer lid on and air fry in the preheated instant pot at 380ºF (193ºC) for sweet potatoes minutes. Flip the 15 when the lid screen indicates TURN FOOD.
4. Taste and adjust the seasonings. Bon appétit!

Carrot and Parsnip Patties

Prep time: 10 minutes | Cook time: 15 minutes | Serves 3

1 carrot, shredded
1 parsnip, shredded
1 onion, chopped
1 garlic clove, minced
½ cup all-purpose flour
1 teaspoon cayenne pepper
Sea salt and ground black pepper, to taste
2 eggs, whisked

1. Mix all ingredients until everything is well combined. Form the mixture into three patties.
2. Arrange the patties in the air fryer basket.
3. Put the air fryer lid on and air fry in the preheated instant pot at 380ºF (193ºC) for 15 minutes or until cooked through.
4. Bon appétit!

Mushrooms and Tomato

Prep time: 10 minutes | Cook time: 7 minutes | Serves 4

1 pound (454 g) cremini mushrooms, sliced
1 large tomato, sliced
2 tablespoons butter, melted
1 teaspoon minced rosemary
1 teaspoon minced parsley
1 teaspoon minced garlic
Coarse sea salt and ground black pepper, to taste

1. Toss the mushrooms and tomatoes with the remaining ingredients. Toss until they are well coated on all sides.
2. Arrange the mushrooms in the air fryer basket.
3. Put the air fryer lid on and air fry in the preheated instant pot at 400ºF (205ºC) for 7 minutes. Flip the mushrooms when the lid screen indicates TURN FOOD.
4. Bon appétit!

Fennel Bulbs with Sesame Seeds

Prep time: 10 minutes | Cook time: 15 minutes | Serves 4

1 pound (454 g) fennel bulbs, trimmed and sliced
2 tablespoons sesame oil
Sea salt and ground black pepper, to taste
1 teaspoon crushed red pepper flakes
1 tablespoon balsamic vinegar
1 tablespoon soy sauce
1 tablespoon lightly toasted sesame seeds

1. Toss the fennel with the sesame oil, salt, black pepper, and red pepper flakes.
2. Arrange the fennel in the air fryer basket.
3. Put the air fryer lid on and air fry in the preheated instant pot at 370ºF (188ºC) for 15 minutes. Flip the fennel when the lid screen indicates TURN FOOD.
4. Toss the warm fennel with the vinegar, soy sauce, and sesame seeds.
5. Bon appétit!

Asparagus with Paprika

Prep time: 5 minutes | Cook time: 6 minutes | Serves 3

¾ pound (340 g) fresh asparagus, trimmed
Coarse sea salt and ground black pepper, to taste
1 teaspoon paprika
2 tablespoons olive oil

1. Toss the asparagus with the salt, black pepper, paprika, and olive oil. Arrange the asparagus spears in the air fryer basket.
2. Put the air fryer lid on and air fry in the preheated instant pot at 400ºF (205ºC) for 6 minutes. Flip the asparagus when the lid screen indicates TURN FOOD.
3. Bon appétit!

Buckwheat Beans Burgers with Walnuts

Prep time: 10 minutes | Cook time: 15 minutes | Serves 4

1 cup buckwheat, soaked overnight and rinsed
1 cup canned kidney beans, drained and well rinsed
¼ cup chopped walnuts
1 tablespoon olive oil
1 small onion, chopped
1 teaspoon smoked paprika
Sea salt and ground black pepper, to taste
½ cup bread crumbs

1. Mix all ingredients until everything is well combined. Form the mixture into four patties and arrange them in a lightly greased air fryer basket.
2. Put the air fryer lid on and air fry in the preheated instant pot at 380ºF (193ºC) for 15 minutes. Flip the burgers when the lid screen indicates TURN FOOD.
3. Bon appétit!

Asparagus with Cheese

Prep time: 5 minutes | Cook time: 6 minutes | Serves 4

1 pound (454 g) asparagus, trimmed
1 tablespoon sesame oil
½ teaspoon onion powder
½ teaspoon granulated garlic
Sea salt and cayenne pepper, to taste
½ cup Pecorino cheese, preferably freshly grated

1. Toss the asparagus with the sesame oil, onion powder, granulated garlic, salt, and cayenne pepper. Arrange the asparagus spears in the air fryer basket.
2. Put the air fryer lid on and air fry in the preheated instant pot at 400ºF (205ºC) for 6 minutes. Flip the asparagus when the lid screen indicates TURN FOOD.
3. Top the asparagus with the cheese. Bon appétit!

Cheesy Green Beans

Prep time: 5 minutes | Cook time: 7 minutes | Serves 2

½ pound (227 g) green beans
1 tablespoon sesame oil
Sea salt and ground black pepper, to taste
2 ounces (57 g) Cheddar cheese, grated

1. Toss the green beans with the sesame oil; then, arrange them in the air fryer basket.
2. Put the air fryer lid on and air fry in the preheated instant pot at 380ºF (193ºC) for 7 minutes. Flip the green beans when the lid screen indicates TURN FOOD.
3. Toss the warm green beans with the salt, black pepper, and cheese; stir to combine well. Enjoy!

Basil Peppers

Prep time: 10 minutes | Cook time: 13 minutes | Serves 3

3 Italian peppers, seeded and halved
1 tablespoon olive oil
Kosher salt and ground black pepper, to taste
1 teaspoon cayenne pepper
1 tablespoon chopped fresh parsley
1 tablespoon chopped fresh basil
1 tablespoon chopped fresh chives

1. Toss the peppers with the olive oil, salt, black pepper, and cayenne pepper; place the peppers in the air fryer basket.
2. Put the air fryer lid on and air fry in the preheated instant pot at 400ºF (205ºC) for 13 minutes. Flip the peppers when the lid screen indicates TURN FOOD.
3. Taste, adjust the seasonings, and serve with the fresh herbs. Bon appétit!

Brussels Sprouts with Ham

Prep time: 5 minutes | Cook time: 13 minutes | Serves 4

1 pound (454 g) Brussels sprouts, trimmed
1 tablespoon peanut oil
Sea salt and freshly ground black pepper, to taste
2 ounces (57 g) ham, diced

1. Toss the Brussels sprouts with the remaining ingredients; then, arrange the Brussels sprouts in the air fryer basket.
2. Put the air fryer lid on and air fry in the preheated instant pot at 380ºF (193ºC) for 13 minutes. Flip the Brussels sprouts when the lid screen indicates TURN FOOD.
3. Serve warm and enjoy!

Buttery Potato

Prep time: 5 minutes | Cook time: 18 minutes | Serves 3

¾ pound (340 g) potatoes, quartered
1 tablespoon butter, melted
1 teaspoon crushed garlic
1 teaspoon dried oregano
Sea salt and ground black pepper, to taste

1. Toss the potatoes with the remaining ingredients until well coated on all sides.
2. Arrange the potatoes in the air fryer basket.
3. Put the air fryer lid on and air fry in the preheated instant pot at 400ºF (205ºC) for 18 minutes. Flip the potatoes when the lid screen indicates TURN FOOD.
4. Serve warm and enjoy!

Chestnut Mushrooms with Cheese

Prep time: 8 minutes | Cook time: 7 minutes | Serves 4

1 pound (454 g) chestnut mushrooms, quartered
1 tablespoon olive oil
1 garlic clove, pressed
Sea salt and ground black pepper, to taste
4 tablespoons shredded Pecorino Romano cheese

1. Toss the mushrooms with the oil, garlic, salt, and black pepper. Toss until they are well coated on all sides.
2. Arrange the mushrooms in the air fryer basket.
3. Put the air fryer lid on and air fry in the preheated instant pot at 400ºF (205ºC) for 7 minutes. Flip the mushrooms when the lid screen indicates TURN FOOD.
4. Afterwards, toss the mushrooms with the cheese and serve immediately!

Sweet Potato with Salsa

Prep time: 5 minutes | Cook time: 35 minutes | Serves 4

1 pound (454 g) sweet potatoes, scrubbed and pricked with a fork
1 tablespoon olive oil
Coarse sea salt and ground black pepper, to taste
½ teaspoon cayenne pepper
4 tablespoons salsa

1. Sprinkle the sweet potatoes with olive oil, salt, black pepper, and cayenne pepper.
2. Place the sweet potatoes in the air fryer basket.
3. Put the air fryer lid on and air fry in the preheated instant pot at 380ºF (193ºC) for 35 minutes. Flip the sweet potatoes when the lid screen indicates TURN FOOD.
4. Split the tops open with a knife. Top each potato with salsa and serve. Bon appétit!

Breaded Cheesy Mushroom Burgers

Prep time: 8 minutes | Cook time: 15 minutes | Serves 3

¾ pound (340 g) brown mushrooms, chopped
1 large eggs, whisked
½ cup bread crumbs
½ cup grated Parmesan cheese
1 small onion, minced
1 garlic clove, minced
Sea salt and ground black pepper, to taste
1 tablespoon olive oil

1. Mix all ingredients until everything is well combined. Form the mixture into three patties.
2. Arrange the patties in the air fryer basket.
3. Put the air fryer lid on and air fry in the preheated instant pot at 380ºF (193ºC) for about 15 minutes or until cooked through.
4. Bon appétit!

Fennel Bulbs Slices

Prep time: 10 minutes | Cook time: 15 minutes | Serves 4

1 pound (454 g) fennel bulbs, trimmed and sliced
2 tablespoons olive oil
1 teaspoon minced fresh garlic
1 teaspoon dried parsley flakes
Kosher salt and ground black pepper, to taste

1. Toss all ingredients in a mixing bowl. Place the fennel in the air fryer basket.
2. Put the air fryer lid on and air fry in the preheated instant pot at 370ºF (188ºC) for 15 minutes. Flip the fennel when the lid screen indicates TURN FOOD.
3. Bon appétit!

Egg Stuffed Bell Peppers

Prep time: 5 minutes | Cook time: 14 minutes | Serves 3

3 bell peppers, seeded and halved
1 tablespoon olive oil
3 eggs
3 tablespoons chopped green onion
Sea salt and ground black pepper, to taste

1. Toss the peppers with the oil; place them in the air fryer basket.
2. Crack an egg into each bell pepper half. Sprinkle the peppers with the salt and black pepper.
3. Put the air fryer lid on and air fry in the preheated instant pot at 400ºF (205ºC) for 10 minutes.
4. Top the peppers with green onions. Continue to cook for 4 minutes more.
5. Bon appétit!

Green Beans with Red Chile Pepper

Prep time: 5 minutes | Cook time: 8 minutes | Serves 3

¾ pound (340 g) fresh green beans, trimmed
1 garlic clove, minced
2 tablespoons olive oil
1 tablespoon soy sauce
1 teaspoon black mustard seeds
1 dried red chile pepper, crushed
Sea salt and ground black pepper, to taste

1. Toss the green beans with the remaining ingredients; then, arrange them in the air fryer basket.
2. Put the air fryer lid on and air fry in the preheated instant pot at 380ºF (193ºC) for 8 minutes. Flip the green beans when the lid screen indicates TURN FOOD.
3. Enjoy!

Glazed Asparagus

Prep time: 5 minutes | Cook time: 6 minutes | Serves 4

1 pound (454 g) asparagus
4 teaspoons Chinese chili oil
½ teaspoon garlic powder
1 tablespoon soy sauce
½ teaspoon crushed red pepper flakes

1. Toss the asparagus with the remaining ingredients. Arrange the asparagus spears in the air fryer basket.
2. Put the air fryer lid on and air fry in the preheated instant pot at 400ºF (205ºC) for 6 minutes. Flip the asparagus when the lid screen indicates TURN FOOD.
3. Bon appétit!

Cheesy Mushrooms

Prep time: 8 minutes | Cook time: 7 minutes | Serves 3

¾ pound (340 g) button mushrooms, halved
1 tablespoon oil
Sea salt and ground black pepper, to taste
½ teaspoon garlic powder
3 ounces (85 g) Cheddar cheese, cubed

1. Toss the mushrooms with the olive oil, salt, black pepper, and garlic powder. Toss until they are well coated on all sides.
2. Arrange the mushrooms in the air fryer basket.
3. Put the air fryer lid on and air fry in the preheated instant pot at 400ºF (205ºC) for 7 minutes. Flip the mushrooms when the lid screen indicates TURN FOOD.
4. Bon appétit!

Brussels Sprouts with Cheese

Prep time: 5 minutes | Cook time: 10 minutes | Serves 4

1 pound (454 g) Brussels sprouts, trimmed
1 tablespoon olive oil
Sea salt and ground black pepper, to taste
4 ounces (113 g) Provolone cheese, crumbled

1. Toss the Brussels sprouts with the olive oil and spices until they are well coated on all sides; then, arrange the Brussels sprouts in the air fryer basket.
2. Put the air fryer lid on and roast in the preheated instant pot at 380ºF (193ºC) for 10 minutes. Flip the Brussels sprouts when the lid screen indicates TURN FOOD.
3. Toss the Brussels sprouts with the cheese and serve warm. Enjoy!

Chapter 10 Poultry

Panko Chicken Tenders

Prep time: 5 minutes | Cook time: 10 minutes | Serves 4

1½ pounds (680 g) chicken tenders
1 tablespoon olive oil
1 egg, whisked
1 teaspoon minced fresh parsley
1 teaspoon minced garlic
Sea salt and black pepper, to taste
1 cup bread crumbs

1. Pat the chicken dry with kitchen towels.
2. In a bowl, thoroughly combine the oil, egg, parsley, garlic, salt, and black pepper.
3. Dip the chicken tenders into the egg mixture. Then, roll the chicken over the bread crumbs.
4. Arrange the chicken tenders in the air fryer basket.
5. Put the air fryer lid on and air fry in the preheated instant pot at 360ºF (182ºC) for 10 minutes. Flip the chicken tenders when the lid screen indicates TURN FOOD.
6. Bon appétit!

Hot Chicken Thighs

Prep time: 5 minutes | Cook time: 22 minutes | Serves 4

1 pound (454 g) chicken thighs, bone-in
Sea salt and freshly ground black pepper, to taste
2 tablespoons olive oil
1 teaspoon stone-ground mustard
¼ cup hot sauce

1. Pat the chicken dry with kitchen towels. Toss the chicken with the remaining ingredients. Arrange the chicken in the air fryer basket.
2. Put the air fryer lid on and air fry in the preheated instant pot at 380ºF (193ºC) for 22 minutes. Flip the chicken when the lid screen indicates TURN FOOD.
3. Bon appétit!

Chicken Breasts with Butter

Prep time: 5 minutes | Cook time: 12 minutes | Serves 4

1 pound (454 g) chicken breasts, boneless and skinless
1 tablespoon butter, room temperature
1 teaspoon garlic powder
Kosher salt and ground black pepper, to taste
1 teaspoon dried parsley flakes
1 teaspoon smoked paprika
½ teaspoon dried oregano

1. Pat the chicken dry with kitchen towels. Toss the chicken breasts with the remaining ingredients. Arrange the chicken breasts in the air fryer basket.
2. Put the air fryer lid on and air fry in the preheated instant pot at 380ºF (193ºC) for 12 minutes. Flip the chicken when the lid screen indicates TURN FOOD.
3. Bon appétit!

Chicken Legs with Cayenne Pepper

Prep time: 5 minutes | Cook time: 30 minutes | Serves 4

4 chicken legs, bone-in
2 tablespoons sesame oil
Coarse sea salt and ground black pepper, to taste
½ teaspoon mustard seeds
1 teaspoon cayenne pepper
½ teaspoon onion powder
½ teaspoon garlic powder

1. Pat the chicken dry with paper towels. Toss the chicken legs with the remaining ingredients. Arrange the chicken legs in the air fryer basket.
2. Put the air fryer lid on and air fry in the preheated instant pot at 380ºF (193ºC) for 30 minutes. Flip the chicken when the lid screen indicates TURN FOOD.
3. Bon appétit!

Turkey Breast with Herb

Prep time: 5 minutes | Cook time: 1 hour | Serves 4

1 tablespoon butter, room temperature
Kosher salt and ground black pepper, to taste
1 teaspoon cayenne pepper
1 teaspoon Italian herb mix
1 pound (454 g) turkey breast, bone-in

1. In a mixing bowl, thoroughly combine the butter, salt, black pepper, cayenne pepper, and herb mix.
2. Rub the mixture all over the turkey breast. Place the turkey breast in the air fryer basket.
3. Put the air fryer lid on and air fry in the preheated instant pot at 350ºF (180ºC) for 1 hour. Flip the turkey breast when the lid screen indicates TURN FOOD.
4. Bon appétit!

Five-Spice Duck Breast

Prep time: 5 minutes | Cook time: 30 minutes | Serves 3

1 pound (454 g) duck breast
1 tablespoon Hoisin sauce
1 tablespoon five-spice powder
Sea salt and black pepper, to taste
¼ teaspoon ground cinnamon

1. Pat the duck breast dry with paper towels. Toss the duck breast with the remaining ingredients. Place the duck breast in the baking dish.
2. Place the baking dish in the air fryer basket. Put the air fryer lid on and bake in the preheated instant pot at 330ºF (166ºC) for 15 minutes. Flip the duck breast when the lid screen indicates TURN FOOD.
3. Increase the temperature to 350ºF (180ºC) and continue to cook for about 15 minutes or until cooked through.
4. Let it rest for 10 minutes before carving and serving. Bon appétit!

Chicken Cheese Burgers

Prep time: 8 minutes | Cook time: 17 minutes | Serves 3

¾ pound (340 g) ground chicken
¼ cup crushed tortilla chips
¼ cup grated Parmesan cheese
1 egg, beaten
2 tablespoons minced onion
2 garlic cloves, minced
1 tablespoon BBQ sauce

1. Mix all ingredients until everything is well combined. Form the mixture into three patties. Arrange the patties in the air fryer basket.
2. Put the air fryer lid on and air fry in the preheated instant pot at 380ºF (193ºC) for 17 minutes. Flip the burgers when the lid screen indicates TURN FOOD.
3. Bon appétit!

Chicken Hawaiian Rolls

Prep time: 5 minutes | Cook time: 17 minutes | Serves 3

¾ pound (340 g) ground chicken
1 teaspoon minced garlic
1 small onion, minced
2 tablespoons minced fresh parsley
2 tablespoons minced fresh cilantro
½ teaspoon mustard seeds
½ teaspoon ground cumin
½ teaspoon paprika
Sea salt and ground black pepper, to taste
2 tablespoons olive oil
6 Hawaiian rolls

1. Mix all ingredients , except for the burger buns, until everything is well combined. Shape the mixture into six patties.
2. Arrange the patties in the air fryer basket.
3. Put the air fryer lid on and air fry in the preheated instant pot at 380ºF (193ºC) for 17 minutes. Flip the burgers when the lid screen indicates TURN FOOD.
4. Serve the burgers over Hawaiian rolls and garnish with toppings of choice. Bon appétit!

Chicken Salad with Carrot

Prep time: 10 minutes | Cook time: 12 minutes | Serves 3

1 pound (454 g) chicken breast
2 tablespoons chopped scallions
1 carrot, shredded
½ cup mayonnaise
1 tablespoon mustard
Sea salt and ground black pepper, to taste

1. Pat the chicken dry with kitchen towels. Place the chicken in a lightly oiled air fryer basket.
2. Put the air fryer lid on and roast in the preheated instant pot at 380ºF (193ºC) for 12 minutes. Flip the chicken when the lid screen indicates TURN FOOD.
3. Chop the chicken breasts and transfer it to a salad bowl; add in the remaining ingredients and toss to combine well. Bon appétit!

Chicken Fillets with Greek Seasoning

Prep time: 5 minutes | Cook time: 12 minutes | Serves 4

1½ pounds (680 g) chicken fillets
1 tablespoon olive oil
1 teaspoon minced garlic
1 tablespoon Greek seasoning mix
½ teaspoon crushed red pepper flakes
Sea salt and ground black pepper, to taste

1. Pat the chicken dry with paper towels. Toss the chicken with the remaining ingredients.
2. Arrange the chicken in the air fryer basket.
3. Put the air fryer lid on and roast in the preheated instant pot at 380ºF (193ºC) for 12 minutes. Flip the chicken fillets when the lid screen indicates TURN FOOD.
4. Bon appétit!

Butter Chicken Cutlets

Prep time: 8 minutes | Cook time: 12 minutes | Serves 4

1 pound (454 g) chicken breasts, boneless, skinless, cut into 4 pieces
1 tablespoon butter, melted
1 teaspoon smoked paprika
Kosher salt and ground black pepper, to taste
1 teaspoon garlic powder

1. Flatten the chicken breasts to ¼-inch thickness.
2. Toss the chicken breasts with the remaining ingredients.
3. Arrange the chicken breasts in the air fryer basket.
4. Put the air fryer lid on and roast in the preheated instant pot at 380ºF (193ºC) for 12 minutes. Flip the chicken when the lid screen indicates TURN FOOD.
5. Bon appétit!

Chicken Legs with Pineapple

Prep time: 5 minutes | Cook time: 35 minutes | Serves 4

1 pound (454 g) chicken legs, boneless
Kosher salt and freshly ground black pepper, to taste
2 tablespoons tamari sauce
1 tablespoon hot sauce
1 cup peeled and diced pineapple
1 tablespoon roughly chopped fresh cilantro

1. Pat the chicken dry with paper towels. Toss the chicken legs with the salt, black pepper, tamari sauce, and hot sauce. Place the chicken in the air fryer basket.
2. Put the air fryer lid on and roast in the preheated instant pot at 380ºF (193ºC) for 30 minutes. Flip the chicken when the lid screen indicates TURN FOOD.
3. Top the chicken with the pineapple and continue to cook for 5 minutes more. Serve warm, garnished with the fresh cilantro.
4. Bon appétit!

Chicken and Pepper Fajitas

Prep time: 10 minutes | Cook time: 30 minutes | Serves 4

1 pound (454 g) chicken legs, boneless, skinless, cut into pieces
2 tablespoons canola oil
1 red bell pepper, sliced
1 yellow bell pepper, sliced
1 jalapeño pepper, sliced
1 onion, sliced
½ teaspoon onion powder
½ teaspoon garlic powder
Sea salt and ground black pepper, to taste

1. Pat the chicken dry with paper towels. Toss the chicken legs with 1 tablespoon of the canola oil. Place the chicken in the air fryer basket.
2. Put the air fryer lid on and air fry in the preheated instant pot at 380ºF (193ºC) for 15 minutes. Flip the chicken when the lid screen indicates TURN FOOD.
3. Add the remaining ingredients to the air fryer basket. Increase the temperature to 400ºF (205ºC) and air fry for 15 minutes more or until cooked through.
4. Bon appétit!

Red Wine Turkey Wings

Prep time: 5 minutes | Cook time: 40 minutes | Serves 5

2 pounds (907 g) turkey wings, bone-in
2 garlic cloves, minced
1 small onion, chopped
1 tablespoon Dijon mustard
½ cup red wine
Sea salt and ground black pepper, to taste
1 teaspoon poultry seasoning

1. Place the turkey wings, garlic, onion, mustard, and wine in a ceramic bowl. Cover the bowl and let the turkey marinate in the refrigerator overnight.
2. Discard the marinade and toss the turkey wings with the salt, black pepper, and poultry seasoning.
3. Arrange the turkey wings in the air fryer basket.
4. Put the air fryer lid on and air fry in the preheated instant pot at 400ºF (205ºC) for 40 minutes. Flip the turkey wings when the lid screen indicates TURN FOOD.
5. Bon appétit!

Quick Chicken Drumettes

Prep time: 5 minutes | Cook time: 22 minutes | Serves 4

1½ pounds (680 g) chicken drumettes
2 tablespoons olive oil
2 tablespoons balsamic vinegar
Kosher salt and ground black pepper, to taste

1. Toss the chicken drumettes with the remaining ingredients.
2. Arrange the chicken drumettes in the air fryer basket.
3. Put the air fryer lid on and roast in the preheated instant pot at 380ºF (193ºC) for 22 minutes. Flip the chicken drumettes when the lid screen indicates TURN FOOD.
4. Bon appétit!

Savory Chicken Drumsticks

Prep time: 5 minutes | Cook time: 20 minutes | Serves 3

3 chicken drumsticks, bone-in
Kosher salt and ground black pepper, to taste
2 tablespoons olive oil
2 tablespoons soy sauce
1 tablespoon rice vinegar
1 teaspoon garlic powder

1. Pat the chicken drumsticks dry with paper towels. Toss the chicken drumsticks with the remaining ingredients.
2. Arrange the chicken drumsticks in the air fryer basket.
3. Put the air fryer lid on and air fry in the preheated instant pot at 370ºF (188ºC) for 20 minutes. Flip the chicken when the lid screen indicates TURN FOOD.
4. Bon appétit!

Chicken Fillets with Coriander

Prep time: 5 minutes | Cook time: 12 minutes | Serves 4

1 pound (454 g) chicken fillets
1 egg
1 tablespoon olive oil
1 cup crushed crackers
1 tablespoon minced fresh coriander
1 tablespoon minced fresh parsley
Sea salt and ground black pepper, to taste
¼ teaspoon ground cumin
¼ teaspoon mustard seeds
1 teaspoon celery seeds

1. Pat the chicken fillets dry with paper towels. Whisk the egg in a shallow bowl.
2. Mix the remaining ingredients in a separate shallow bowl.
3. Dip the chicken fillets into the egg mixture. Then, roll the chicken fillets over the bread crumb mixture.
4. Arrange the chicken fillets in the air fryer basket.
5. Put the air fryer lid on and air fry in the preheated instant pot at 380ºF (193ºC) for 12 minutes. Flip the chicken when the lid screen indicates TURN FOOD.
6. Bon appétit!

Breaded Chicken Schnitzel

Prep time: 5 minutes | Cook time: 20 minutes | Serves 3

3 chicken legs, boneless and skinless
2 tablespoons olive oil
1 teaspoon dried basil
1 teaspoon dried oregano
1 teaspoon dried sage
Sea salt and freshly cracked black pepper
½ cup bread crumbs

1. Pat the chicken dry with paper towels. Toss the chicken legs with the remaining ingredients.
2. Arrange the chicken legs in the air fryer basket.
3. Put the air fryer lid on and air fry in the preheated instant pot at 370ºF (188ºC) for 20 minutes. Flip the chicken when the lid screen indicates TURN FOOD.
4. Bon appétit!

Panko Cheese Chicken

Prep time: 10 minutes | Cook time: 12 minutes | Serves 4

1 egg, whisked
½ cup all-purpose flour
1 teaspoon garlic powder
1 teaspoon cayenne pepper
Sea salt and ground black pepper, to taste
¼ cup bread crumbs
¼ cup grated Parmesan cheese
1½ pounds (680 g) chicken breast, boneless, skinless, cut into strips

1. Mix the egg and flour in a shallow bowl. In a separate bowl, whisk the garlic powder, cayenne pepper, salt, black pepper, bread crumbs, and Parmesan cheese.
2. Dip the chicken breasts into the egg mixture. Then, roll the chicken breasts over the bread crumb mixture.
3. Arrange the chicken in the air fryer basket.
4. Put the air fryer lid on and air fry in the preheated instant pot at 380ºF (193ºC) for 12 minutes. Flip the chicken when the lid screen indicates TURN FOOD.
5. Bon appétit!

Chicken Patties with Chili Sauce

Prep time: 5 minutes | Cook time: 17 minutes | Serves 4

1 pound (454 g) ground chicken
1 tablespoon olive oil
1 small onion, chopped
1 teaspoon minced garlic
1 tablespoon chili sauce
Kosher salt and ground black pepper, to taste

1. Mix all ingredients until everything is well combined. Form the mixture into four patties.
2. Arrange the patties in the air fryer basket.
3. Put the air fryer lid on and air fry in the preheated instant pot at 380ºF (193ºC) for 17 minutes. Flip the patties when the lid screen indicates TURN FOOD.
4. Bon appétit!

Soy Sauce Duck Fillet

Prep time: 5 minutes | Cook time: 30 minutes | Serves 4

1½ pounds (680 g) duck fillet
1 tablespoon honey
2 tablespoons dark soy sauce
1 tablespoon soybean paste

1. Toss the duck fillet with the remaining ingredients. Place the duck fillet in the baking dish.
2. Place the baking dish in the air fryer basket. Put the air fryer lid on and bake in the preheated instant pot at 330ºF (166ºC) for 15 minutes. Flip the duck fillet when the lid screen indicates TURN FOOD.
3. Increase the temperature to 350ºF (180ºC) and continue to cook for about 15 minutes or until cooked through.
4. Let it rest for 10 minutes before carving and serving. Bon appétit!

Breaded Butter Chicken

Prep time: 5 minutes | Cook time: 12 minutes | Serves 4

1 pound (454 g) chicken breasts, boneless and skinless
1 tablespoon butter, room temperature
1 egg, whisked
1 teaspoon cayenne pepper
1 teaspoon garlic powder
Kosher salt and ground black pepper, to taste
½ cup bread crumbs

1. Pat the chicken dry with paper towels.
2. In a bowl, thoroughly combine the butter, egg, cayenne pepper, garlic powder, kosher salt, black pepper.
3. Dip the chicken breasts into the egg mixture. Then, roll the chicken breasts over the bread crumbs.
4. Arrange the chicken breasts in the air fryer basket.
5. Put the air fryer lid on and air fry in the preheated instant pot at 380ºF (193ºC) for 12 minutes. Flip the chicken when the lid screen indicates TURN FOOD.
6. Bon appétit!

Cheesy Chicken Wings

Prep time: 5 minutes | Cook time: 22 minutes | Serves 3

1 pound (454 g) chicken wings, bone-in
Sea salt and red pepper flakes, to taste
2 tablespoons olive oil
½ cup grated Parmesan cheese
2 cloves garlic, pressed

1. Pat the chicken wings dry with kitchen towels. Toss the chicken wings with the remaining ingredients.
2. Arrange the chicken wings in the air fryer basket.
3. Put the air fryer lid on and air fry in the preheated instant pot at 380ºF (193ºC) for 22 minutes. Flip the chicken wings when the lid screen indicates TURN FOOD.
4. Bon appétit!

Turkey Breasts with Mustard

Prep time: 5 minutes | Cook time: 1 hour | Serves 5

2 tablespoons olive oil
Sea salt and freshly cracked black pepper, to taste
1 tablespoon Dijon mustard
1 tablespoon hot sauce
1 teaspoon smoked paprika
1 teaspoon dried basil
1 teaspoon dried thyme
2 pounds (907 g) turkey breast, bone-in

1. In a mixing bowl, thoroughly combine the olive oil, salt, black pepper, mustard, hot sauce, paprika, basil, and thyme.
2. Rub the mixture all over the turkey breast. Place the turkey breast in the air fryer basket.
3. Put the air fryer lid on and roast in the preheated instant pot at 350ºF (180ºC) for 1 hour, turning them over every 20 minutes.
4. Bon appétit!

Turkey Drumettes

Prep time: 5 minutes | Cook time: 40 minutes | Serves 4

1½ pounds (680 g) turkey drumettes
1 tablespoon sesame oil
1 teaspoon poultry seasoning mix
Sea salt and ground black pepper, to taste

1. Toss the turkey drumettes with the remaining ingredients. Arrange the turkey drumettes in the air fryer basket.
2. Put the air fryer lid on and air fry in the preheated instant pot at 400ºF (205ºC) for 40 minutes. Flip the turkey drumettes when the lid screen indicates TURN FOOD.
3. Let the turkey rest for 10 minutes before carving and serving. Bon appétit!

Chicken Salad with Cucumber

Prep time: 10 minutes | Cook time: 12 minutes | Serves 4

1 pound (454 g) chicken breasts, boneless, skinless
1 red onion, thinly sliced
1 bell pepper, sliced
4 Kalamata olives, pitted and minced
1 small Greek cucumber, grated and squeezed
4 tablespoons Greek yogurt
4 tablespoons mayonnaise
1 tablespoon fresh lemon juice
Coarse sea salt and red pepper flakes, to taste

1. Pat the chicken dry with paper towels. Place the chicken breasts in a lightly oiled air fryer basket.
2. Put the air fryer lid on and roast in the preheated instant pot at 380ºF (193ºC) for 12 minutes. Flip the chicken when the lid screen indicates TURN FOOD.
3. Chop the chicken breasts and transfer it to a salad bowl; add in the remaining ingredients and toss to combine well.
4. Serve chilled.

Chicken Cheese Muffins

Prep time: 5 minutes | Cook time: 12 minutes | Serves 4

1 pound (454 g) chicken breasts
1 tablespoon olive oil
Sea salt and black pepper, to taste
4 slices Cheddar cheese
4 teaspoons yellow mustard
4 English muffins, lightly toasted

1. Pat the chicken dry with kitchen towels. Toss the chicken breasts with the olive oil, salt, and pepper. Place the chicken in the air fryer basket.
2. Put the air fryer lid on and roast in the preheated instant pot at 380ºF (193ºC) for 12 minutes. Flip the chicken when the lid screen indicates TURN FOOD.
3. Shred the chicken using two forks and serve with cheese, mustard, and English muffins. Bon appétit!

Bacon and Cheese Stuffed Chicken

Prep time: 5 minutes | Cook time: 20 minutes | Serves 4

1 pound (454 g) chicken breasts
4 tablespoons goat cheese
4 tablespoons bacon
1 tablespoon olive oil
½ teaspoon garlic powder
1 teaspoon dried basil
1 teaspoon dried oregano
1 teaspoon dried parsley flakes

1. Flatten the chicken breasts with a mallet.
2. Stuff each piece of chicken with cheese and bacon. Roll them up and secure with toothpicks.
3. Then, sprinkle the chicken with olive oil, garlic powder, basil, oregano, and parsley.
4. Place the stuffed chicken breasts in the air fryer basket. Put the air fryer lid on and air fry in the preheated instant pot at 400ºF (205ºC) for 20 minutes. Flip the chicken when the lid screen indicates TURN FOOD.
5. Bon appétit!

Panko Chicken with Olives

Prep time: 10 minutes | Cook time: 12 minutes | Serves 4

1 pound (454 g) chicken fillets, boneless, skinless
2 eggs, whisked
1 teaspoon dried basil
½ teaspoon dried rosemary
½ teaspoon dried oregano
½ teaspoon crushed red pepper flakes
½ cup seasoned bread crumbs
2 ounces (57 g) Kalamata olives, pitted and sliced

1. Pat the chicken dry with paper towels.
2. In a shallow bowl, thoroughly combine the eggs and spices. Place the bread crumbs in a separate shallow bowl.
3. Dip the chicken fillets into the egg mixture. Then, roll the chicken fillets over the bread crumbs. Arrange the chicken fillets in the air fryer basket.
4. Put the air fryer lid on and air fry in the preheated instant pot at 380ºF (193ºC) for 12 minutes. Flip the chicken fillets when the lid screen indicates TURN FOOD.
5. Serve with Kalamata olives and enjoy!

Chicken Drumsticks

Prep time: 5 minutes | Cook time: 22 minutes | Serves 3

3 chicken drumsticks
2 tablespoons sesame oil
Kosher salt and ground black pepper, to taste
1 tablespoon soy sauce
1 teaspoon five-spice powder

1. Pat the chicken drumsticks dry with paper towels. Toss the chicken drumsticks with the remaining ingredients. Place the chicken drumsticks in the air fryer basket.
2. Put the air fryer lid on and roast in the preheated instant pot at 370ºF (188ºC) for 22 minutes. Flip the chicken drumsticks when the lid screen indicates TURN FOOD.
3. Bon appétit!

Duck Breast with Lime

Prep time: 5 minutes | Cook time: 30 minutes | Serves 4

2 tablespoons fresh lime juice
1½ pounds (680 g) duck breast
2 tablespoons olive oil
1 teaspoon cayenne pepper
Kosher salt and freshly ground black pepper, to taste

1. Pat the duck breast dry with paper towels. Toss the duck breast with the remaining ingredients. Place the duck breast in the baking dish.
2. Place the baking dish in the air fryer basket. Put the air fryer lid on and bake in the preheated instant pot at 330ºF (166ºC) for 15 minutes. Flip the duck breast when the lid screen indicates TURN FOOD.
3. Increase the temperature to 350ºF (180ºC) and continue to cook for about 15 minutes or until cooked through.
4. Let the duck breast rest for 10 minutes before carving and serving. Bon appétit!

Chicken Fillets with Cheese

Prep time: 5 minutes | Cook time: 12 minutes | Serves 4

1½ pounds (680 g) chicken fillets
2 tablespoons olive oil
1 teaspoon smoked paprika
1 teaspoon Italian seasoning mix
Sea salt and ground black pepper, to taste
½ cup grated Pecorino Romano cheese

1. Pat the chicken fillets dry with paper towels. Toss the chicken fillets with the olive oil and spices. Place the chicken fillets in the air fryer basket.
2. Put the air fryer lid on and air fry in the preheated instant pot at 380ºF (193ºC) for 12 minutes. Flip the chicken fillets when the lid screen indicates TURN FOOD.
3. Top the chicken fillets with grated cheese and serve warm. Bon appétit!

Tomato and Cheese Stuffed Chicken

Prep time: 10 minutes | Cook time: 20 minutes | Serves 4

1 pound (454 g) chicken breasts, boneless, skinless, cut into 4 pieces
2 tablespoons chopped sun-dried tomatoes
1 garlic clove, minced
2 ounces (57 g) Mozzarella cheese, crumbled
Sea salt and ground black pepper, to taste
1 tablespoon olive oil

1. Flatten the chicken breasts with a mallet.
2. Stuff each piece of chicken with the sun-dried tomatoes, garlic, and cheese. Roll them up and secure with toothpicks.
3. Season the chicken with the salt and pepper and drizzle the olive oil over them.
4. Place the stuffed chicken in the air fryer basket. Put the air fryer lid on and air fry in the preheated instant pot at 400ºF (205ºC) for 20 minutes. Flip the chicken when the lid screen indicates TURN FOOD.
5. Bon appétit!

Spinach and Cheese Stuffed Chicken

Prep time: 10 minutes | Cook time: 20 minutes | Serves 4

1 pound (454 g) chicken breasts, skinless, boneless, and cut into pieces
2 tablespoons chopped olives
1 garlic clove, minced
2 cups spinach, torn into pieces
2 ounces (57 g) feta cheese
Sea salt and ground black pepper, to taste
2 tablespoons olive oil

1. Flatten the chicken breasts with a mallet.
2. Stuff each piece of chicken with olives, garlic, spinach, and cheese. Roll them up and secure with toothpicks.
3. Sprinkle the chicken with the salt, black pepper, and olive oil.
4. Place the stuffed chicken breasts in the air fryer basket. Put the air fryer lid on and air fry in the preheated instant pot at 400ºF (205ºC) for 20 minutes. Flip the chicken when the lid screen indicates TURN FOOD.
5. Bon appétit!

Chicken Wings with Mustard

Prep time: 5 minutes | Cook time: 18 minutes | Serves 2

¾ pound (340 g) chicken wings, boneless
1 tablespoon butter, room temperature
½ teaspoon garlic powder
½ teaspoon shallot powder
½ teaspoon mustard powder

1. Toss the chicken wings with the remaining ingredients.
2. Arrange the chicken wings in the air fryer basket.
3. Put the air fryer lid on and air fry in the preheated instant pot at 380ºF (193ºC) for 18 minutes. Flip the chicken wings when the lid screen indicates TURN FOOD.
4. Bon appétit!

Buttery Turkey Breasts

Prep time: 5 minutes | Cook time: 1 hour | Serves 5

2 pounds (907 g) turkey breasts, rib bones trimmed
4 tablespoons butter, melted
1 teaspoon Sriracha sauce
1 tablespoon chopped fresh cilantro
1 tablespoon chopped fresh parsley
1 tablespoon chopped fresh thyme
Kosher salt and freshly ground black pepper, to taste

1. Pat the turkey breasts dry with paper towels. Toss the turkey breasts with the remaining ingredients. Place the turkey breasts in the air fryer basket.
2. Put the air fryer lid on and roast in the preheated instant pot at 350ºF (180ºC) for 1 hour. Flip the turkey breasts when the lid screen indicates TURN FOOD.
3. Bon appétit!

Chicken Drumsticks with Hot Sauce

Prep time: 5 minutes | Cook time: 20 minutes | Serves 4

½ cup all-purpose flour
1 tablespoon Ranch seasoning mix
1 pound (454 g) chicken drumsticks
1 tablespoon hot sauce
Sea salt and ground black pepper, to taste

1. Pat the chicken drumsticks dry with paper towels. Toss the chicken drumsticks with the remaining ingredients. Arrange the chicken drumsticks in the air fryer basket.
2. Put the air fryer lid on and air fry in the preheated instant pot at 370ºF (188ºC) for 20 minutes. Flip the chicken drumsticks when the lid screen indicates TURN FOOD.
3. Bon appétit!

Duck with Miso Paste

Prep time: 5 minutes | Cook time: 30 minutes | Serves 5

2 pounds (907 g) duck breasts
1 tablespoon butter, melted
2 tablespoons pomegranate molasses
2 tablespoons miso paste
1 teaspoon minced garlic
1 teaspoon peeled and minced ginger
1 teaspoon five-spice powder

1. Pat the duck breasts dry with paper towels. Toss the duck breasts with the remaining ingredients. Place the duck breasts in the baking dish.
2. Place the baking dish in the air fryer basket. Put the air fryer lid on and bake in the preheated instant pot at 330ºF (166ºC) for 15 minutes. Flip the duck breasts when the lid screen indicates TURN FOOD.
3. Increase the temperature to 350ºF (180ºC) and continue to cook for about 15 minutes or until cooked through.
4. Let it rest for 10 minutes before carving and serving. Bon appétit!

Golden Breaded Chicken Nuggets

Prep time: 5 minutes | Cook time: 12 minutes | Serves 4

1 egg, whisked
¼ cup all-purpose flour
1 cup seasoned bread crumbs
1 tablespoon olive oil
Sea salt and ground black pepper, to taste
1½ pounds (680 g) chicken breasts, cut into small pieces

1. Mix the egg and flour in a shallow bowl. In a separate bowl, whisk the bread crumbs, olive oil, salt, and black pepper.
2. Dip the chicken breasts into the egg mixture. Then, roll the chicken breasts over the bread crumb mixture.
3. Arrange the chicken breasts in the air fryer basket.
4. Put the air fryer lid on and air fry in the preheated instant pot at 380ºF (193ºC) for 12 minutes. Flip the chicken when the lid screen indicates TURN FOOD.
5. Bon appétit!

Lemony Turkey Wings

Prep time: 5 minutes | Cook time: 40 minutes | Serves 5

2 pounds (907 g) turkey wings
2 tablespoons olive oil
½ teaspoon garlic powder
½ teaspoon onion powder
1 teaspoon poultry seasoning mix
2 tablespoons roughly chopped fresh parsley
1 lemon, cut into slices

1. Toss the turkey wings with the olive oil, garlic powder, onion powder, and poultry seasoning mix. Arrange the turkey wings in the air fryer basket.
2. Put the air fryer lid on and air fry in the preheated instant pot at 400ºF (205ºC) for 40 minutes. Flip the turkey wings when the lid screen indicates TURN FOOD.
3. Let the turkey rest for 10 minutes before carving and serving. Garnish the turkey wings with the parsley and lemon slices.
4. Bon appétit!

Tangy Duck Legs

Prep time: 5 minutes | Cook time: 40 minutes | Serves 4

1 pound (454 g) duck legs
¼ cup orange sauce
Sea salt and red pepper flakes, to taste

1. Toss the duck legs with the remaining ingredients. Place the duck legs in the air fryer basket.
2. Put the air fryer lid on and roast in the preheated instant pot at 400ºF (205ºC) for 40 minutes. Flip the duck legs when the lid screen indicates TURN FOOD.
3. Bon appétit!

Baked Turkey Cheese Taquitos

Prep time: 5 minutes | Cook time: 24 minutes | Serves 6

1 pound (454 g) turkey breasts, boneless and skinless
Kosher salt and freshly ground black pepper, to taste
1 clove garlic, minced
1 habanero pepper, minced
4 ounces (113 g) Mexican cheese blend, shredded
6 small corn tortillas
½ cup salsa

1. Pat the turkey breasts dry with kitchen towels. Toss the turkey breasts with the salt and black pepper. Arrange the turkey breasts in the air fryer basket.
2. Put the air fryer lid on and air fry in the preheated instant pot at 380ºF (193ºC) for 18 minutes. Flip the turkey breasts when the lid screen indicates TURN FOOD.
3. Place the shredded chicken, garlic, habanero pepper, and cheese on one end of each tortilla. Roll them up tightly and transfer them to a lightly oiled baking dish.
4. Reduce the temperature to 360ºF (182ºC). Place the baking dish in the air fryer basket. Put the air fryer lid on and bake the taquitos in the preheated instant pot for 6 minutes.
5. Serve the taquitos with salsa and enjoy!

Chicken Cheese Tortilla

Prep time: 8 minutes | Cook time: 12 minutes | Serves 4

1 egg, whisked
½ cup grated Parmesan cheese
½ cup crushed tortilla chips
½ teaspoon onion powder
½ teaspoon garlic powder
1 teaspoon red chili powder
1½ pounds (680 g) chicken breasts, boneless, skinless, cut into strips

1. Whisk the egg in a shallow bowl. In a separate bowl, whisk the Parmesan cheese, tortilla chips, onion powder, garlic powder, and red chili powder.
2. Dip the chicken pieces into the egg mixture. Then, roll the chicken pieces over the bread crumb mixture. Place the chicken in the air fryer basket.
3. Put the air fryer lid on and air fry in the preheated instant pot at 380ºF (193ºC) for 12 minutes. Flip the chicken when the lid screen indicates TURN FOOD.
4. Bon appétit!

Creamy Chicken Salad

Prep time: 5 minutes | Cook time: 12 minutes | Serves 4

1 pound (454 g) chicken breasts, skinless and boneless
¼ cup mayonnaise
¼ cup sour cream
1 tablespoon lemon juice
Sea salt and ground black pepper, to taste
½ cup chopped celery

1. Pat the chicken dry with paper towels. Place the chicken in a lightly oiled air fryer basket.
2. Put the air fryer lid on and roast in the preheated instant pot at 380ºF (193ºC) for 12 minutes. Flip the chicken breasts when the lid screen indicates TURN FOOD.
3. Shred the chicken breasts using two forks; transfer it to a salad bowl and add in the remaining ingredients.
4. Toss to combine and serve chilled. Bon appétit!

Golden Breaded Turkey Schnitzel

Prep time: 5 minutes | Cook time: 22 minutes | Serves 3

1½ pounds (680 g) turkey thighs, skinless, boneless
1 egg, beaten
½ cup all-purpose flour
½ cup seasoned bread crumbs
½ teaspoon crushed red pepper flakes
Sea salt and ground black pepper, to taste
1 tablespoon olive oil

1. Flatten the turkey thighs with a mallet.
2. Whisk the egg in a shallow bowl. Place the flour in a second bowl.
3. Then, in a third shallow bowl, place the bread crumbs, red pepper, salt, and black pepper. Dip the turkey first in the flour, then, in the beaten egg, and roll them in the bread crumb mixture.
4. Place the breaded turkey thighs in the air fryer basket and mist them with the olive oil.
5. Put the air fryer lid on and air fry in the preheated instant pot at 380ºF (193ºC) for 22 minutes. Flip the schnitzel when the lid screen indicates TURN FOOD.
6. Bon appétit!

Turkey Drumsticks with Thyme

Prep time: 5 minutes | Cook time: 40 minutes | Serves 5

2 pounds (907 g) turkey drumsticks, bone-in
2 tablespoons olive oil
Kosher salt and freshly ground black pepper, to taste
1 teaspoon dried thyme
1 teaspoon dried rosemary
1 teaspoon minced garlic

1. Toss the turkey drumsticks with the remaining ingredients. Place the turkey drumsticks in the air fryer basket.
2. Put the air fryer lid on and air fry in the preheated instant pot at 400ºF (205ºC) for 40 minutes. Flip the turkey drumsticks when the lid screen indicates TURN FOOD.
3. Bon appétit!

Hot Chicken with Mustard

Prep time: 5 minutes | Cook time: 12 minutes | Serves 2

¾ pound (340 g) chicken breasts, boneless, skinless
1 teaspoon minced garlic
½ cup red wine
¼ cup hot sauce
1 tablespoon Dijon mustard
Sea salt and cayenne pepper, to taste

1. Place the chicken, garlic, red wine, hot sauce, and mustard in a ceramic bowl. Cover the bowl and let the chicken marinate for about 3 hours in the refrigerator.
2. Discard the marinade and place the chicken breasts in the air fryer basket.
3. Put the air fryer lid on and roast in the preheated instant pot at 380ºF (193ºC) for 12 minutes. Flip the chicken breasts when the lid screen indicates TURN FOOD.
4. Season the chicken with the salt and cayenne pepper to taste. Bon appétit!

Chicken Cheese Dinner Rolls

Prep time: 5 minutes | Cook time: 17 minutes | Serves 4

1 pound (454 g) ground chicken
½ cup crushed tortilla chips
2 ounces (57 g) Cheddar cheese, grated
1 teaspoon dried parsley flakes
1 teaspoon cayenne pepper
½ teaspoon paprika
Kosher salt and ground black pepper, to taste
4 dinner rolls

1. Mix the chicken, tortilla chips, cheese, and spices until everything is well combined. Now, roll the mixture into four patties.
2. Arrange the patties in the air fryer basket.
3. Put the air fryer lid on and air fry in the preheated instant pot at 380ºF (193ºC) for 17 minutes. Flip the burgers when the lid screen indicates TURN FOOD.
4. Serve the burgers in dinner rolls. Bon appétit!

Butter Chicken Fillets

Prep time: 5 minutes | Cook time: 15 minutes | Serves 4

1 pound (454 g) chicken fillets
2 tablespoons butter
2 bell peppers, seeded and sliced
1 teaspoon minced garlic
Sea salt and ground black pepper, to taste
1 teaspoon red pepper flakes

1. Toss the chicken fillets with the butter and place them in the air fryer basket. Top the chicken with bell peppers, garlic, salt, black pepper, and red pepper flakes.
2. Put the air fryer lid on and air fry in the preheated instant pot at 380ºF (193ºC) for 15 minutes. Flip the chicken when the lid screen indicates TURN FOOD.
3. Serve warm and enjoy!

Ham and Cheese Stuffed Chicken

Prep time: 6 minutes | Cook time: 22 minutes | Serves 4

1 pound (454 g) chicken breasts, skinless, boneless, and cut into 4 slices
4 ounces (113 g) goat cheese, crumbled
4 ounces (113 g) ham, chopped
1 egg
¼ cup all-purpose flour
¼ cup grated Parmesan cheese
½ teaspoon onion powder
½ teaspoon garlic powder

1. Flatten the chicken breasts with a mallet.
2. Stuff each piece of chicken with cheese and ham. Roll them up and secure with toothpicks.
3. In a shallow bowl, mix the remaining ingredients until well combined. Dip the chicken rolls into the egg mixture.
4. Place the stuffed chicken in the air fryer basket. Put the air fryer lid on and air fry in the preheated instant pot at 400ºF (205ºC) for 22 minutes. Flip the stuffed chicken breasts when the lid screen indicates TURN FOOD.
5. Bon appétit!

Chicken Cutlets with Broccoli

Prep time: 5 minutes | Cook time: 12 minutes | Serves 4

1 pound (454 g) chicken cutlets
1 pound (454 g) broccoli florets
1 tablespoon olive oil
Sea salt and ground black pepper, to taste

1. Pat the chicken dry with kitchen towels. Place the chicken cutlets in a lightly greased air fryer basket.
2. Put the air fryer lid on and air fry in the preheated instant pot at 380ºF (193ºC) for 6 minutes. Flip the chicken cutlets when the lid screen indicates TURN FOOD.
3. Increase the temperature to 400ºF (205ºC) and add in the remaining ingredients. Continue to cook for 6 minutes more.
4. Bon appétit!

Rice Wine Chicken Breasts

Prep time: 5 minutes | Cook time: 12 minutes | Serves 4

1 pound (454 g) chicken breasts, boneless, skinless
½ cup rice wine
1 tablespoon stone-ground mustard
1 teaspoon minced garlic
1 teaspoon whole black peppercorns
1 teaspoon chili powder
¼ teaspoon sea salt, or more to taste

1. Place the chicken, wine, mustard, garlic, and whole peppercorns in a ceramic bowl. Cover the bowl and let the chicken marinate for about 3 hours in the refrigerator.
2. Discard the marinade and place the chicken breasts in the air fryer basket.
3. Put the air fryer lid on and roast in the preheated instant pot at 380ºF (193ºC) for 12 minutes. Flip the chicken breasts when the lid screen indicates TURN FOOD.
4. Season the chicken with the chili powder and salt. Serve immediately and enjoy!

Chicken with Ranch Seasoning

Prep time: 5 minutes | Cook time: 22 minutes | Serves 3

1 pound (454 g) chicken wings, boneless
2 tablespoons olive oil
1 teaspoon Ranch seasoning mix
Kosher salt and ground black pepper, to taste

1. Pat the chicken dry with kitchen towels. Toss the chicken with the remaining ingredients.
2. Arrange the chicken in the air fryer basket.
3. Put the air fryer lid on and air fry in the preheated instant pot at 380ºF (193ºC) for 22 minutes. Flip the chicken wings when the lid screen indicates TURN FOOD.
4. Bon appétit!

Buttermilk Chicken

Prep time: 5 minutes | Cook time: 12 minutes | Serves 4

1 pound (454 g) chicken breast halves
Sea salt and ground black pepper, to taste
1 cup buttermilk
1 cup all-purpose flour
½ teaspoon onion powder
1 teaspoon garlic powder
1 teaspoon smoked paprika

1. Toss together the chicken pieces, salt, and black pepper in a large bowl to coat. Stir in the buttermilk until the chicken is coated on all sides. Place the chicken in the refrigerator for about 6 hours.
2. In a shallow bowl, thoroughly combine the flour, onion powder, garlic powder, and smoked paprika.
3. Then, dredge the chicken in the seasoned flour; shake off any excess and transfer them to a lightly oiled air fryer basket.
4. Put the air fryer lid on and air fry in the preheated instant pot at 380ºF (193ºC) for 12 minutes. Flip the chicken breasts when the lid screen indicates TURN FOOD.
5. Enjoy!

Turkey Legs with Butter

Prep time: 5 minutes | Cook time: 40 minutes | Serves 4

1½ pounds (680 g) turkey legs
1 tablespoon butter, melted
1 teaspoon hot paprika
1 teaspoon crushed garlic
Sea salt and ground black pepper, to taste
2 tablespoons chopped scallions

1. Toss the turkey legs with the remaining ingredients, except for the scallions. Place the turkey legs in the air fryer basket.
2. Put the air fryer lid on and roast in the preheated instant pot at 400ºF (205ºC) for 40 minutes. Flip the turkey legs when the lid screen indicates TURN FOOD.
3. Garnish the roasted turkey legs with the fresh scallions and enjoy!

Chicken Sandwich Buns with Mayo

Prep time: 10 minutes | Cook time: 12 minutes | Serves 4

1 pound (454 g) chicken breasts, boneless and skinless
1 stalks celery, chopped
1 carrot, chopped
1 small onion, chopped
1 cup mayonnaise
Sea salt and ground black pepper, to taste
4 sandwich buns

1. Pat the chicken dry with paper towels. Place the chicken in a lightly oiled air fryer basket.
2. Put the air fryer lid on and roast in the preheated instant pot at 380ºF (193ºC) for 12 minutes. Flip the chicken breasts when the lid screen indicates TURN FOOD.
3. Shred the chicken breasts using two forks; transfer it to a salad bowl and add in the celery, carrot, onion, mayo, salt, and pepper.
4. Toss to combine and serve in sandwich buns. Enjoy!

Chicken Drumsticks with Butter

Prep time: 5 minutes | Cook time: 20 minutes | Serves 4

4 chicken drumsticks, bone-in
1 tablespoon butter
½ teaspoon cayenne pepper
1 teaspoon Italian herb mix
Sea salt and ground black pepper, to taste

1. Pat the chicken drumsticks dry with paper towels. Toss the chicken drumsticks with the remaining ingredients. Place the chicken drumsticks in the air fryer basket.
2. Put the air fryer lid on and air fry in the preheated instant pot at 370ºF (188ºC) for 20 minutes. Flip the chicken drumsticks when the lid screen indicates TURN FOOD.
3. Bon appétit!

Chicken Drumettes with Hot Sauce

Prep time: 5 minutes | Cook time: 22 minutes | Serves 3

1 pound (454 g) chicken drumettes, bone-in
Sea salt and freshly ground black pepper, to taste
¼ cup Thai hot sauce
2 tablespoons sesame oil
1 teaspoon tamari sauce

1. Toss the chicken drumettes with the remaining ingredients. Place the chicken drumettes in the air fryer basket.
2. Put the air fryer lid on and roast in the preheated instant pot at 380ºF (193ºC) for 22 minutes. Flip the chicken drumettes when the lid screen indicates TURN FOOD.
3. Bon appétit!

Avocado and Turkey Rolls

Prep time: 8 minutes | Cook time: 20 minutes | Serves 4

1 pound (454 g) ground turkey
1 tablespoon olive oil
1 avocado, peeled, pitted, and chopped
2 garlic cloves, minced
½ cup bread crumbs
Kosher salt and ground black pepper, to taste
8 small rolls

1. Mix the turkey, olive oil, avocado, garlic, bread crumbs, salt, and black pepper until everything is well combined. Form the mixture into eight small patties.
2. Arrange the patties in the air fryer basket.
3. Put the air fryer lid on and air fry in the preheated instant pot at 380ºF (193ºC) for 20 minutes. Flip the patties when the lid screen indicates TURN FOOD.
4. Serve the patties in the prepared rolls and enjoy!

Chapter 11 Desserts

Cocoa Butter Brownies

Prep time: 5 minutes | Cook time: 20 minutes | Serves 6

1 stick butter, melted
1 cup brown sugar
2 eggs
¾ cup all-purpose flour
½ teaspoon baking powder
¼ cup cocoa powder
2 tablespoons coconut oil
1 teaspoon coconut extract
A pinch of sea salt

1. Spritz the sides and bottom of a baking dish with nonstick cooking spray.
2. In a mixing bowl, beat the melted butter and sugar until fluffy. Next, fold in the eggs and beat again until well combined.
3. After that, add in the remaining ingredients. Mix until everything is well incorporated. Transfer to the baking dish.
4. Place the baking dish in the air fryer basket. Put the air fryer lid on and bake in the preheated instant pot at 340ºF (171ºC) for 20 minutes. Enjoy!

Danish Pastry with Apple Pie

Prep time: 5 minutes | Cook time: 20 minutes | Serves 5

12 ounces (340 g) refrigerated puff pastry
1 cup apple pie filling

1. Roll out the puff pastry sheet into a large rectangle; cut the pastry sheet into triangles.
2. Spoon the filling into each triangle; fold the pastry over and seal the edges with the fingers. Transfer to the baking dish.
3. Place the baking dish in the air fryer basket. Put the air fryer lid on and bake in the preheated instant pot at 350ºF (180ºC) for 20 minutes, or until the top is golden brown.
4. Bon appétit!

Gulgulas with Yogurt

Prep time: 5 minutes | Cook time: 10 minutes | Serves 4

½ cup all-purpose flour
½ teaspoon baking powder
½ cup sugar
¼ teaspoon ground cardamom
¼ teaspoon sea salt
1 tablespoon ghee
2 eggs, whisked
2 tablespoons Indian yogurt

1. In a mixing bowl, thoroughly combine all the ingredients.
2. Drop a spoonful of batter onto the greased baking dish.
3. Place the baking dish in the air fryer basket. Put the air fryer lid on and bake in the preheated instant pot at 360ºF (182ºC) for 10 minutes. Flip them when the lid screen indicates TURN FOOD.
4. Repeat with the remaining batter and serve warm. Enjoy!

Vanilla Pancake Cups

Prep time: 5 minutes | Cook time: 5 minutes | Serves 4

½ cup flour
2 eggs
⅓ cup coconut milk
1 tablespoon coconut oil, melted
1 teaspoon vanilla paste
¼ teaspoon ground cinnamon
A pinch of ground cardamom

1. Mix all the ingredients until well combined.
2. Let the batter stand for 20 minutes. Spoon the batter into a greased muffin tin. Transfer to the baking dish.
3. Place the baking dish in the air fryer basket. Put the air fryer lid on and bake in the preheated instant pot at 330ºF (166ºC) for 5 minutes, or until golden brown. Serve with toppings of choice.
4. Bon appétit!

Baked Apples with Pecans

Prep time: 5 minutes | Cook time: 17 minutes | Serves 2

2 medium apples
4 tablespoons chopped pecans
4 tablespoons Sultanas
2 tablespoons butter, at room temperature
½ teaspoon cinnamon
¼ teaspoon grated nutmeg

1. Cut the apples in halves and spoon out some of the flesh.
2. In a mixing bowl, thoroughly combine the remaining ingredients. Stuff the apple halves and transfer them to the baking dish. Pour ¼ cup of water into the baking dish.
3. Place the baking dish in the air fryer basket. Put the air fryer lid on and bake in the preheated instant pot at 340ºF (171ºC) for 17 minutes. Serve at room temperature. Bon appétit!

Butter Toast

Prep time: 5 minutes | Cook time: 8 minutes | Serves 3

1 egg, whisked
¼ cup coconut milk
2 tablespoons butter, melted
1 teaspoon vanilla paste
½ teaspoon ground cinnamon
A pinch of grated nutmeg
3 slices bread

1. In a mixing bowl, thoroughly combine the eggs, milk, butter, vanilla, cinnamon, and nutmeg.
2. Then dip each piece of bread into the egg mixture; place the bread slices in a lightly greased baking dish.
3. Place the baking dish in the air fryer basket. Put the air fryer lid on and bake in the preheated instant pot at 330ºF (166ºC) for 8 minutes. Flip the bread slices when the lid screen indicates TURN FOOD. Enjoy!

Raisin Butter Scones

Prep time: 5 minutes | Cook time: 17 minutes | Serves 5

1 cup all-purpose flour
½ teaspoon baking powder
½ cup granulated sugar
2 tablespoons raisins
A pinch of coarse sea salt
A pinch of grated nutmeg
1 teaspoon lemon zest
1 teaspoon vanilla extract
¼ cup cold butter
2 eggs, whisked

1. Mix all the ingredients until everything is well incorporated. Spoon the batter into baking cups; lower the cups into the baking dish.
2. Place the baking dish in the air fryer basket. Put the air fryer lid on and bake in the preheated instant pot at 360ºF (182ºC) for 17 minutes, or until a tester comes out dry and clean.
3. Bon appétit!

Churros with Butter

Prep time: 5 minutes | Cook time: 20 minutes | Serves 4

¾ cup all-purpose flour
½ teaspoon baking powder
¾ cup water
4 tablespoons butter
1 tablespoon granulated sugar
½ teaspoon vanilla extract
½ teaspoon sea salt
1 large egg

1. In a mixing bowl, thoroughly combine all ingredients. Place the batter in a piping bag fitted with a large open star tip.
2. Pipe the churros into 6-inch long ropes and lower them onto the greased baking dish.
3. Place the baking dish in the air fryer basket. Put the air fryer lid on and bake in the preheated instant pot at 360ºF (182ºC) for 10 minutes. Flip the churros when the lid screen indicates TURN FOOD.
4. Repeat with the remaining batter and serve warm. Enjoy!

Cocoa Butter Cupcakes

Prep time: 5 minutes | Cook time: 15 minutes | Serves 6

¾ cup all-purpose flour
1 teaspoon baking powder
¼ teaspoon ground cinnamon
¼ teaspoon ground cardamom
¾ cup granulated sugar
¼ cup unsweetened cocoa powder
A pinch of sea salt
1 stick butter, room temperature
¾ cup milk
2 eggs, beaten

1. Mix all the ingredients in a bowl. Scrape the batter into silicone baking molds; place them in the baking dish.
2. Place the baking dish in the air fryer basket. Put the air fryer lid on and bake in the preheated instant pot at 330ºF (166ºC) for 15 minutes, or until a tester comes out dry and clean.
3. Allow the cupcakes to cool before unmolding and serving. Bon appétit!

Coconut and Chocolate Cake

Prep time: 5 minutes | Cook time: 20 minutes | Serves 6

½ cup coconut oil, room temperature
1 cup brown sugar
2 chia eggs (2 tablespoons ground chia seeds plus 4 tablespoons water)
¼ cup all-purpose flour
¼ cup coconut flour
½ cup cocoa powder
½ cup dark chocolate chips
A pinch of grated nutmeg
A pinch of sea salt
2 tablespoons coconut milk

1. Spritz the sides and bottom of a baking dish with nonstick cooking spray.
2. In a mixing bowl, beat the coconut oil and brown sugar until fluffy. Next, fold in the chia eggs and beat again until well combined.
3. After that, add in the remaining ingredients. Mix until everything is well incorporated. Transfer to the baking dish.
4. Place the baking dish in the air fryer basket. Put the air fryer lid on and bake in the preheated instant pot at 340ºF (171ºC) for 20 minutes. Enjoy!

Apple Pie

Prep time: 8 minutes | Cook time: 35 minutes | Serves 4

12 ounces (340 g) refrigerated 2 pie crusts
3 cups peeled and thinly sliced apples
¼ cup brown sugar
1 tablespoon lemon juice
1 teaspoon pure vanilla extract
½ teaspoon cinnamon
A pinch of ground cardamom
A pinch of kosher salt

1. Place the first pie crust in a lightly greased baking dish.
2. In a mixing bowl, thoroughly combine the remaining ingredients to make the filling. Spoon the filling into the prepared pie crust.
3. Unroll the second pie crust and place it on top of the filling.
4. Place the baking dish in the air fryer basket. Put the air fryer lid on and bake in the preheated instant pot at 350ºF (180ºC) for 35 minutes, or until the top is golden brown. Bon appétit!

Yogurt Beignets

Prep time: 5 minutes | Cook time: 20 minutes | Serves 4

¾ cup all-purpose flour
1 teaspoon baking powder
¼ teaspoon kosher salt
¼ cup yogurt
2 eggs, beaten
¼ cup granulated sugar
2 tablespoons coconut oil, melted

1. In a mixing bowl, thoroughly combine all the ingredients.
2. Drop a spoonful of batter onto the greased baking dish.
3. Place the baking dish in the air fryer basket. Put the air fryer lid on and bake in the preheated instant pot at 360ºF (182ºC) for 10 minutes. Flip them when the lid screen indicates TURN FOOD.
4. Repeat with the remaining batter and serve warm. Enjoy!

Apple Pancake

Prep time: 8 minutes | Cook time: 13 minutes | Serves 3

1 small apple, peeled, cored, and sliced
1 tablespoon coconut oil, melted
1 egg, whisked
¼ cup plain flour
¼ teaspoon baking powder
¼ cup full-fat coconut milk
A pinch of granulated sugar
A pinch of kosher salt
½ teaspoon vanilla paste

1. Drizzle the apple slices with the melted coconut oil; arrange the apple slices in a baking dish.
2. Mix the remaining ingredients to make the batter. Pour the batter over the apples.
3. Place the baking dish in the air fryer basket. Put the air fryer lid on and bake in the preheated instant pot at 350ºF (180ºC) for 13 minutes, or until it is golden brown around the edges.
4. Bon appétit!

Pumpkin and Walnuts Pie

Prep time: 5 minutes | Cook time: 35 minutes | Serves 4

12 ounces (340 g) refrigerated pie crusts
½ cup canned pumpkin purée
1 ounce (28 g) walnuts, coarsely chopped
½ cup granulated sugar
1 teaspoon pumpkin pie spice mix
1 teaspoon peeled and grated fresh ginger

1. Place the first pie crust in a lightly greased baking dish.
2. In a mixing bowl, thoroughly combine the remaining ingredients to make the filling. Spoon the filling into the prepared pie crust.
3. Unroll the second pie crust and place it on top of the filling.
4. Place the baking dish in the air fryer basket. Put the air fryer lid on and bake in the preheated instant pot at 350ºF (180ºC) for 35 minutes, or until the top is golden brown. Bon appétit!

Cinnamon Donuts

Prep time: 5 minutes | Cook time: 20 minutes | Serves 4

12 ounces (340 g) flaky large biscuits
¼ cup granulated sugar
1 teaspoon ground cinnamon
¼ teaspoon grated nutmeg
2 tablespoons coconut oil

1. Separate the dough into biscuits and place them in a lightly oiled baking dish.
2. Mix the sugar, cinnamon, nutmeg, and coconut oil until well combined.
3. Drizzle the donuts with the cinnamon mixture.
4. Place the baking dish in the air fryer basket. Put the air fryer lid on and bake in the preheated instant pot at 340ºF (171ºC) for 10 minutes, or until golden. Repeat with the remaining donuts.
5. Bon appétit!

Banana Goreng Pisang

Prep time: 6 minutes | Cook time: 13 minutes | Serves 2

4 tablespoons rice flour
4 tablespoons all-purpose flour
¼ teaspoon ground cinnamon
A pinch of sea salt
A pinch of grated nutmeg
4 tablespoons coconut flakes
2 teaspoons coconut oil
2 eggs, whisked
2 bananas, peeled and sliced

1. In a mixing dish, thoroughly combine the flour, cinnamon, salt, nutmeg, and coconut flakes.
2. Now, add in the coconut oil and eggs. Roll each slice of banana over the egg mixture. Transfer to the baking dish.
3. Place the baking dish in the air fryer basket. Put the air fryer lid on and bake in the preheated instant pot at 390ºF (199ºC) for 13 minutes. Flip the bananas when the lid screen indicates TURN FOOD. Bon appétit!

Cocoa Cupcakes with Raisins

Prep time: 5 minutes | Cook time: 15 minutes | Serves 4

¾ cup all-purpose flour
½ teaspoon baking powder
½ cup unsweetened cocoa powder
A pinch of kosher salt
¼ teaspoon grated nutmeg
½ teaspoon ground cinnamon
4 tablespoons coconut oil
¾ cup brown sugar
2 eggs, whisked
½ teaspoon vanilla extract
¾ cup yogurt
2 tablespoons raisins

1. Mix all the ingredients in a bowl. Scrape the batter into silicone baking molds; place them in the baking dish.
2. Place the baking dish in the air fryer basket. Put the air fryer lid on and bake in the preheated instant pot at 330ºF (166ºC) for 15 minutes, or until a tester comes out dry and clean.
3. Allow the cupcakes to cool before unmolding and serving. Bon appétit!

Apple Fritters

Prep time: 8 minutes | Cook time: 20 minutes | Serves 4

1 apple, peeled and grated
¼ cup coconut oil, melted
¾ cup all-purpose flour
1¼ teaspoons baking powder
¼ teaspoon ground cinnamon
1 egg
½ cup milk
2 tablespoons granulated sugar

1. In a mixing bowl, thoroughly combine all the ingredients.
2. Drop a spoonful of batter onto the greased baking dish.
3. Place the baking dish in the air fryer basket. Put the air fryer lid on and bake in the preheated instant pot at 360ºF (182ºC) for 10 minutes. Flip them when the lid screen indicates TURN FOOD.
4. Repeat with the remaining batter and serve warm. Enjoy!

Cocoa Cake

Prep time: 5 minutes | Cook time: 20 minutes | Serves 6

½ cup coconut oil
1 cup white granulated sugar
2 eggs
½ cup all-purpose flour
¼ cup coconut flour
½ teaspoon baking powder
½ cup unsweetened cocoa powder
¼ teaspoon salt
¼ teaspoon grated nutmeg
½ teaspoon ground cinnamon
¼ cup milk
½ teaspoon pure vanilla extract

1. Brush the sides and bottom of a baking dish with nonstick cooking spray.
2. In a mixing bowl, beat the coconut oil and sugar until fluffy. Next, fold in the eggs and beat again until well combined.
3. After that, add in the remaining ingredients. Mix until everything is well combined. Transfer to the baking dish.
4. Place the baking dish in the air fryer basket. Put the air fryer lid on and bake in the preheated instant pot at 340ºF (171ºC) for 20 minutes. Bon appétit!

Walnuts and Yogurt Stuffed Pears

Prep time: 5 minutes | Cook time: 17 minutes | Serves 2

2 pears
¼ teaspoon cloves
⅛ teaspoon grated nutmeg
¼ teaspoon ground cinnamon
2 tablespoons honey
2 tablespoons chopped walnuts
2 ounces (57 g) Greek yogurt

1. Cut the pears in half and spoon out some of the flesh.
2. In a mixing bowl, thoroughly combine the remaining ingredients. Stuff the pear halves.
3. Pour ¼ cup of water into the baking dish. Place the pears in the baking dish.
4. Place the baking dish in the air fryer basket. Put the air fryer lid on and bake in the preheated instant pot at 340ºF (171ºC) for 17 minutes. Serve at room temperature. Bon appétit!

Purple Plum Pies Cups

Prep time: 8 minutes | Cook time: 20 minutes | Serves 6

1 cup pitted and coarsely chopped purple plums
½ cup brown sugar
½ teaspoon ground cinnamon
12 ounces (340 g) refrigerated flaky cinnamon rolls

1. Toss the plums with the sugar and cinnamon.
2. Spray the muffin cups with nonstick cooking spray. Separate dough into 6 rolls and press them into the prepared muffin cups.
3. Spoon the filling into each dough-lined cup. Transfer the cups to the baking dish.
4. Place the baking dish in the air fryer basket. Put the air fryer lid on and bake in the preheated instant pot at 350ºF (180ºC) for 20 minutes, or until the top is golden brown. Bon appétit!

Apple and Oats Cakes

Prep time: 5 minutes | Cook time: 20 minutes | Serves 4

½ cup all-purpose flour
½ cup ground oats
½ teaspoon baking powder
1 apple, peeled and grated
¼ cup dried cranberries
2 tablespoons butter
½ teaspoon ground cinnamon
½ cup full-fat milk
1 egg, whisked

1. In a mixing bowl, thoroughly combine all the ingredients.
2. Drop a spoonful of batter onto the greased baking dish.
3. Place the baking dish in the air fryer basket. Put the air fryer lid on and bake in the preheated instant pot at 360ºF (182ºC) for 10 minutes. Flip them when the lid screen indicates TURN FOOD.
4. Repeat with the remaining batter and serve warm. Enjoy!

Pear Pancake

Prep time: 10 minutes | Cook time: 13 minutes | Serves 4

1 pear, peeled, cored, and sliced
1 tablespoon lemon juice
1 tablespoon coconut oil
½ cup all-purpose flour
½ teaspoon baking powder
2 tablespoons brown sugar
½ teaspoon cinnamon
2 eggs, whisked
½ cup milk
½ teaspoon vanilla extract

1. Drizzle the pear slices with the lemon juice and melted coconut oil; arrange the pear slices in the baking dish.
2. Mix the remaining ingredients to make the batter. Pour the batter over the pears.
3. Place the baking dish in the air fryer basket. Put the air fryer lid on and bake in the preheated instant pot at 350ºF (180ºC) for 13 minutes, or until it is golden brown around the edges.
4. Bon appétit!

Chocolate Fudge Cake

Prep time: 5 minutes | Cook time: 20 minutes | Serves 5

½ cup butter, melted
1 cup turbinado sugar
3 eggs
1 teaspoon vanilla extract
¼ teaspoon salt
¼ teaspoon ground cloves
½ teaspoon ground cinnamon
½ cup all-purpose flour
¼ cup almond flour
5 ounces (142 g) chocolate chips

1. Spritz the sides and bottom of a baking dish with nonstick cooking spray.
2. In a mixing bowl, beat the butter and sugar until fluffy. Next, fold in the eggs and beat again until well combined.
3. After that, add in the remaining ingredients. Mix until everything is well combined.
4. Place the baking dish in the air fryer basket. Put the air fryer lid on and bake in the preheated instant pot at 340ºF (171ºC) for 20 minutes. Enjoy!

Buttery Almonds Rolls

Prep time: 5 minutes | Cook time: 20 minutes | Serves 4

12 ounces (340 g) refrigerated dinner roll dough
½ cup brown sugar
1 teaspoon ground cinnamon
¼ cup chopped almonds
¼ cup butter, melted

1. Spritz muffin cups with nonstick cooking spray.
2. Separate the dough into biscuits. In a shallow bowl, thoroughly combine the sugar, cinnamon, almonds, and butter.
3. Roll the biscuits over the sugar mixture. Divide them between muffin cups. Transfer the muffin cups to the baking dish.
4. Place the baking dish in the air fryer basket. Put the air fryer lid on and bake in the preheated instant pot at 340ºF (171ºC) for 20 minutes, or until golden brown. Turn them upside down and serve.

Chocolate Chips Mug Cake

Prep time: 5 minutes | Cook time: 20 minutes | Serves 2

2 tablespoons coconut flour
2 tablespoons almond flour
2 tablespoons all-purpose flour
½ teaspoon baking powder
4 tablespoons unsweetened cocoa powder
2 ounces (57 g) chocolate chips
A pinch of salt
A pinch of grated nutmeg
2 tablespoons coconut oil
4 tablespoons coconut milk
½ teaspoon pure almond extract

1. Thoroughly combine all the ingredients; mix until well combined.
2. Divide the mixture between two mugs and place them in the baking dish.
3. Place the baking dish in the air fryer basket. Put the air fryer lid on and bake in the preheated instant pot at 350ºF (180ºC) for 20 minutes. Bon appétit!

Vettu Cake

Prep time: 5 minutes | Cook time: 13 minutes | Serves 4

¾ cup all-purpose flour
½ teaspoon baking powder
¼ teaspoon cardamom powder
¼ teaspoon cinnamon powder
2 eggs, whisked
½ cup caster sugar
2 tablespoons coconut oil

1. Mix all the ingredients to make the batter. Pour the batter into a lightly oiled baking dish.
2. Place the baking dish in the air fryer basket. Put the air fryer lid on and bake in the preheated instant pot at 350ºF (180ºC) for 13 minutes, or until they are golden brown around the edges.
3. Bon appétit!

Cherry Pies

Prep time: 8 minutes | Cook time: 20 minutes | Serves 6

½ cup pitted Maraschino cherries
½ cup granulated sugar
½ teaspoon ground cardamom
1 teaspoon pure vanilla extract
2 tablespoons chopped hazelnuts
12 ounces (340 g) refrigerated flaky cinnamon rolls

1. Toss the cherries with the sugar, cardamom, vanilla, and hazelnuts.
2. Spray muffin cups with nonstick cooking spray. Separate the dough into 6 rolls and press them into the prepared muffin cups.
3. Spoon the filling into each dough-lined cup. Transfer the muffin cups to the baking dish.
4. Place the baking dish in the air fryer basket. Put the air fryer lid on and bake in the preheated instant pot at 350ºF (180ºC) for 20 minutes, or until the top is golden brown. Bon appétit!

Banana Fritters

Prep time: 5 minutes | Cook time: 10 minutes | Serves 1

1 banana, mashed
1 egg, beaten
1 tablespoon coconut oil
¼ teaspoons ground cinnamon
1 tablespoon brown sugar

1. In a mixing bowl, thoroughly combine all the ingredients.
2. Ladle the batter into a lightly greased baking dish.
3. Place the baking dish in the air fryer basket. Put the air fryer lid on and bake in the preheated instant pot at 360ºF (182ºC) for 10 minutes. Flip the fritter when the lid screen indicates TURN FOOD. Enjoy!

Roasted Cherries

Prep time: 10 minutes | Cook time: 20 minutes | Serves 4

2 cups pitted cherries
4 tablespoons brown sugar
1 tablespoon coconut oil
2 tablespoons bourbon
¼ teaspoon ground cinnamon

1. Toss the cherries with the remaining ingredients; place the cherries in a lightly greased air fryer basket.
2. Put the air fryer lid on and roast in the preheated instant pot at 370ºF (188ºC) for 20 minutes.
3. Serve at room temperature. Bon appétit!

Pears with Vanilla Pod

Prep time: 5 minutes | Cook time: 17 minutes | Serves 3

3 pears, peeled and cored
1 vanilla pod
1 cinnamon stick
2 to 3 cloves
1 cup caster sugar
1 cup red wine

1. Place the pears, vanilla, cinnamon, cloves, sugar, and wine in the baking dish.
2. Place the baking dish in the air fryer basket. Put the air fryer lid on and bake in the preheated instant pot at 340ºF (171ºC) for 17 minutes. Serve at room temperature. Bon appétit!

Banana with Cinnamon

Prep time: 6 minutes | Cook time: 13 minutes | Serves 1

1 banana, peeled and sliced
1 tablespoon coconut oil
2 tablespoons granulated sugar
½ teaspoon ground cloves
½ teaspoon ground cinnamon

1. Toss banana slices with the remaining ingredients. Transfer to the baking dish.
2. Place the baking dish in the air fryer basket. Put the air fryer lid on and bake in the preheated instant pot at 390ºF (199ºC) for 13 minutes. Flip the banana slices when the lid screen indicates TURN FOOD.
3. Bon appétit!

Coconut Plantain Boats

Prep time: 6 minutes | Cook time: 7 minutes | Serves 2

2 plantains, peeled
½ cup shredded coconut
1 tablespoon coconut oil
4 tablespoons brown sugar
½ teaspoon cinnamon powder
½ teaspoon cardamom powder
4 tablespoons raisins

1. In the peel, slice the plantains lengthwise; make sure not to slice all the way through the plantains.
2. Divide the remaining ingredients between the plantain pockets.
3. Place the plantain boats in the baking dish.
4. Place the baking dish in the air fryer basket. Put the air fryer lid on and bake in the preheated instant pot at 395ºF (202ºC) for 7 minutes. Eat with a spoon and enjoy!

Pumpkin Cake with Butter

Prep time: 5 minutes | Cook time: 13 minutes | Serves 2

1/3 cup pumpkin purée
½ cup peanut butter
2 eggs, beaten
1 teaspoon vanilla extract
½ teaspoon pumpkin pie spice
½ teaspoon baking powder

1. Mix all the ingredients to make the batter. Pour the batter into a lightly oiled baking dish.
2. Place the baking dish in the air fryer basket. Put the air fryer lid on and bake in the preheated instant pot at 350ºF (180ºC) for 13 minutes, or until it is golden brown around the edges.
3. Bon appétit!

Cranberry Cupcakes with Chocolate

Prep time: 5 minutes | Cook time: 15 minutes | Serves 6

Cupcakes:
¾ cup self-raising flour
¾ cup caster sugar
¼ cup cocoa powder
A pinch of sea salt
A pinch of grated nutmeg
2 eggs, whisked
½ cup buttermilk
½ stick butter, melted
2 ounces (57 g) dried cranberries

Frosting:
½ cup butter, room temperature
1 teaspoon vanilla extract
3 ounces (85 g) chocolate chips, melted
4 tablespoons heavy whipping cream

1. Mix all the ingredients for the cupcakes. Scrape the batter into silicone baking molds; place them in the baking dish.
2. Place the baking dish in the air fryer basket. Put the air fryer lid on and bake in the preheated instant pot at 330ºF (166ºC) for 15 minutes, or until a tester comes out dry and clean.
3. Beat all the ingredients for the frosting using an electric mixer. Pipe the frosting onto the cupcakes. Bon appétit!

Cinnamon Apple Wedges

Prep time: 5 minutes | Cook time: 17 minutes | Serves 2

2 apples, peeled, cored, and cut into wedges
2 teaspoons coconut oil
2 tablespoons brown sugar
1 teaspoon pure vanilla extract
1 teaspoon ground cinnamon
¼ cup water

1. Toss the apples with the coconut oil, sugar, vanilla, and cinnamon.
2. Pour ¼ cup of water into the baking dish. Place the apples in the baking dish.
3. Place the baking dish in the air fryer basket. Put the air fryer lid on and bake in the preheated instant pot at 340ºF (171ºC) for 17 minutes. Serve at room temperature. Bon appétit!

Cranberries Scones

Prep time: 5 minutes | Cook time: 17 minutes | Serves 4

1 cup all-purpose flour
1 teaspoon baking powder
¼ cup caster sugar
A pinch of sea salt
¼ teaspoon ground cinnamon
4 tablespoons butter
1 egg, beaten
¼ cup milk
2 ounces (57 g) dried cranberries

1. Mix all the ingredients until everything is well incorporated. Spoon the batter into baking cups; lower the cups into the baking dish.
2. Place the baking dish in the air fryer basket. Put the air fryer lid on and bake in the preheated instant pot at 360ºF (182ºC) for 17 minutes, or until a tester comes out dry and clean.
3. Bon appétit!

Eggs Donuts

Prep time: 5 minutes | Cook time: 20 minutes | Serves 4

1 cup all-purpose flour
½ teaspoon baking powder
¼ teaspoon sea salt
½ cup white sugar
2 large eggs, whisked
2 tablespoons canola oil
¼ cup milk
½ teaspoon cinnamon powder

1. In a mixing bowl, thoroughly combine all-purpose flour with baking powder, salt, and sugar.
2. In a separate bowl, beat the eggs until frothy using a hand mixer; add in the oil and milk and beat again; lastly, stir in cinnamon powder and mix again until everything is well combined.
3. Then, stir the egg mixture into the flour mixture and continue mixing until a dough ball forms. Try not to over-mix the dough. Transfer to a lightly floured surface.
4. Roll out the dough to a ¼-inch thickness using a rolling pin. Cut out doughnuts using a 3-inch round cutter; now, use a 1-inch round cutter to remove the center. Transfer the donuts to the baking dish.
5. Place the baking dish in the air fryer basket. Put the air fryer lid on and bake in the preheated instant pot at 340ºF (171ºC) for 10 minutes, or until golden. Repeat with the remaining doughnuts.
6. Bon appétit!

Plums with Star Anise

Prep time: 10 minutes | Cook time: 17 minutes | Serves 4

1 pound (454 g) plums, halved and pitted
2 tablespoons coconut oil
4 tablespoons brown sugar
4 whole cloves
1 cinnamon stick
4 whole star anise

1. Toss the plums with the remaining ingredients.
2. Pour ¼ cup of water into the baking dish. Place the plums in the baking dish.
3. Place the baking dish in the air fryer basket. Put the air fryer lid on and bake in the preheated instant pot at 340ºF (171ºC) for 17 minutes. Serve at room temperature. Bon appétit!

Chocolate Chip Butter Cupcakes

Prep time: 5 minutes | Cook time: 15 minutes | Serves 6

¾ cup plain flour
½ teaspoon baking powder
¼ cup cocoa powder
¾ cup caster sugar
1 egg, whisked
2 ounces (57 g) butter, room temperature
¾ cup whole milk
2 ounces (57 g) chocolate chips
½ teaspoon vanilla extract

1. Mix all the ingredients in a bowl. Scrape the batter into silicone baking molds; place them in the baking dish.
2. Place the baking dish in the air fryer basket. Put the air fryer lid on and bake in the preheated instant pot at 330ºF (166ºC) for 15 minutes, or until a tester comes out dry and clean.
3. Allow the cupcakes to cool before unmolding and serving. Bon appétit!

Apricots with Star Anise

Prep time: 10 minutes | Cook time: 16 minutes | Serves 3

5 ripe apricots, halved and pitted
½ cup caster sugar
½ cup rosé wine
½ vanilla bean, split
½ cinnamon stick
3 to 4 whole star anise
1 tablespoon butter
1 teaspoon lemon peel

1. Toss the apricots with the caster sugar.
2. Pour the wine into the baking dish. Place the apricots along with the spices and butter in the baking dish.
3. Place the baking dish in the air fryer basket. Put the air fryer lid on and bake in the preheated instant pot at 340ºF (171ºC) for 16 minutes. Serve at room temperature. Bon appétit!

French Baguette

Prep time: 5 minutes | Cook time: 8 minutes | Serves 2

2 eggs
2 tablespoons coconut oil, melted
¼ cup milk
½ teaspoon vanilla extract
¼ teaspoon ground cinnamon
⅛ teaspoon ground nutmeg
4 thick slices baguette

1. In a mixing bowl, thoroughly combine the eggs, coconut oil, milk, vanilla, cinnamon, and nutmeg.
2. Then, dip each piece of bread into the egg mixture; place the bread slices in a lightly greased baking dish.
3. Place the baking dish in the air fryer basket. Put the air fryer lid on and bake in the preheated instant pot at 330ºF (166ºC) for 8 minutes. Flip the bread slices when the lid screen indicates TURN FOOD. Enjoy!

Eggs and Butter Crullers

Prep time: 5 minutes | Cook time: 20 minutes | Serves 4

¾ cup all-purpose flour
¼ cup butter
¼ cup water
½ cup full-fat milk
¼ teaspoon kosher salt
A pinch of grated nutmeg
3 eggs, beaten

1. In a mixing bowl, thoroughly combine all ingredients. Place the batter in a piping bag fitted with a large open star tip.
2. Pipe the crullers into circles and lower them onto the greased baking dish.
3. Place the baking dish in the air fryer basket. Put the air fryer lid on and bake in the preheated instant pot at 360ºF (182ºC) for 10 minutes. Flip the crullers when the lid screen indicates TURN FOOD.
4. Repeat with the remaining batter and serve immediately. Enjoy!

Strawberry Fritters

Prep time: 5 minutes | Cook time: 15 minutes | Serves 4

¾ cup all-purpose flour
½ teaspoon baking powder
2 tablespoons butter, melted
¼ cup coconut milk
2 eggs, whisked
1 teaspoon lime juice
½ cup strawberries
2 tablespoons powdered sugar

1. In a mixing bowl, thoroughly combine all the ingredients.
2. Drop a spoonful of batter onto the greased baking dish.
3. Place the baking dish in the air fryer basket. Put the air fryer lid on and bake in the preheated instant pot at 360ºF (182ºC) for 10 minutes. Flip them when the lid screen indicates TURN FOOD.
4. Repeat with the remaining batter and serve warm. Enjoy!

Buttery Chocolate Fudge Brownie

Prep time: 5 minutes | Cook time: 20 minutes | Serves 6

½ cup butter, melted
½ cup granulated sugar
2 eggs, whisked
¾ cup self-raising flour
¼ cup cocoa powder
1 teaspoon vanilla extract
½ cup chocolate chips

1. Spritz the sides and bottom of a baking dish with nonstick cooking spray.
2. In a mixing bowl, beat the melted butter and sugar until fluffy. Next, fold in the eggs and beat again until well combined.
3. After that, add in the remaining ingredients. Mix until everything is well incorporated. Transfer to the baking dish.
4. Place the baking dish in the air fryer basket. Put the air fryer lid on and bake in the preheated instant pot at 340ºF (171ºC) for 20 minutes. Enjoy!

Butter Pears

Prep time: 10 minutes | Cook time: 17 minutes | Serves 2

2 pears, peeled, cored, and cut into sticks
2 tablespoons butter
A pinch of grated nutmeg
A pinch of sea salt
½ teaspoon ground cinnamon
1 teaspoon grated fresh ginger

1. Toss the pears with the remaining ingredients.
2. Pour ¼ cup of water into the baking dish. Place the pears in the baking dish.
3. Place the baking dish in the air fryer basket. Put the air fryer lid on and bake in the preheated instant pot at 340ºF (171ºC) for 17 minutes. Serve at room temperature. Bon appétit!

Chocolate Cream Eclairs

Prep time: 5 minutes | Cook time: 20 minutes | Serves 4

Choux Pastry:
¾ cup all-purpose flour
¼ cup almond milk
½ cup water
6 tablespoons butter, room temperature
1 teaspoon brown sugar
¼ teaspoon kosher salt
¼ teaspoon grated nutmeg
3 eggs

Chocolate Glaze:
⅓ cup heavy whipping cream
2 ounces (57 g) semi-sweet chocolate chips

1. In a mixing bowl, thoroughly combine all the ingredients for the pastry. Place the batter in a piping bag fitted with a large open star tip.
2. Pipe the eclairs into strips and lower them onto the greased baking dish.
3. Place the baking dish in the air fryer basket. Put the air fryer lid on and bake in the preheated instant pot at 360ºF (182ºC) for 10 minutes. Flip the eclairs when the lid screen indicates TURN FOOD.
4. Repeat with the remaining batter. Place the eclairs in the refrigerator while making the chocolate glaze.
5. Heat the whipping cream in a microwave; add in the chocolate and whisk until smooth sauce forms.
6. Top the chilled eclairs with the chocolate glaze and let it sit for about 30 minutes before serving. Bon appétit!

Fruity Kabobs

Prep time: 15 minutes | Cook time: 10 minutes | Serves 4

1 cup melon, cut into 1-inch chunks
1 cup pineapple, cut into 1-inch chunks
1 banana, cut into 1-inch chunks
1 peach, cut into 1-inch chunks
2 tablespoons coconut oil, melted
2 tablespoons honey

1. Toss the fruits with the coconut oil and honey.
2. Thread the fruits onto skewers and place them in the air fryer basket.
3. Put the air fryer lid on and air fry in the preheated instant pot at 400ºF (205ºC) for 10 minutes. Flip the skewers when the lid screen indicates TURN FOOD.
4. Bon appétit!

Almond Butter Cupcakes

Prep time: 5 minutes | Cook time: 15 minutes | Serves 6

¾ cup self-raising flour
¼ cup cocoa powder
2 eggs, beaten
1 stick butter, room temperature
1 cup granulated sugar
½ cup almond milk
2 ounces (57 g) almonds, slivered

1. Mix all the ingredients in a bowl. Scrape the batter into silicone baking molds; place them in the baking dish.
2. Place the baking dish in the air fryer basket. Put the air fryer lid on and bake in the preheated instant pot at 330ºF (166ºC) for 15 minutes, or until a tester comes out dry and clean.
3. Allow the cupcakes to cool before unmolding and serving. Bon appétit!

Apple Cake

Prep time: 10 minutes | Cook time: 13 minutes | Serves 3

$^1/_3$ cup all-purpose flour
¼ cup coconut flour
½ teaspoon baking powder
½ teaspoon ground cinnamon
3 tablespoons brown sugar
A pinch of kosher salt
2 eggs, beaten
½ teaspoon pure vanilla extract
¼ cup full-fat milk
2 small apples, peeled, cored, and grated

1. Mix all the ingredients to make the batter. Pour the batter into a lightly oiled baking dish.
2. Place the baking dish in the air fryer basket. Put the air fryer lid on and bake in the preheated instant pot at 350ºF (180ºC) for 13 minutes, or until it is golden brown around the edges.
3. Bon appétit!

Blueberry Fritters

Prep time: 5 minutes | Cook time: 15 minutes | Serves 4

¾ cup all-purpose flour
1 teaspoon baking powder
½ cup coconut milk
2 tablespoons coconut sugar
A pinch of sea salt
1 egg
2 tablespoons melted butter
2 ounces (57 g) fresh blueberries

1. In a mixing bowl, thoroughly combine all the ingredients.
2. Drop a spoonful of batter onto the greased baking dish.
3. Place the baking dish in the air fryer basket. Put the air fryer lid on and bake in the preheated instant pot at 360ºF (182ºC) for 10 minutes. Flip them when the lid screen indicates TURN FOOD.
4. Repeat with the remaining batter and serve warm. Enjoy!

Unnakai Malabar with Coconut

Prep time: 5 minutes | Cook time: 13 minutes | Serves 1

1 plantain, peeled
¼ cup coconut flakes
¼ teaspoon cinnamon powder
¼ teaspoon cardamom powder
1 tablespoon ghee
2 tablespoons brown sugar

1. Toss the plantain with the remaining ingredients. Transfer to the baking dish.
2. Place the baking dish in the air fryer basket. Put the air fryer lid on and bake in the preheated instant pot at 390ºF (199ºC) for 13 minutes. Flip it when the lid screen indicates TURN FOOD.
3. Bon appétit!

Pumpkin Cake

Prep time: 5 minutes | Cook time: 13 minutes | Serves 3

4 tablespoons all-purpose flour
4 tablespoons almond flour
1 teaspoon baking powder
4 tablespoons honey
1 teaspoon pumpkin pie spice blend
A pinch of Himalayan salt
¼ cup milk
¼ cup canned pumpkin
1 egg, beaten

1. Mix all the ingredients to make the batter. Pour the batter into a lightly oiled baking dish.
2. Place the baking dish in the air fryer basket. Put the air fryer lid on and bake in the preheated instant pot at 350ºF (180ºC) for 13 minutes, or until it is golden brown around the edges.
3. Bon appétit!

Butternut Squash Cake

Prep time: 10 minutes | Cook time: 15 minutes | Serves 4

2 cups shredded butternut squash
½ cup all-purpose flour
2 eggs, beaten
1 tablespoon coconut oil
1 teaspoon pumpkin pie spice mix

1. In a mixing bowl, thoroughly combine all the ingredients.
2. Drop a spoonful of batter onto the greased baking dish.
3. Place the baking dish in the air fryer basket. Put the air fryer lid on and bake in the preheated instant pot at 360ºF (182ºC) for 10 minutes. Flip them when the lid screen indicates TURN FOOD.
4. Repeat with the remaining batter and serve warm. Enjoy!

Apricots with Cheese

Prep time: 10 minutes | Cook time: 16 minutes | Serves 4

8 apricots, halved and pitted
1 tablespoon coconut oil, melted
2 tablespoons honey
1 teaspoon ground cinnamon
2 ounces (57 g) mascarpone cheese
1 tablespoon coconut flakes

1. Toss the apricots with the coconut oil, honey, and cinnamon.
2. Place the apricots in a lightly oiled air fryer basket.
3. Put the air fryer lid on and air fry in the preheated instant pot at 340ºF (171ºC) for 16 minutes. Top the fried apricots with mascarpone cheese and coconut flakes.
4. Bon appétit!

Cinnamon Rolls

Prep time: 5 minutes | Cook time: 10 minutes | Serves 4

9 ounces (255 g) refrigerated crescent rolls
1 tablespoon coconut oil
4 tablespoons caster sugar
1 teaspoon ground cinnamon

1. Separate the dough into rectangles. Mix the remaining ingredients until well combined.
2. Spread each rectangle with the cinnamon mixture; roll them up tightly.
3. Place the rolls in the baking dish.
4. Place the baking dish in the air fryer basket. Put the air fryer lid on and bake in the preheated instant pot at 300ºF (150ºC) for 10 minutes. Flip the rolls when the lid screen indicates TURN FOOD.
5. Bon appétit!

Banana Fritters

Prep time: 5 minutes | Cook time: 20 minutes | Serves 4

¾ cup all-purpose flour
¾ cup water
1 tablespoon rum
4 tablespoons butter
1 banana, mashed
1 tablespoon caster sugar
¼ teaspoon salt
¼ teaspoon grated nutmeg

1. In a mixing bowl, thoroughly combine all the ingredients.
2. Drop a spoonful of batter onto the greased baking dish.
3. Place the baking dish in the air fryer basket. Put the air fryer lid on and bake in the preheated instant pot at 360ºF (182ºC) for 10 minutes. Flip them when the lid screen indicates TURN FOOD.
4. Repeat with the remaining batter and serve warm. Enjoy!

Homemade Mug Cake

Prep time: 5 minutes | Cook time: 20 minutes | Serves 1

2 tablespoons all-purpose flour
2 tablespoons almond flour
2 tablespoons unsweetened cocoa powder
2 tablespoons agave nectar
¼ teaspoon baking powder
1 teaspoon pure vanilla extract
A pinch of kosher salt
A pinch of grated nutmeg
2 tablespoons coconut oil, room temperature
2 tablespoons full-fat milk

1. Thoroughly combine all the ingredients; mix until well combined.
2. Spoon the mixture into a mug and place it in the baking dish.
3. Place the baking dish in the air fryer basket. Put the air fryer lid on and bake in the preheated instant pot at 350ºF (180ºC) for 20 minutes. Bon appétit!

Baked Peaches with Brown Sugar

Prep time: 5 minutes | Cook time: 15 minutes | Serves 3

3 peaches, halved
1 tablespoon fresh lime juice
½ teaspoon ground cinnamon
½ teaspoon grated nutmeg
½ cup brown sugar
4 tablespoons coconut oil

1. Toss the peaches with the remaining ingredients.
2. Pour ¼ cup of water into the baking dish. Place the peaches in the baking dish.
3. Place the baking dish in the air fryer basket. Put the air fryer lid on and bake in the preheated instant pot at 340ºF (171ºC) for 15 minutes. Serve at room temperature. Bon appétit!

Chapter 12 Other Air Fryer Favorites

Tomato and Cheese Frittata

Prep time: 5 minutes | Cook time: 15 minutes | Serves 3

4 tablespoons sour cream
5 eggs
¼ cup crumbled Mozzarella cheese
2 tablespoons olive oil
1 medium tomato, chopped
¼ cup chopped fresh parsley
¼ cup chopped fresh chives
½ teaspoon dried oregano
Sea salt and ground black pepper, to taste

1. Spritz the sides and bottom of the baking dish with nonstick cooking oil.
2. In a mixing bowl, thoroughly combine all the ingredients.
3. Pour the mixture into the prepared baking dish.
4. Place the baking dish in the air fryer basket. Put the air fryer lid on and bake in the preheated instant pot at 350ºF (180ºC) for 15 minutes, or until a toothpick comes out dry and clean. Bon appétit!

Beef and Sausage Rissoles

Prep time: 5 minutes | Cook time: 15 minutes | Serves 4

1 slice bread, crusts removed and soaked
1 shallot, chopped
2 cloves garlic, minced
½ pound (227 g) ground beef
½ pound (227 g) pork sausage, crumbled
1 egg, beaten
Sea salt and ground black pepper, to taste

1. Mix all the ingredients until everything is well combined. Form the mixture into balls. Transfer to the air fryer basket.
2. Put the air fryer lid on and air fry in the preheated instant pot at 380ºF (193ºC) for 15 minutes. Flip the meatballs when the lid screen indicates TURN FOOD.
3. Bon appétit!

Air Fried Eggs

Prep time: 2 minutes | Cook time: 15 minutes | Serves 2

4 eggs
Sea salt, to taste

1. Place the eggs in the air fryer basket.
2. Put the air fryer lid on and air fry in the preheated instant pot at 270ºF (132ºC) for 15 minutes.
3. Peel the eggs and season them with the salt. Bon appétit!

Black Beans Hoagie

Prep time: 8 minutes | Cook time: 15 minutes | Serves 4

Burgers:
14 ounces (397 g) canned black beans, drained and rinsed
1 chia egg (1 tablespoon ground chia seeds plus 2 tablespoons lukewarm water)
Sea salt and ground black pepper, to taste
½ teaspoon ground cumin
2 tablespoons olive oil
1 medium onion, chopped
2 garlic cloves, minced
Hoagie:
2 hoagie rolls, halved
4 tablespoons ketchup
4 teaspoons mustard

1. Thoroughly combine all the ingredients for the burgers. Form the mixture into sausages and arrange them in a lightly greased air fryer basket.
2. Put the air fryer lid on and air fry in the preheated instant pot at 380ºF (193ºC) for 15 minutes. Flip the sausages when the lid screen indicates TURN FOOD.
3. Assemble the sandwiches with black bean sausages, hoagie rolls, ketchup, and mustard.
4. Bon appétit!

Corn Kernels Cheese Cakes

Prep time: 5 minutes | Cook time: 15 minutes | Serves 4

1 cup all-purpose flour
½ teaspoon baking powder
1 cup canned sweet corn kernels, drained
2 eggs
¼ cup buttermilk
½ teaspoon sea salt
¼ teaspoon freshly ground black pepper, or more to taste
1 garlic clove, minced
1 tablespoon butter, melted
2 ounces (57 g) Swiss cheese, shredded

1. Mix all the ingredients until everything is well combined. Form the mixture into patties. Transfer to the air fryer basket.
2. Put the air fryer lid on and air fry in the preheated instant pot at 380ºF (193ºC) for 15 minutes. Flip them when the lid screen indicates TURN FOOD.
3. Bon appétit!

Potato Cheese Croquettes

Prep time: 10 minutes | Cook time: 14 minutes | Serves 4

½ cup all-purpose flour
¾ pound (340 g) potatoes, peeled and grated
2 eggs, whisked
2 tablespoons butter
2 ounces (57 g) Parmesan cheese, grated
2 ounces (57 g) bread crumbs
2 tablespoons olive oil
1 teaspoon paprika
Kosher salt and freshly ground black pepper, to taste

1. Mix all the ingredients in a bowl. Shape the mixture into bite-sized balls and place them in a lightly oiled air fryer basket.
2. Put the air fryer lid on and air fry in the preheated instant pot at 400ºF (205ºC) for 14 minutes. Flip the croquettes when the lid screen indicates TURN FOOD.
3. Bon appétit!

Yogurt Griddlecake

Prep time: 5 minutes | Cook time: 15 minutes | Serves 4

¾ cup all-purpose flour
½ teaspoon baking powder
2 tablespoons brown sugar
½ cup yogurt
2 eggs, whisked
½ teaspoon ground cinnamon
½ teaspoon vanilla extract

1. In a mixing bowl, thoroughly combine all the ingredients.
2. Drop a spoonful of batter onto the greased baking dish.
3. Place the baking dish in the air fryer basket. Put the air fryer lid on and bake in the preheated instant pot at 360ºF (182ºC) for 10 minutes. Flip them when the lid screen indicates TURN FOOD.
4. Repeat with the remaining batter and serve warm. Enjoy!

Spinach and Egg Cheese Cups

Prep time: 6 minutes | Cook time: 15 minutes | Serves 4

4 eggs
4 tablespoons cream cheese
1 tablespoon butter, melted
Sea salt and ground black pepper, to taste
½ teaspoon cayenne pepper
1 cup chopped baby spinach
1 small tomato, chopped
2 garlic cloves, minced

1. Spritz silicone molds with nonstick cooking oil.
2. In a mixing bowl, thoroughly combine all the ingredients.
3. Pour the mixture into the prepared silicone molds and lower them into the baking dish.
4. Place the baking dish in the air fryer basket. Put the air fryer lid on and bake in the preheated instant pot at 350ºF (180ºC) for 15 minutes, or until a toothpick comes out dry and clean.
5. Bon appétit!

Roti Canai

Prep time: 5 minutes | Cook time: 20 minutes | Serves 4

¾ cup flour
½ teaspoons baking soda
A pinch of kosher salt
A pinch of grated nutmeg
¾ cup milk
1 egg
2 tablespoons brown sugar
1 tablespoon coconut oil, melted

1. Thoroughly combine all the ingredients in a mixing bowl.
2. Drop a spoonful of batter onto the greased baking dish.
3. Place the baking dish in the air fryer basket. Put the air fryer lid on and bake in the preheated instant pot at 360ºF (182ºC) for 10 minutes. Flip them when the lid screen indicates TURN FOOD.
4. Repeat with the remaining batter and serve warm.
5. Bon appétit!

French Toast

Prep time: 5 minutes | Cook time: 8 minutes | Serves 2

2 tablespoons butter, melted
2 eggs, whisked
4 tablespoons coconut milk
½ teaspoon ground cinnamon
½ teaspoon vanilla extract
4 tablespoons brown sugar
4 slices stale French bread

1. In a mixing bowl, thoroughly combine the butter, eggs, coconut milk, cinnamon, vanilla, and brown sugar.
2. Then dip each piece of bread into the egg mixture; place the bread slices in a lightly greased baking dish.
3. Place the baking dish in the air fryer basket. Put the air fryer lid on and bake in the preheated instant pot at 330ºF (166ºC) for 8 minutes. Flip the bread slices when the lid screen indicates TURN FOOD. Enjoy!

Sausage Cheese Rolls

Prep time: 5 minutes | Cook time: 10 minutes | Serves 4

6 ounces (170 g) refrigerated crescent dinner rolls
½ pound (227 g) smoked sausage, chopped
4 ounces (113 g) Swiss cheese, shredded
½ teaspoon dried oregano
2 tablespoons tomato paste

1. Separate the dough into rectangles. In a bowl, combine the remaining ingredients.
2. Spread each rectangle with the sausage mixture; roll them up tightly.
3. Place the rolls in the baking dish.
4. Place the baking dish in the air fryer basket. Put the air fryer lid on and bake in the preheated instant pot at 300ºF (150ºC) for 10 minutes. Flip the rolls when the lid screen indicates TURN FOOD.
5. Bon appétit!

Sausage Rolls with Mustard

Prep time: 5 minutes | Cook time: 8 minutes | Serves 4

4 ounces (113 g) refrigerated crescent rolls
1 tablespoon Dijon mustard
8 cocktail sausages

1. Separate the dough into triangles. Cut them lengthwise into triangles. Spread each triangle with the mustard.
2. Place a cocktail sausage on the shortest side of each triangle and roll it up.
3. Place the rolls in the baking dish.
4. Place the baking dish in the air fryer basket. Put the air fryer lid on and bake in the preheated instant pot at 320ºF (160ºC) for 8 minutes. Flip the rolls when the lid screen indicates TURN FOOD.
5. Bon appétit!

Spinach Cheese Frittata

Prep time: 5 minutes | Cook time: 15 minutes | Serves 3

6 eggs
6 tablespoons half-and-half
¼ teaspoon salt
¼ teaspoon ground black pepper
3 ounces (85 g) ricotta cheese, crumbled
2 cups baby spinach
1 tablespoon chopped fresh cilantro
2 tablespoons olive oil

1. Spritz the sides and bottom of the baking dish with nonstick cooking oil.
2. In a mixing bowl, thoroughly combine all the ingredients.
3. Pour the mixture into the prepared baking dish.
4. Place the baking dish in the air fryer basket. Put the air fryer lid on and bake in the preheated instant pot at 350ºF (180ºC) for 15 minutes, or until a toothpick comes out dry and clean.
5. Bon appétit!

Rosemary Butter Popovers

Prep time: 5 minutes | Cook time: 15 minutes | Serves 4

6 large-sized eggs
½ cup all-purpose flour
½ teaspoon baking powder
4 tablespoons butter, melted
½ cup milk
½ teaspoon granulated sugar
¼ teaspoon kosher salt
1 teaspoon dried rosemary

1. Spritz mini muffin cups with nonstick cooking oil.
2. In a mixing bowl, thoroughly combine all the ingredients.
3. Pour the mixture into the prepared mini muffin cups and lower them into the baking dish.
4. Place the baking dish in the air fryer basket. Put the air fryer lid on and bake in the preheated instant pot at 350ºF (180ºC) for 15 minutes, or until a toothpick comes out dry and clean.
5. Bon appétit!

Zucchini Chickpeas Cheese Croquettes

Prep time: 5 minutes | Cook time: 14 minutes | Serves 4

2 eggs, whisked
½ cup chickpea flour
2 ounces (57 g) feta cheese, crumbled
2 ounces (57 g) Swiss cheese, shredded
1 bell pepper, chopped
1 small zucchini, chopped
1 clove garlic, minced
½ teaspoon smoked paprika
Kosher salt and freshly ground black pepper, to taste
2 tablespoons butter, melted

1. Mix all the ingredients in a bowl. Shape the mixture into bite-sized balls and place them in a lightly oiled air fryer basket.
2. Put the air fryer lid on and air fry in the preheated instant pot at 400ºF (205ºC) for 14 minutes. Flip the croquettes when the lid screen indicates TURN FOOD.
3. Bon appétit!

Broccoli Salad

Prep time: 5 minutes | Cook time: 9 minutes | Serves 4

1 pound (454 g) broccoli florets
2 tablespoons sunflower seeds
2 tablespoons pepitas
2 tablespoons Sultanas
1 small shallot, chopped
1 teaspoon minced garlic
¼ cup extra-virgin olive oil
1 tablespoon yellow mustard
Sea salt and ground black pepper, to taste

1. Place the broccoli florets in a lightly greased air fryer basket.
2. Put the air fryer lid on and air fry in the preheated instant pot at 395ºF (202ºC) for 9 minutes. Flip the broccoli florets when the lid screen indicates TURN FOOD.
3. Toss the broccoli florets with the remaining ingredients. Serve at room temperature and enjoy!

Quinoa and Beans Sausage with Walnuts

Prep time: 5 minutes | Cook time: 15 minutes | Serves 4

1 cup cooked quinoa
10 ounces (283 g) canned red kidney beans, rinsed and dried
½ cup ground walnuts
1 red onion, chopped
2 cloves garlic, minced
1 teaspoon smoked paprika
Sea salt and ground black pepper, to taste

1. Mix all the ingredients in the blender or food processor. Form the mixture into logs and arrange them in a lightly greased air fryer basket.
2. Put the air fryer lid on and air fry in the preheated instant pot at 380ºF (193ºC) for 15 minutes. Flip the sausages when the lid screen indicates TURN FOOD.
3. Bon appétit!

Cauliflower Cheese Balls

Prep time: 5 minutes | Cook time: 15 minutes | Serves 4

2 cups cauliflower florets
4 tablespoons butter
1 teaspoon dried parsley flakes
1 teaspoon dried rosemary
2 garlic cloves, minced
Sea salt and ground black pepper, to taste
½ cup feta cheese

1. Arrange the cauliflower florets in a lightly greased air fryer basket.
2. Put the air fryer lid on and air fry in the preheated instant pot at 400ºF (205ºC) for 15 minutes. Flip the cauliflower florets when the lid screen indicates TURN FOOD.
3. Chop the roasted cauliflower and combine it with the remaining ingredients. Shape the mixture into balls.
4. Bon appétit!

Cheese Toast with Yogurt

Prep time: 5 minutes | Cook time: 8 minutes | Serves 3

2 ounces (57 g) goat cheese, crumbled
1 ounce (28 g) butter, melted
1 ounce (28 g) yogurt
2 eggs
¼ teaspoon sea salt
3 stale Brioche bread slices

1. In a mixing bowl, thoroughly combine the cheese, butter, yogurt, eggs, and sea salt.
2. Then dip each piece of bread into the egg mixture; place the bread slices in a lightly greased baking dish.
3. Place the baking dish in the air fryer basket. Put the air fryer lid on and bake in the preheated instant pot at 330ºF (166ºC) for 8 minutes. Flip the bread slices when the lid screen indicates TURN FOOD.
4. Enjoy!

Breaded Potato Tater Tots

Prep time: 8 minutes | Cook time: 14 minutes | Serves 4

¾ cup all-purpose flour
1 cup mashed boiled potatoes
2 eggs, whisked
1 tablespoon chopped fresh parsley
1 tablespoon chopped fresh cilantro
2 tablespoons chopped fresh scallions
Sea salt and ground black pepper, to taste
½ cup fresh bread crumbs
2 tablespoons olive oil

1. Mix all the ingredients in a bowl. Shape the mixture into bite-sized balls and place them in a lightly oiled air fryer basket.
2. Put the air fryer lid on and air fry in the preheated instant pot at 400ºF (205ºC) for 14 minutes. Flip the tater tots when the lid screen indicates TURN FOOD.
3. Bon appétit!

Creamy Mushroom Cheese Frittata

Prep time: 6 minutes | Cook time: 15 minutes | Serves 3

6 eggs
¼ cup sour cream
½ cup shredded Swiss cheese
Kosher salt and ground black pepper, to taste
1 teaspoon hot paprika
2 tablespoons olive oil
2 cloves garlic, crushed
6 ounces (170 g) brown mushrooms, sliced
2 tablespoons roughly chopped fresh parsley

1. Spritz the sides and bottom of the baking dish with nonstick cooking oil.
2. In a mixing bowl, thoroughly combine all the ingredients.
3. Pour the mixture into the prepared baking dish.
4. Place the baking dish in the air fryer basket. Put the air fryer lid on and bake in the preheated instant pot at 350ºF (180ºC) for 15 minutes, or until a toothpick comes out dry and clean.
5. Bon appétit!

Pork and Turkey Cheese Meatballs

Prep time: 5 minutes | Cook time: 15 minutes | Serves 4

½ pound (227 g) ground pork
½ pound (227 g) ground turkey
1 onion, minced
2 garlic cloves, minced
¼ cup Italian-style bread crumbs
¼ cup grated Parmesan cheese
1 large-sized egg, whisked
Sea salt and ground black pepper, to taste

1. Mix all the ingredients until everything is well combined. Form the mixture into balls. Transfer to the air fryer basket.
2. Put the air fryer lid on and air fry in the preheated instant pot at 380ºF (193ºC) for 15 minutes. Flip the meatballs when the lid screen indicates TURN FOOD.
3. Bon appétit!

Potato Cheese Sticks

Prep time: 6 minutes | Cook time: 14 minutes | Serves 4

1 cup mashed boiled potato
1 cup grated Cheddar cheese
1 tablespoon miso paste
1 cup all-purpose flour
½ teaspoon coriander seeds
Sea salt and ground black pepper, to taste
1 egg, beaten
1 cup bread crumbs
2 tablespoons Kewpie Japanese mayonnaise

1. Mix all the ingredients, except for the bread crumbs, in a bowl. Press the mixture into a parchment-lined baking dish and allow it to freeze until firm.
2. Cut the mixture into sticks and roll them into the bread crumbs; place the sticks in a lightly oiled air fryer basket.
3. Put the air fryer lid on and air fry in the preheated instant pot at 400ºF (205ºC) for 14 minutes. Flip the sticks when the lid screen indicates TURN FOOD.
4. Bon appétit!

Eggs Salad with Yogurt

Prep time: 5 minutes | Cook time: 15 minutes | Serves 4

6 eggs
4 tablespoons Greek-style yogurt
4 tablespoons mayonnaise
3 tablespoons chopped scallions
1 tablespoon Dijon mustard
Sea salt and ground black pepper, to taste

1. Place the eggs in the air fryer basket.
2. Put the air fryer lid on and air fry in the preheated instant pot at 270ºF (132ºC) for 15 minutes.
3. Peel and chop the eggs; place them in a salad bowl and add in the remaining ingredients. Gently toss to combine.
4. Place the salad in the refrigerator until ready to serve. Bon appétit!

Cauliflower Steaks

Prep time: 5 minutes | Cook time: 20 minutes | Serves 4

1 pound (454 g) cauliflower, cut into 4 steaks
4 tablespoons olive oil
1 teaspoon minced garlic
1 teaspoon cayenne pepper
½ teaspoon cumin seeds
Coarse sea salt and ground black pepper, to taste

1. Toss the cauliflower steaks with the remaining ingredients.
2. Place the cauliflower steaks in a lightly greased air fryer basket.
3. Put the air fryer lid on and air fry in the preheated instant pot at 390ºF (199ºC) for 20 minutes. Flip the cauliflower steaks when the lid screen indicates TURN FOOD.
4. Bon appétit!

Spinach Frittata with Bacon

Prep time: 10 minutes | Cook time: 15 minutes | Serves 4

6 eggs, whisked
6 tablespoons all-purpose flour
½ teaspoon baking soda
6 tablespoons full-fat milk
4 ounces (113 g) Canadian bacon, diced
1 tablespoon olive oil
2 cups baby spinach
1 tomato, chopped
1 Serrano pepper, chopped
Kosher salt and freshly ground black pepper, to taste

1. Spritz the sides and bottom of the baking dish with nonstick cooking oil.
2. In a mixing bowl, thoroughly combine all the ingredients.
3. Pour the mixture into the prepared baking dish.
4. Place the baking dish in the air fryer basket. Put the air fryer lid on and bake in the preheated instant pot at 350ºF (180ºC) for 15 minutes, or until a toothpick comes out dry and clean.
5. Bon appétit!

Dosas Cakes

Prep time: 5 minutes | Cook time: 20 minutes | Serves 4

½ cup all-purpose flour
½ cup rice flour
½ teaspoon baking powder
½ cup water
1 clove garlic, minced
½ teaspoon ground turmeric
½ teaspoon ground cumin
½ teaspoon mustard seeds

1. Thoroughly combine all the ingredients in a mixing bowl.
2. Drop a spoonful of batter onto the greased baking dish.
3. Place the baking dish in the air fryer basket. Put the air fryer lid on and bake in the preheated instant pot at 360ºF (182ºC) for 10 minutes. Flip the cakes when the lid screen indicates TURN FOOD.
4. Repeat with the remaining batter and serve warm.
5. Bon appétit!

Beef and Turkey Cheese Meatballs

Prep time: 6 minutes | Cook time: 15 minutes | Serves 4

⅓ pound (136 g) ground beef
½ pound (227 g) ground turkey
1 egg, slightly beaten
¼ cup crushed tortilla chips
½ cup grated Cheddar cheese
1 small onion, chopped
1 teaspoon minced garlic
Sea salt and freshly ground black pepper, to taste
1 teaspoon dried parsley flakes
1 teaspoon dried oregano
1 teaspoon dried basil

1. Mix all the ingredients until everything is well combined. Form the mixture into balls. Transfer to the air fryer basket.
2. Put the air fryer lid on and air fry in the preheated instant pot at 380ºF (193ºC) for 15 minutes. Flip the meatballs when the lid screen indicates TURN FOOD.
3. Bon appétit!

Cauliflower and Mushroom Cheese Balls

Prep time: 10 minutes | Cook time: 14 minutes | Serves 4

1 pound (454 g) cauliflower, grated
1 small onion, chopped
1 teaspoon minced garlic cloves
2 teaspoons butter, room temperature
1 pound (454 g) brown mushrooms, chopped
2 ounces (57 g) Cheddar cheese, grated
Sea salt and ground black pepper, to taste
1 cup Japanese bread crumbs

1. Mix all the ingredients in a bowl. Shape the mixture into bite-sized balls and place them in a lightly oiled air fryer basket.
2. Put the air fryer lid on and air fry in the preheated instant pot at 400ºF (205ºC) for 14 minutes. Flip the balls when the lid screen indicates TURN FOOD.
3. Bon appétit!

Buttermilk Cornbread Muffins

Prep time: 5 minutes | Cook time: 15 minutes | Serves 4

½ cup corn flour
½ cup plain flour
1 teaspoon baking soda
½ teaspoon salt
A pinch of grated nutmeg
2 eggs, whisked
2 tablespoons lard, melted
1 cup buttermilk

1. Spritz mini muffin cups with nonstick cooking oil.
2. In a mixing bowl, thoroughly combine all the ingredients.
3. Pour the mixture into the prepared mini muffin cups and lower them into the baking dish.
4. Place the baking dish in the air fryer basket. Put the air fryer lid on and bake in the preheated instant pot at 350ºF (180ºC) for 15 minutes, or until a toothpick comes out dry and clean.
5. Bon appétit!

Eggs Muffins with Bacon

Prep time: 6 minutes | Cook time: 15 minutes | Serves 4

6 eggs
6 tablespoons crumbled cottage cheese
2 tablespoons chopped scallions
1 teaspoon minced garlic
3 ounces (85 g) bacon, chopped
1 teaspoon paprika
Sea salt and ground black pepper, to taste

1. Spritz the silicone molds with nonstick cooking oil.
2. In a mixing bowl, thoroughly combine all the ingredients.
3. Pour the mixture into the prepared silicone molds and lower them into the baking dish.
4. Place the baking dish in the air fryer basket. Put the air fryer lid on and bake in the preheated instant pot at 350ºF (180ºC) for 15 minutes, or until a toothpick comes out dry and clean.
5. Bon appétit!

Brussels Sprout Salad with Apple

Prep time: 10 minutes | Cook time: 10 minutes | Serves 4

1 pound (454 g) fresh Brussels sprouts, trimmed
1 Vidalia onion, peeled and thinly sliced
1 garlic clove, minced
1 apple, cored and sliced
¼ cup pomegranate arils
2 ounces (57 g) goat cheese, crumbled
1 tablespoon fresh lemon juice
¼ cup extra-virgin olive oil
2 tablespoons honey
1 tablespoon Dijon mustard

1. Arrange the Brussels sprouts in the air fryer basket.
2. Put the air fryer lid on and air fry in the preheated instant pot at 380ºF (193ºC) for 10 minutes. Flip the Brussels sprouts when the lid screen indicates TURN FOOD.
3. Toss the Brussels sprouts with the remaining ingredients and serve at room temperature. Enjoy!

Zucchini Cheese Frittata

Prep time: 10 minutes | Cook time: 15 minutes | Serves 4

8 eggs
6 tablespoons sour cream
Coarse sea salt and ground black pepper, to taste
1 teaspoon cayenne pepper
½ teaspoon dried oregano
1 teaspoon dried basil
4 ounces (113 g) Gouda cheese, shredded
2 tablespoons olive oil
1 small zucchini, shredded
1 small shallot, chopped

1. Spritz the sides and bottom of the baking dish with nonstick cooking oil.
2. In a mixing bowl, thoroughly combine all the ingredients.
3. Pour the mixture into the prepared baking dish.
4. Place the baking dish in the air fryer basket. Put the air fryer lid on and bake in the preheated instant pot at 350ºF (180ºC) for 15 minutes, or until a toothpick comes out dry and clean.
5. Bon appétit!

Lentils and Carrot Burgers

Prep time: 8 minutes | Cook time: 15 minutes | Serves 4

12 ounces (340 g) canned lentils, drained and rinsed
1 medium carrot, grated
1 medium onion, grated
1 garlic clove, minced
1 teaspoon smoked paprika
Sea salt and ground black pepper, to taste
2 tablespoons olive oil

1. Mix all the ingredients until everything is well combined. Form the mixture into four patties and arrange them in a lightly greased air fryer basket.
2. Put the air fryer lid on and air fry in the preheated instant pot at 380ºF (193ºC) for 15 minutes. Flip the burgers when the lid screen indicates TURN FOOD.
3. Bon appétit!

Cauliflower Salad

Prep time: 5 minutes | Cook time: 13 minutes | Serves 4

1 pound (454 g) cauliflower florets
Sea salt and ground black pepper, to taste
4 tablespoons freshly squeezed lemon juice
¼ cup extra-virgin olive oil
1 teaspoon minced fresh garlic
1 tablespoon chopped fresh parsley
2 tablespoons chopped fresh scallions

1. Arrange the cauliflower florets in a lightly greased air fryer basket.
2. Put the air fryer lid on and air fry in the preheated instant pot at 400ºF (205ºC) for 13 minutes. Flip the cauliflower florets when the lid screen indicates TURN FOOD.
3. Toss the cauliflower florets with the remaining ingredients.
4. Bon appétit!

Bacon Frittata

Prep time: 8 minutes | Cook time: 15 minutes | Serves 4

7 eggs
4 tablespoons sour cream
1 teaspoon paprika
Kosher salt and ground black pepper, to taste
2 tablespoons olive oil
2 ounces (57 g) bacon, diced
1 bell pepper, seeded and diced
2 garlic cloves, minced

1. Spritz the sides and bottom of the baking dish with nonstick cooking oil.
2. In a mixing bowl, thoroughly combine all the ingredients.
3. Pour the mixture into the prepared baking dish.
4. Place the baking dish in the air fryer basket. Put the air fryer lid on and bake in the preheated instant pot at 350ºF (180ºC) for 15 minutes, or until a toothpick comes out dry and clean.
5. Bon appétit!

Milk Rabanadas

Prep time: 5 minutes | Cook time: 8 minutes | Serves 2

4 slices baguette
½ cup full-fat milk
4 tablespoons granulated sugar
2 eggs, beaten
½ teaspoon ground cinnamon
2 tablespoons coconut oil

1. Toss the bread slices with the remaining ingredients. Transfer to the air fryer basket.
2. Put the air fryer lid on and air fry in the preheated instant pot at 330ºF (166ºC) for 8 minutes. Flip the bread slices when the lid screen indicates TURN FOOD.
3. Bon appétit!

Beef Cheese Sandwich

Prep time: 5 minutes | Cook time: 10 minutes | Serves 2

4 slices sourdough bread
2 tablespoons butter, room temperature
4 slices Cheddar cheese
½ pound (227 g) corned beef

1. Butter one side of each slice of bread.
2. Assemble the sandwiches with cheese and corned beef. Transfer to the air fryer basket.
3. Put the air fryer lid on and air fry in the preheated instant pot at 380ºF (193ºC) for 10 minutes.
4. Bon appétit!

Buckwheat Cheese Balls

Prep time: 5 minutes | Cook time: 15 minutes | Serves 4

1½ cups cooked buckwheat
1 cup rice flour
½ teaspoon baking powder
½ cup grated Parmesan cheese
2 eggs, beaten
2 tablespoons olive oil
Sea salt and ground black pepper, to taste

1. Mix all the ingredients until everything is well combined. Form the mixture into balls. Transfer to the air fryer basket.
2. Put the air fryer lid on and air fry in the preheated instant pot at 380ºF (193ºC) for 15 minutes. Flip the balls when the lid screen indicates TURN FOOD.
3. Bon appétit!

Potato Sinkers

Prep time: 5 minutes | Cook time: 14 minutes | Serves 4

1 cup mashed boiled potatoes
1 cup all-purpose flour
½ teaspoon baking powder
2 eggs, beaten
½ teaspoon cayenne pepper
¼ teaspoon dried dill weed
½ teaspoon salt
¼ teaspoon ground black pepper

1. Mix all the ingredients in a bowl. Shape the mixture into bite-sized balls and place them in a lightly oiled air fryer basket.
2. Put the air fryer lid on and air fry in the preheated instant pot at 400ºF (205ºC) for 14 minutes. Flip the sinkers when the lid screen indicates TURN FOOD.
3. Bon appétit!

Eggs Salad with Mayo

Prep time: 5 minutes | Cook time: 15 minutes | Serves 4

5 eggs
4 tablespoons sour cream
¼ cup mayonnaise
1 tablespoon Dijon mustard
2 tablespoons snipped fresh basil
Sea salt and ground black pepper, to taste

1. Place the eggs in the air fryer basket.
2. Put the air fryer lid on and air fry in the preheated instant pot at 270ºF (132ºC) for 15 minutes.
3. Peel and chop the eggs; place them in a salad bowl and add in the remaining ingredients. Gently toss to combine.
4. Place the salad in the refrigerator until ready to serve. Bon appétit!

Spinach and Cheese Tartlets

Prep time: 5 minutes | Cook time: 15 minutes | Serves 4

5 eggs
2 tablespoons butter, room temperature
1 cup baby spinach
1 bell pepper, chopped
1 shallot, chopped
Kosher salt ground black pepper, to taste
½ teaspoon dried basil
½ teaspoon dried oregano
3 ounces (85 g) feta cheese, crumbled

1. Spritz mini muffin cups with nonstick cooking oil.
2. In a mixing bowl, thoroughly combine all the ingredients.
3. Pour the mixture into the prepared mini muffin cups and lower them into the baking dish.
4. Place the baking dish in the air fryer basket. Put the air fryer lid on and bake in the preheated instant pot at 350ºF (180ºC) for 15 minutes, or until a toothpick comes out dry and clean.
5. Bon appétit!

Bulgur and Mushrooms Fritters

Prep time: 8 minutes | Cook time: 15 minutes | Serves 4

1½ cups cooked bulgur
1 cup chopped brown mushrooms
1 medium onion, chopped
2 cloves garlic, finely chopped
1 cup crushed crackers
2 tablespoons butter
2 tablespoons chopped fresh parsley
Sea salt and ground black pepper, to taste

1. Mix all the ingredients until everything is well combined. Form the mixture into balls. Transfer to the air fryer basket.
2. Put the air fryer lid on and air fry in the preheated instant pot at 380ºF (193ºC) for 15 minutes. Flip the balls when the lid screen indicates TURN FOOD.
3. Bon appétit!

Green Beans Cheese Salad

Prep time: 6 minutes | Cook time: 7 minutes | Serves 4

1 pound (454 g) green beans, trimmed
Sea salt and ground black pepper, to taste
1 shallot, finely chopped
1 teaspoon minced garlic
¼ cup extra-virgin olive oil
2 tablespoons white wine vinegar
¼ cup chopped fresh parsley
2 ounces (57 g) feta cheese, crumbled

1. Arrange the green beans in a lightly greased air fryer basket.
2. Put the air fryer lid on and air fry in the preheated instant pot at 375ºF (190ºC) for 7 minutes. Flip the green beans when the lid screen indicates TURN FOOD.
3. Add the green beans to a salad bowl; add in the remaining ingredients and stir to combine well. Enjoy!

Sweet Potato and Lentil Patties

Prep time: 8 minutes | Cook time: 15 minutes | Serves 4

1 cup red lentils
2 tablespoons tomato paste
1 sweet potato, peeled and grated
Sea salt and ground black pepper, to taste
1 small onion, chopped
1 tablespoon chopped fresh parsley
1 tablespoon chopped fresh coriander
2 tablespoons olive oil

1. Mix all the ingredients until everything is well combined. Form the mixture into four patties and arrange them in a lightly greased air fryer basket.
2. Put the air fryer lid on and air fry in the preheated instant pot at 380ºF (193ºC) for 15 minutes. Flip the burgers when the lid screen indicates TURN FOOD.
3. Bon appétit!

Chili Chickpeas

Prep time: 5 minutes | Cook time: 13 minutes | Serves 4

10 ounces (283 g) chickpeas, drained and rinsed
1 tablespoon olive oil
Coarse sea salt and ground black pepper, to taste
½ teaspoon garlic powder
1 teaspoon cayenne pepper
½ teaspoon red chili powder

1. Toss the chickpeas with the other ingredients in the air fryer basket.
2. Put the air fryer lid on and air fry in the preheated instant pot at 390ºF (199ºC) for 13 minutes.
3. Bon appétit!

Waffle with Blueberries

Prep time: 2 minutes | Cook time: 7 minutes | Serves 1

1 frozen waffle
1 tablespoon blueberries
1 tablespoon whipped cream

1. Place the frozen waffle in a lightly greased air fryer basket.
2. Put the air fryer lid on and air fry in the preheated instant pot at 360ºF (182ºC) for 7 minutes. Flip the waffle when the lid screen indicates TURN FOOD.
3. Serve the waffle with blueberries and whipped cream. Bon appétit!

Corn Salad

Prep time: 10 minutes | Cook time: 10 minutes | Serves 2

2 corn on the cob, husked and halved
2 teaspoons ghee
Sea salt and ground black pepper, to taste
1 Vidalia onion, thinly sliced
1 bell pepper, thinly sliced
2 tablespoons lime juice
2 tablespoons extra-virgin olive oil

1. Toss the ears of corn with the ghee, salt, and pepper. Arrange the ears of corn in the air fryer basket.
2. Put the air fryer lid on and air fry in the preheated instant pot at 390ºF (199ºC) for 10 minutes.
3. Next, cut the kernels off the cob. Toss the corn kernels with the remaining ingredients. Bon appétit!

Air Fried Beans

Prep time: 5 minutes | Cook time: 13 minutes | Serves 4

12 ounces (340 g) canned garbanzo beans, drained and rinsed
1 tablespoon olive oil
1 tablespoon Ranch seasoning mix

1. Toss the garbanzo beans with the other ingredients in the air fryer basket.
2. Put the air fryer lid on and air fry in the preheated instant pot at 390ºF (199ºC) for 13 minutes. Flip the garbanzo beans when the lid screen indicates TURN FOOD.
3. Bon appétit!

Panko Cheese Arancini

Prep time: 5 minutes | Cook time: 15 minutes | Serves 4

1½ cups cooked Arborio rice
½ cup grated Parmesan cheese
1 cup panko crumbs
2 large eggs, whisked
1 teaspoon dried parsley flakes
Kosher salt and freshly ground black pepper, to taste
2 tablespoons butter

1. Mix all the ingredients until everything is well combined. Form the mixture into balls. Transfer to the air fryer basket.
2. Put the air fryer lid on and air fry in the preheated instant pot at 380ºF (193ºC) for 15 minutes. Flip the balls when the lid screen indicates TURN FOOD.
3. Bon appétit!

Potato Cheese Croquettes

Prep time: 5 minutes | Cook time: 14 minutes | Serves 4

½ cup flour
1 teaspoon baking powder
¾ pound (340 g) potatoes, grated
2 eggs, whisked
½ cup grated Parmesan cheese
1 tablespoon chopped parsley
1 tablespoon chopped cilantro
1 tablespoon chopped chives
1 teaspoon smoked paprika
Kosher salt and ground black pepper, to taste
2 tablespoons olive oil

1. Mix all the ingredients in a bowl. Shape the mixture into bite-sized balls and place them in a lightly oiled air fryer basket.
2. Put the air fryer lid on and air fry in the preheated instant pot at 400ºF (205ºC) for 14 minutes. Flip the croquettes when the lid screen indicates TURN FOOD.
3. Bon appétit!

Corn with Butter

Prep time: 8 minutes | Cook time: 10 minutes | Serves 2

2 ears corn, husked and halved
1 teaspoon olive oil
Coarse sea salt and cayenne pepper, to taste
2 tablespoons cold butter
½ teaspoon crushed garlic
1 tablespoon chopped fresh scallions

1. Toss the ears of corn with the oil, salt, and cayenne pepper. Arrange the ears of corn in the air fryer basket.
2. Put the air fryer lid on and air fry in the preheated instant pot at 390ºF (199ºC) for 10 minutes.
3. Garnish the ears of corn with the butter, garlic, and fresh scallions. Bon appétit!

Sweet Potato Salad Bowl with Spinach

Prep time: 10 minutes | Cook time: 15 minutes | Serves 2

1 (5-inch) long sweet potato, peeled and cut into slices
2 tablespoons extra-virgin olive oil
Sea salt and ground black pepper, to taste
2 cups baby spinach
1 tomato, diced
1 bell pepper, seeded and sliced
1 tablespoon white wine vinegar

1. Toss the sweet potato with 1 tablespoon of olive oil and place them in the air fryer basket.
2. Put the air fryer lid on and air fry in the preheated instant pot at 360ºF (182ºC) for 15 minutes. Flip the sweet potato when the lid screen indicates TURN FOOD.
3. Toss the roasted potatoes with the remaining ingredients and serve immediately.
4. Enjoy!

Eggplant Rice Patties

Prep time: 10 minutes | Cook time: 15 minutes | Serves 4

1 cup cooked brown rice
2 eggs, beaten
1 cup peeled and chopped eggplant
1 cup bread crumbs
1 bell pepper, chopped
1 small onion, chopped
2 cloves garlic, minced
Sea salt and ground black pepper, to taste
2 tablespoons olive oil

1. Mix all the ingredients until everything is well combined. Form the mixture into patties. Transfer to the air fryer basket.
2. Put the air fryer lid on and air fry in the preheated instant pot at 380ºF (193ºC) for 15 minutes. Flip the patties when the lid screen indicates TURN FOOD.
3. Bon appétit!

Cinnamon Butter Toast

Prep time: 2 minutes | Cook time: 8 minutes | Serves 2

2 bread slices
1 teaspoon ground cinnamon
2 tablespoons butter, softened

1. Toss the bread slices with cinnamon and butter. Transfer to the air fryer basket.
2. Put the air fryer lid on and air fry in the preheated instant pot at 330ºF (166ºC) for 8 minutes. Flip the bread slices when the lid screen indicates TURN FOOD.
3. Bon appétit!

Barley and Walnuts Croquettes

Prep time: 5 minutes | Cook time: 15 minutes | Serves 4

1½ cups cooked barley
2 large eggs, beaten
1 cup bread crumbs
Kosher salt and cayenne pepper, to taste
1 teaspoon red chili powder
2 ounces (57 g) ground walnuts
2 tablespoons olive oil

1. Mix all the ingredients until everything is well combined. Form the mixture into balls. Transfer to the air fryer basket.
2. Put the air fryer lid on and air fry in the preheated instant pot at 380ºF (193ºC) for 15 minutes. Flip the balls when the lid screen indicates TURN FOOD.
3. Bon appétit!

Appendix 1 Measurement Conversion Chart

VOLUME EQUIVALENTS(DRY)

US STANDARD	METRIC (APPROXIMATE)
1/8 teaspoon	0.5 mL
1/4 teaspoon	1 mL
1/2 teaspoon	2 mL
3/4 teaspoon	4 mL
1 teaspoon	5 mL
1 tablespoon	15 mL
1/4 cup	59 mL
1/2 cup	118 mL
3/4 cup	177 mL
1 cup	235 mL
2 cups	475 mL
3 cups	700 mL
4 cups	1 L

WEIGHT EQUIVALENTS

US STANDARD	METRIC (APPROXIMATE)
1 ounce	28 g
2 ounces	57 g
5 ounces	142 g
10 ounces	284 g
15 ounces	425 g
16 ounces (1 pound)	455 g
1.5 pounds	680 g
2 pounds	907 g

VOLUME EQUIVALENTS(LIQUID)

US STANDARD	US STANDARD (OUNCES)	METRIC (APPROXIMATE)
2 tablespoons	1 fl.oz.	30 mL
1/4 cup	2 fl.oz.	60 mL
1/2 cup	4 fl.oz.	120 mL
1 cup	8 fl.oz.	240 mL
1 1/2 cup	12 fl.oz.	355 mL
2 cups or 1 pint	16 fl.oz.	475 mL
4 cups or 1 quart	32 fl.oz.	1 L
1 gallon	128 fl.oz.	4 L

TEMPERATURES EQUIVALENTS

FAHRENHEIT(F)	CELSIUS(C) (APPROXIMATE)
225 °F	107 °C
250 °F	120 °C
275 °F	135 °C
300 °F	150 °C
325 °F	160 °C
350 °F	180 °C
375 °F	190 °C
400 °F	205 °C
425 °F	220 °C
450 °F	235 °C
475 °F	245 °C
500 °F	260 °C

Appendix 2 Air Fryer Cooking Chart

Beef

Item	Temp (°F)	Time (mins)	Item	Temp (°F)	Time (mins)
Beef Eye Round Roast (4 lbs.)	400 °F	45 to 55	Meatballs (1-inch)	370 °F	7
Burger Patty (4 oz.)	370 °F	16 to 20	Meatballs (3-inch)	380 °F	10
Filet Mignon (8 oz.)	400 °F	18	Ribeye, bone-in (1-inch, 8 oz)	400 °F	10 to 15
Flank Steak (1.5 lbs.)	400 °F	12	Sirloin steaks (1-inch, 12 oz)	400 °F	9 to 14
Flank Steak (2 lbs.)	400 °F	20 to 28			

Chicken

Item	Temp (°F)	Time (mins)	Item	Temp (°F)	Time (mins)
Breasts, bone in (1 ¼ lb.)	370 °F	25	Legs, bone-in (1 ¾ lb.)	380 °F	30
Breasts, boneless (4 oz)	380 °F	12	Thighs, boneless (1 ½ lb.)	380 °F	18 to 20
Drumsticks (2 ½ lb.)	370 °F	20	Wings (2 lb.)	400 °F	12
Game Hen (halved 2 lb.)	390 °F	20	Whole Chicken	360 °F	75
Thighs, bone-in (2 lb.)	380 °F	22	Tenders	360 °F	8 to 10

Pork & Lamb

Item	Temp (°F)	Time (mins)	Item	Temp (°F)	Time (mins)
Bacon (regular)	400 °F	5 to 7	Pork Tenderloin	370 °F	15
Bacon (thick cut)	400 °F	6 to 10	Sausages	380 °F	15
Pork Loin (2 lb.)	360 °F	55	Lamb Loin Chops (1-inch thick)	400 °F	8 to 12
Pork Chops, bone in (1-inch, 6.5 oz)	400 °F	12	Rack of Lamb (1.5 – 2 lb.)	380 °F	22

Fish & Seafood

Item	Temp (°F)	Time (mins)	Item	Temp (°F)	Time (mins)
Calamari (8 oz)	400 °F	4	Tuna Steak	400 °F	7 to 10
Fish Fillet (1-inch, 8 oz)	400 °F	10	Scallops	400 °F	5 to 7
Salmon, fillet (6 oz)	380 °F	12	Shrimp	400 °F	5
Swordfish steak	400 °F	10			

Vegetables

INGREDIENT	AMOUNT	PREPARATION	OIL	TEMP	COOK TIME
Asparagus	2 bunches	Cut in half, trim stems	2 Tbsp	420°F	12-15 mins
Beets	1½ lbs	Peel, cut in ½-inch cubes	1Tbsp	390°F	28-30 mins
Bell peppers (for roasting)	4 peppers	Cut in quarters, remove seeds	1Tbsp	400°F	15-20 mins
Broccoli	1 large head	Cut in 1-2-inch florets	1Tbsp	400°F	15-20 mins
Brussels sprouts	1lb	Cut in half, remove stems	1Tbsp	425°F	15-20 mins
Carrots	1lb	Peel, cut in ¼-inch rounds	1 Tbsp	425°F	10-15 mins
Cauliflower	1 head	Cut in 1-2-inch florets	2 Tbsp	400°F	20-22 mins
Corn on the cob	7 ears	Whole ears, remove husks	1 Tbps	400°F	14-17 mins
Green beans	1 bag (12 oz)	Trim	1 Tbps	420°F	18-20 mins
Kale (for chips)	4 oz	Tear into pieces,remove stems	None	325°F	5-8 mins
Mushrooms	16 oz	Rinse, slice thinly	1 Tbps	390°F	25-30 mins
Potatoes, russet	1½ lbs	Cut in 1-inch wedges	1 Tbps	390°F	25-30 mins
Potatoes, russet	1lb	Hand-cut fries, soak 30 mins in cold water, then pat dry	½ -3 Tbps	400°F	25-28 mins
Potatoes, sweet	1lb	Hand-cut fries, soak 30 mins in cold water, then pat dry	1 Tbps	400°F	25-28 mins
Zucchini	1lb	Cut in eighths lengthwise, then cut in half	1 Tbps	400°F	15-20 mins

Appendix 3 Recipe Index

C

D

E

F

G

H

J-K

L

M-O

P

Q

R

S

T-U

V-W

Y

Z

Milton Keynes UK
Ingram Content Group UK Ltd.
UKHW030105160124
436086UK00002B/56

9 781637 332160